TRANSFORMING MINISTRY FORMATION

TRANSFORMING
MINISTRY FORMATION

Edited by Edward P. Hahnenberg, Marti R. Jewell,
and Theodore James Whapham

Paulist Press
New York / Mahwah, NJ

Cover image by aohovector/Shutterstock.com
Cover design by Joe Gallagher
Book design by Lynn Else

Library of Congress Cataloging-in-Publication Data
Names: Hahnenberg, Edward P., editor. | Jewell, Marti R., editor. | Whapham, Theodore James, 1974– editor.
Title: Transforming ministry formation / edited by Edward P. Hahnenberg, Marti R. Jewell, and Theodore James Whapham.
Description: New York / Mahwah, NJ : Paulist Press, 2021. | Includes bibliographical references. | Summary: "Transforming Ministry Formation is a theological and practical exploration of ministry formation. Drawing on thirty years of experience from the Association of Graduate Programs in Ministry (AGPIM), these essays survey the changing ministerial landscape of Catholicism in the United States, identifying important challenges and best opportunities facing ministers, ministry students, and those responsible for their initial and ongoing formation."— Provided by publisher.
Identifiers: LCCN 2020027716 (print) | LCCN 2020027717 (ebook) | ISBN 9780809155101 (paperback) | ISBN 9781587689093 (ebook)
Subjects: LCSH: Lay ministry—Catholic Church—Training of—United States—History—21st century. | Laity—Catholic Church—Training of—United States—History—21st century
Classification: LCC BX932 .T73 2021 (print) | LCC BX932 (ebook) | DDC 230.07/3273—dc23
LC record available at https://lccn.loc.gov/2020027716
LC ebook record available at https://lccn.loc.gov/2020027717

ISBN 978-0-8091-5510-1 (paperback)
ISBN 978-1-58768-909-3 (e-book)

Published by Paulist Press
997 Macarthur Boulevard
Mahwah, New Jersey 07430
www.paulistpress.com

Printed and bound in the
United States of America

CONTENTS

CONTENTS

PART TWO
THE PRACTICES OF MINISTERIAL FORMATION

ACKNOWLEDGMENTS

A project such as this volume is the product of collaboration by a wide group of scholars. We thank the members of AGPIM for choosing to dedicate their annual gathering to this topic, and especially the authors in this volume for their dedication to their writing, scholarship, and furtherance of the field of practical theology. We would also like to thank AGPIM's leadership team over the past several years. In particular, Tom Ryan played a pivotal role in helping to organize the conference and champion this project during his term as president. Debbie Sargo provided outstanding administrative expertise in helping to communicate with authors and in keeping us organized. We also greatly appreciate the help of the staff and editors at Paulist Press, especially Diane Vescovi, Patrick McNamara, and Donna Crilly.

ABBREVIATIONS

ORGANIZATIONS

AGPIM—Association of Graduate Programs in Ministry
ATS—Association of Theological Schools
ITC—International Theological Commission
NALM—National Association for Lay Ministry
NACC—National Association of Catholic Chaplains
NCCL—National Conference of Catechetical Leaders
NFCYM—National Federation for Catholic Youth Ministers
NPLC—National Pastoral Life Center
USCCB—United States Conference of Catholic Bishops

DOCUMENTS

AA—*Apostolicam Actuositatem*
CCC—*Catechism of the Catholic Church*
CG—*Called and Gifted: The American Catholic Laity. Reflections of the
    American Bishops Commemorating the Fifteenth Anniversary of the
    Issuance of the Decree on the Apostolate of the Laity*
CG3—*Called and Gifted for the Third Millennium*
CL—*Christifideles Laici*
Co-Workers—*Co-Workers in the Vineyard of the Lord*
GS—*Guadium et Spes*
LG—*Lumen Gentium*
NCS—National Certification Standards

INTRODUCTION

Fifteen years after Vatican II, the United States Bishops looked back and celebrated the many ways lay Catholics had embraced the Council's call to become active participants in the life and mission of the Church. Their 1980 statement "Called and Gifted" (CG) recognized a new maturity among the people of God, as the baptized claimed their vocation to serve the reign of God in the family, the world of work, culture, and society, and in the Church. Within this early, energetic affirmation, the bishops noted a new development: laypeople who had "prepared for professional ministry in the Church."[1] Laywomen and laymen had begun to do ministry for a living. And they were seeking out the theological education and pastoral training needed to do it more effectively.

The emergence of professional, committed lay ministers—what the bishops have since come to call *lay ecclesial ministers*—was sudden, widespread, and lasting. Indeed, the "ministry explosion" that followed Vatican II stands out in Church history as one of the three or four most important ministerial transformations of the past two thousand years.[2] It can be compared to the changes in the Church brought on by the rise of communal forms of monasticism in the fifth century, the birth of mendicant orders in the thirteenth century, and the proliferation of active women's religious communities in the seventeenth century. Like these earlier movements, lay ecclesial ministry has transformed the Catholic experience of the Church in our own day, challenging past models of an active clergy and a passive laity, and broadening our appreciation for the many ways Christians are called to serve.

As lay Catholics swept into ministry, schools and diocesan offices scrambled to provide training for ministerial roles that had never existed before, but the needs and circumstances of these new lay ministers did not fit neatly into longstanding structures and practices of ministerial formation in the United States, which had focused almost exclusively on teaching future priests in seminaries. Lay ministry brought a distinctive set of challenges. First, there was little direction from the hierarchy above. The emergence of professional forms of lay ministry was not the result of a Vatican decree or a national pastoral plan. Instead, new ministerial roles emerged at the grassroots, as pastors created positions on the parish staff to help coordinate expanding religious education programs, implement liturgical changes, or lead the newly introduced RCIA. Second, the men and women who were hired to fill these positions came from a variety of different backgrounds, with a range of experiences and exposure to the theological tradition. Women religious seeking more direct ministry in the parish, former seminarians and men leaving the priesthood, trusted volunteers asked by their pastors to lead new programs—these diverse groups had different needs in terms of ministerial formation. A single program or uniform model would not suffice. Finally, the thoroughly pastoral nature of their work stretched an educational system that emphasized doctrine, deductive argumentation, and abstract ideas. As seminaries experimented with "coeducation" and universities raced to launch new summer programs in theology, they had no guidelines or competency standards to direct their curricular choices.

It was within this context that the Association of Graduate Programs in Ministry (AGPIM) came into existence. The early organizers recognized the challenges they faced in developing common curricular expectations, in integrating personal and spiritual formation into academic programs, and in responding to new ministerial configurations brought about by the presence of laypersons, both men and women, on parish staffs. They met to explore a new formational paradigm that could address the unique needs of lay ecclesial ministers, and to ask how such a paradigm would shape theology itself. Since its first meeting in

Introduction

1987, AGPIM has met annually to continue the work and vision of that initial gathering. While the themes of these annual meetings have varied over the years, there has been a constant focus on the relationship between the academy and the Church, as well as a deep commitment to *practical theology.*

At their sixth annual meeting in 1992, AGPIM members approved the following position statement, which would come to define the association's self-understanding:

> The Association of Graduate Programs in Ministry (AGPIM), an organization of Roman Catholic graduate programs, recognizes and supports the emergence of a new theological paradigm in graduate education for ministry. This theology, commonly referred to as practical or pastoral theology, is a mutually interpretive, critical, and transforming conversation between the Christian tradition and contemporary experience. Historical, hermeneutical, and socio-cultural analyses are integral to this method of theology. Pastoral or practical theology takes place in a community of faith, implies a spirituality that is both personal and liturgical, and is directed toward individual and social transformation in Christ.[3]

While practical theology has had a long history within Protestantism, dating back at least to Friedrich Schleiermacher's classic description of the discipline in his *Brief Outline to Theology as a Field of Study,* the field did not have wide acceptance in Catholic circles until well into the twentieth century.[4] Important movements of the post–World War II period—including the catechetical renewal in Europe (e.g., the Munich method) and Catholic Action, with its praxis-oriented methods (e.g., "see-judge-act")—began to call into question an exclusively deductive framework for understanding ministerial education. However, it was St. John XXIII's vision of Vatican II as a "pastoral council" that brought front and center the question of the relationship between doctrine and life, theory and practice. This emphasis resonated with some of the more influential theological developments of the postconciliar period, including Karl Rahner's turn to experience, Bernard Lonergan's "theological empirical method," and David Tracy's revised correlation method.[5] The explosion of liberation, feminist, and Latinx theologies, as well as the pedagogical moves of religious educators inspired by Paulo Freire, further confirmed the centrality of praxis for theologians teaching in ministry programs in the decades after Vatican II.[6]

In its emphasis on *praxis*—understood as the dynamic interchange between action and theory that fuels purposeful human activity—practical theology is not simply the one-directional, one-dimensional attempt to apply theological ideas to pastoral realities. As the position statement quoted above indicates, practical theology is a mutually interpretive, critical conversation between the Christian tradition and contemporary experience. This dialogical dynamic requires a community of faith as the necessary context for theological reflection. No practical theology is done alone. While this volume is primarily concerned with the formation of lay ecclesial ministers, it rejects a "clerical paradigm" in which practical theology is oriented *exclusively* to the tasks of church leadership.[7] The goal of adopting a practical theological approach to ministerial formation is not to polish a set of tools that belong to the ministers alone. Rather the goal is to cultivate a Christian mode of thinking and acting in the world that can pollinate the whole people of God. Thus, the paradigm of practical theology that takes shape in what follows is not only *dialogical* and *communal,* it is profoundly *transformative.* It involves critical thinking about what we do and how we live out our faith, precisely in order to deepen discipleship and further our commitment to Christ's work of bringing about the reign of God.

Working at the intersection of the academy and the Church, AGPIM members have been on the frontlines of this dialogical, communal, and transformative work. In consulting with the USCCB on drafts of the 2005 statement *Co-Workers in the Vineyard of the Lord* (*Co-Workers*), in helping to develop a framework for national certification standards for lay ecclesial ministry, and, most importantly, in training a generation of liturgists, catechetical leaders, chaplains, and Catholic social activists, AGPIM has lived into and lived out the practical theological paradigm described in this volume.

Introduction

In recent years, the members of AGPIM increasingly expressed the conviction that the association has made an important contribution to theological and ministerial education and to the life of the Church in the United States. AGPIM members determined that these contributions needed to be documented and their implications explored. In February 2018, the association dedicated its thirty-first annual meeting to discussing the state of ministerial formation in the United States and to advancing the work of Catholic practical theology. Twenty-six papers were presented on a variety of topics, which in different ways expressed the association's common vision of the role of practical theology in ministerial education.

This volume is a collection of select papers presented at that gathering and is offered as a series of reflections on the work of AGPIM and its member schools. The essays are presented with the conviction that the experience of lay ministry formation articulated in these chapters will be of concrete value to many who are engaged in the work of forming men and women for a variety of ministerial roles in the Church. To this end, the work is organized into two major sections. Part 1 lays out some of the most important contexts for the work of ministerial formation today. Part 2 offers more specific insights of AGPIM members into the various practices of ministerial education and formation.

The opening chapter by William H. Johnston provides a thematic history of the Association of Graduate Programs in Ministry. This chapter discusses the founding of the Association, its view of practical theology, and six features characteristic of its work. It provides greater context for understanding the commitments of those involved in ministerial formation at the graduate level and the challenges AGPIM member schools have encountered in the midst of their formation work.

Marti R. Jewell provides an in-depth narrative of AGPIM's involvement in the development of the National Certification Standards for Lay Ecclesial Ministers (NCS), which are now used by universities for curricular development and regional assessment. These standards developed in interaction with discussions about accreditation standards, competency-based standards, and practical theology. In this context, a debate between theologians Joseph Merkt and Bernard Lee played a central role in the history of this significant development. At the root of the discussion was the tension between competency-based education and assessment, on the one hand, and apprenticeship models of education, on the other.

William H. Johnston revisits the 2005 statement of the U.S. Bishops, *Co-Workers in the Vineyard of the Lord*. He engages in a critical-constructive reading of the text that asks the question, What next? In light of the teaching of Vatican II, Johnston concludes that lay ecclesial ministers ought to have greater agency in discerning their charisms and in maintaining their relationships with the ordained than *Co-Workers* seems to allow. His reasoning develops out of the concrete experience of many lay ecclesial ministers and relies upon a reflection on the spiritual works of mercy to allow improved ministerial relationships to develop out of concrete situations.

Howard Ebert argues that Vatican II's recovery of the ancient concept of the "sense of the faith" (*sensus fidei*) offers the potential for a more inclusive, dialogical, and participatory church. However, given its nature as a kind of spiritual "sense" or supernatural "instinct," the *sensus fidei* is notoriously difficult to pin down. With the help of the French social theorist Pierre Bourdieu, Ebert suggests that the lay ecclesial minister can play an important role in helping the Church discern the implicit, intuitive wisdom spread throughout the faithful lives of all the baptized. In particular, he draws upon the social location of lay ecclesial ministers, viewing it through the lens of prophetic power and the capacity of the prophet to transform structures from a position of liminality.

The chapters of part 2 turn to explore questions that face ministerial formation in light of various ministerial practices. Hosffman Ospino highlights the incredible cultural diversity that marks the Catholic Church in the United States. He challenges those responsible for ministry formation to attend to this reality and to reimagine educational models in light of these increasingly diverse communities. He articulates this challenge with the category of "interculturality." The term highlights the importance of embedded cultural contexts for the life of the Church and the impact that the cultural frameworks can have on our interactions with others. The cultural diversity of our Church thus not only poses a challenge, but also an opportunity to realize more fully the Church's call to be the Body of Christ.

In her chapter on catechists as storytellers, timone davis (she uses lowercase) applies a narrative approach influenced by African American traditions of storytelling. Davis adapts Thomas Groome's shared Christian praxis approach in light of a dialogical method of storytelling that she refers to as "my story—your story." This approach is then applied to the catechetical model presented by three archetypes—the preacher, the emcee, and the catechist—to exemplify ways in which this method can be enacted, thus bringing young adults into contact with the story of Christianity.

Tracey Lamont confronts head-on the widely accepted and deeply discouraging diagnosis of young adults as beholden to a "moralistic therapeutic deism," with its corrosive effects on the life of faith. She asks whether the conclusions coming out of research by the sociologist Christian Smith ultimately reflects a "theory-to-practice" set of assumptions that miss important dynamics at play in the lives of emerging adult Catholics. A more nuanced picture emerges when the qualitative and interdisciplinary methods of practical theology begin to uncover the moral development and deep culture of young adults.

Drawing on her extensive work in health care ministry, Celeste Mueller discusses the importance of ministerial formation for administrative boards in Catholic nonprofit organizations. She makes a case for the centrality of forming lay executives in Catholic health care for their work in directing the administration of hospital networks and other care facilities. She outlines a curricular approach for the formation of those involved in administrative ministry. Her work with health care executives and board members draws out the importance of this distinctive form of lay formation for the Catholic identity of a variety of important ministries, including schools, health care systems, and Catholic Charities.

Diana Dudoit Raiche's chapter reflects on the Rite of Christian Initiation of Adults as a paradigm for theological education and ministerial formation. The emphasis in the RCIA on the integration of content and method provides a model drawn from the heart of the Church for overcoming debates regarding the relationship between theory and practice that have rankled much of theological education. She argues that the praxis-oriented model inherent in the RCIA process provides the key to integrating personal conversion to Christ with the desire to know, accept, and appropriate gospel values.

Maureen O'Brien surfaces the contributions that the broader field of religious education can make toward a practical theological approach to ministerial formation. In particular, it is at the borders—between disciplines, between cultures, between religious traditions—that some of the most important insights emerge. Those preparing for lay ecclesial ministry, which itself exists in a kind of "in-between" space, have much to learn by the "border crossing" practical theology encourages. At the same time, she challenges ministry formation providers to engage in interdisciplinary, intercultural, and interreligious pedagogical practices to foster these intellectual and cultural migrations.

Wayne Cavalier illustrates the importance of supervised ministry in the process of ministerial formation. He demonstrates how the praxis of supervised ministry can be particularly effective in facilitating the transformation of meaning—the conversion—undergone by new ministers. In particular, he focuses on adult learning theory, as developed by Jack Mezirow and others, to articulate the transformative and integrative power of field education experiences for those in ministerial formation. This process has the structure of a *community of practice* seeking *critical intersubjectivity*, which culminates in *reflection-in-action*.

In the conclusion, Nathaniel G. Samuel and Theodore Whapham briefly reflect on all these contributions in order to discuss developing trends in ministerial formation. They highlight issues related to diversity and access, interdisciplinarity, and crosscurrents to established norms in ministerial formation, and the need to foster greater trust and reconciliation within the Church. These issues provide both new challenges and opportunities for the work of ministerial formation that will help shape the future of this vital work.

Each chapter demonstrates the author's engagement and critique of various theoretical frameworks[8]—clerical, ecclesial, public, praxis—based on insights drawn from their own experience in lay ministry formation. Some essays, like Johnson's rereading of the *Co-Workers* document, focus on the ways that traditional doctrinal formations can be developed and refined in light of pastoral practice. Others, like O'Brien's and Cavalier's essays, show the significance of theoretical frameworks for pastoral practice. Therefore, the overall contribution of this volume is its specific focus on ministerial formation as the concrete site for doing practical theology.

Discussions in practical theological methodology have also given substantial attention to interdisciplinarity.[9] While philosophical and historical methods continue to be important theological conversation partners for the contributors to this volume, the following chapters reflect the tendency among practical theologians to engage the social sciences. Lamont's chapter on young adults engages directly with psychological and sociological research. Ebert's work on the *sensus fidei* draws on the field of social theory. Several authors engage educational research and theory. Thus, the volume as a whole reflects the broad engagement of practical theologians with the social sciences, as well as engaging explicitly theological sources.

Finally, each of the chapters in this volume reflects the current emphasis in practical theology on hermeneutics and context. Ospino's chapter on the challenge of intercultural ministry in the U.S. Catholic Church and davis's use of call and response dialectic in African American storytelling reflect the embeddedness of theological thinking and the richness of one's context for theological reflection. Raiche's chapter on the relationship between theory and practice is firmly located in her experience with the implementation of RCIA and the interplay between content and method in pedagogy. Above all, each of the contributions reflects a need to read "the signs of the times" and respond to our present challenges with the prophetic call of the gospel.

NOTES

1. National Conference of Catholic Bishops, "Called and Gifted: The American Catholic Laity, 1980," *Origins* 10.4 (November 27, 1980): 369–73, at 372.

2. See Edward P. Hahnenberg, *Theology for Ministry: An Introduction for Lay Ministers* (Collegeville, MN: Liturgical Press, 2014), 11–14; Robert J. Hater, *The Ministry Explosion: A New Awareness of*

Every Christian's Call to Minister (Dubuque, IA: Wm. C. Brown, 1979).

3. AGPIM, Meeting Minutes, 1992.

4. Friedrich Schleiermacher, *Brief Outline of Theology as a Field of Study*, 3rd ed., trans. Terrence Tice (Louisville: Westminster John Knox Press, 2011).

5. Kathleen A. Cahalan and Bryan Froehle, "A Developing Discipline: The Catholic Voice in Practical Theology," in *Invitation to Practical Theology: Catholic Voices and Visions*, ed. Claire E. Wolfteich (New York: Paulist Press, 2014), 27–51, at 37.

6. See Paulo Freire, *Pedagogy of the Oppressed*, trans. Myra Bergman Ramos (New York: Seabury, 1970); Daniel S. Schipani, *Religious Education Encounters Liberation Theology* (Birmingham, AL: Religious Education Press, 1988); Thomas H. Groome, *Sharing Faith: A Comprehensive Approach to Religious Education and Pastoral Ministry: The Way of Shared Praxis* (San Francisco: HarperSanFrancisco, 1991).

7. See "Introduction," in *Invitation to Practical Theology*, ed. Claire E. Wolfteich (New York: Paulist Press, 2014), 1–24, at 5–6. Wolfteich cites the critique of Edward Farley, *Theologia: The Fragmentation and Unity of Theological Education* (Philadelphia: Fortress Press, 1983).

8. Kathleen Cahalan, "Roman Catholic Pastoral Theology," in *Opening the Field of Practical Theology: An Introduction*, ed. Kathleen A. Cahalan and Gordon S. Mikoski (New York: Rowman & Littlefield, 2014), 217–32.

9. For a discussion of the interaction between theology and the social sciences, particularly as it relates to practical theology, see Richard H. Roberts, "Theology and the Social Sciences," in *The Modern Theologians: An Introduction to Christian Theology since 1918*, ed. David F. Ford with Rachael Muers (Oxford: Blackwell, 2005), 370–88.

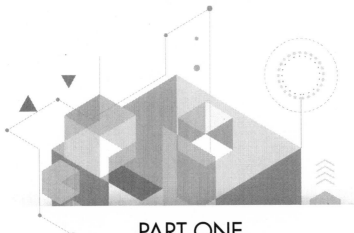

PART ONE

THE CONTEXTS OF MINISTERIAL FORMATION

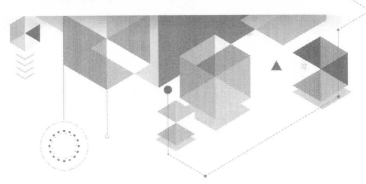

Chapter One

SERVING LAY ECCLESIAL MINISTRY PAST AND PRESENT

Thirty Years of Preparing Workers for the Vineyard

William H. Johnston

This chapter offers reflections on the history, identity, and future of the Association of Graduate Programs in Ministry (AGPIM). AGPIM is "an organization of educators, theologians and administrators representing Roman Catholic institutions that offer graduate programs in ministry."[1]

The first gathering of representatives of such U.S. institutions of higher learning took place in 1987 with thirty-nine attendees. Meetings have continued annually since then, offering participants the opportunity to

- Connect and confer with professional colleagues;
- Explore issues and questions of common concern;

- Stay informed about and actively contribute to emerging trends and resources in the field; and
- Celebrate ministerial developments in the postconciliar Church and the role of graduate education in service to those developments, with special attention to lay ecclesial ministry.[2]

AGPIM is one of the many national organizations formed in the years after Vatican II in response to initiatives arising from the Council's call for renewal of the Church. In particular, to implement the 1965 decree on the renewal of consecrated life, *Perfectae Caritatis*, religious communities sought to rediscover and embrace the distinctive charisms of their founders. They also sought to absorb the broad range of theological developments enshrined in the various conciliar documents, exploring their implications for the Church and its mission in the modern world, with special concern for their own updated role in that mission. This effort sent many religious men and women back to graduate school for retooling, to acquire the knowledge and skills needed to meet new priorities and enter new fields of endeavor. Laypersons soon joined them, eager to prepare and qualify for new or expanding opportunities opening for them in Catholic parishes, schools, and agencies. In response to this sign of the times and new educational market, many Catholic universities launched or enlarged their graduate-level theology and ministry programs in both the regular academic year and summer school. It was a thriving era for such programs.

In 1980, the U.S. Catholic bishops acknowledged these developments in *Called and Gifted*, their document marking the fifteenth anniversary of the Council's decree on the apostolate of the laity, *Apostolicam Actuositatem*. After thanking those laity serving the Church as "volunteers and part-time workers" in various capacities, the bishops then took note that "growing numbers of lay women and men are also preparing themselves professionally to work in the Church. In this regard, religious sisters and brothers have shown the way with their initiative and creativity."[3] The bishops used the term *ecclesial ministers* to designate "lay persons who have prepared for professional ministry in the Church," and welcomed this "new development" as "a gift to the Church."[4]

4

To understand better how these ministry professionals were being prepared for their roles, the Bishops' Committee on the Laity commissioned a study, with funding support from the Lilly Endowment. The result was *Preparing Laity for Ministry: A Report on the Progress in Catholic Dioceses throughout the United States* (1986) by Suzanne E. Elsesser and Eugene F. Hemrick. An outcome of this report—also made possible with support from the Lilly Endowment—was the first meeting of leaders of academic programs providing such preparation. They gathered at the Julie Penrose Center in Colorado Springs, February 25–27, 1987, with David Thomas (then of Regis College) and Robert Ludwig (then of the Loyola Institute for Ministry, Loyola University New Orleans) cofacilitating.

The thirty-nine attendees represented twenty-three academic institutions and four other formation providers, with observers from the Lilly Endowment and from the Raskob Foundation for Catholic Activities. One participant recalled the positive spirit pervading this gathering: "The sounds of laughter and conversations about dreams, concerns, and hopes were charged with enthusiasm and energy."[5]

When these new colleagues met, all of them engaged in or concerned about this distinctly postconciliar academic enterprise of graduate ministry education for laity, they shared their experiences, hopes, and challenges, and discussed a range of topics. Among these were the following, reflected in the detailed "Final Report" of that meeting:

Students: Who are the laypersons, women and men, enrolling in these graduate ministry programs? What academic and other relevant experience do they bring or lack; what are their distinct goals and needs, and in that light; and what admission criteria (including equivalencies) make sense?

Curriculum: Given what students are preparing for, what curricular content and educational methods are appropriate? What academic standards apply? What range of competencies do students need to develop and programs need to teach? What place should be given formational features such as mentoring, spiritual direction, or personal counseling?

External relations: How should these programs and faculty relate with the Church in their own dioceses and beyond? How can they best be of service to the Church and its mission and ministries? How is academic freedom to be protected?

Internal relations: How should these programs and faculty relate with others in the academy, such as to explain or even defend their work to those who "view professional education as a compromise," as "watered-down academic[s]" or even "a kind of 'side show'" to the real work of the university?[6]

Looking to the future, the participants decided on a name, defining themselves as an association of educational programs with a common mission. They set up a steering committee to organize future meetings and a research committee to gather data relevant to this new form of graduate education—data, for example, on students and graduates, financing procedures, competency requirements, and an inventory of programs. They also agreed they did not want a program of "outside speakers" at future meetings but simply the opportunity for "organizational reflection, interaction of participants, [and] collaboration, in order to generate research, share information, etc." Trusting in each other's experience and expertise, they wanted the "face-to-face collaboration of a homogenous group."[7]

Already at this first gathering, we can see features of AGPIM that have remained characteristic of the organization throughout its history. Let us consider six features, briefly describing each, with selected examples to illustrate.

AGPIM MEETINGS OFFER MUTUAL SUPPORT FOR COLLABORATIVE COLLEAGUES

A defining feature of AGPIM is the positive spirit of support and understanding experienced in gathering with true disciplinary colleagues. While those who attend the meetings may have much in common with departmental colleagues at their home institutions who teach students in *theology* degree programs, as many AGPIM attendees do as well, there are other and distinctive responsibilities they share with those who teach students in *ministry* degree programs. These responsibilities include shaping curricular components and providing academic and career advising designed for that particular student population with their particular formational needs and vocational aspirations. Because of that shared distinctive work, AGPIM attendees feel themselves to be with colleagues who genuinely understand their unique work.[8] They are "insiders" to each other, constituting in effect a distinct professional guild or "community of practice."[9]

The sentiment was well expressed in the 1987 meeting minutes, which described an opening session of "personal introductions," with participants sharing what kept them going and gave them joy in their work. This created "a certain sense of solidarity in a shared ministry," forming the basis for subsequent discussion of "common concerns." As the minutes noted, the "opportunity to listen to one another in the management and stewardship of institutionally based programs of pastoral preparation for lay ministry was a precious moment for providers," and has become a regular feature of the Association's opening session.[10]

What is especially noteworthy here—and this applies both to the culture of the Association as a whole and the character of its annual meetings—is the spirit of collaboration rather than competition. While some ministry students enroll in the AGPIM program closest to home, others may apply to multiple member schools, in effect putting programs in competition with each other. Nonetheless, AGPIM meetings are characterized by open sharing of information and practices, offered to colleagues in a spirit of mutual helpfulness and collaboration in a common and valued cause to which all are committed.[11] This is truly a "precious" feature of the meetings, an enduring characteristic to recognize, honor, and maintain.

AGPIM ATTENDEES GATHER TO EDUCATE THEMSELVES

Those who work in Catholic academic graduate ministry programs for laity attend AGPIM meetings to learn how to do what they do better, exploring various dimensions of the role, including the theological, spiritual, pedagogical, sociological, and administrative.[12] For the first fifteen or so years, meetings were mostly resourced internally. One regular feature of the schedule was time for "interest groups," allowing time for those with concern for a particular topic to share how they handle it, exploring together how to do so more effectively. Topics over the years included accreditation, admissions, assessment, the bishops' *mandatum*, competencies, curriculum content and outcomes, diversity, the ecumenical dimension, finances, marketing, pastoral administration, pedagogical method, practical theology, recruitment, and spiritual formation.

Meetings also had general sessions on topics of shared interest led by regular AGPIM participants. In 1990, for example, while affirming that ministry students need both "general [theological] knowledge" and skills for "specialization" in ministry, Bernard Lee proposed "the method of praxis" as the distinctive "emerging educational method for ministry education," contrasting "Practical Theology with Classical Western Theology…(praxis vs. theory)." He highlighted four "moments" in the process of practical theology: knowing the tradition (Scripture, Church history) with critical reflective understanding; acquiring skills to probe our present context (social analysis); cultivating the ability to put the two in "disciplined conversation"; leading to the concrete practice of ministry (historical agency).[13]

In 1995, Joseph Merkt addressed the "Current Challenge of Professionalization in Ministry," discussing the emergence of competency standards in national ministry organizations. Participants then developed a SWOT analysis regarding the potential of this trend for graduate ministry education.[14] The following year, Merkt presented "A Proposal for a Listing of Common Competencies for Ecclesial Ministry," the initial fruit of the mammoth task he and Margaret Cooper had undertaken to synthesize over a thousand competencies for different ministerial positions into the workable format of a manageable number of common and specialized competencies—a format that structured the National Certification Standards for Lay Ecclesial Ministers approved by the United States Conference of Catholic Bishops (USCCB) Commission on Certification and Accreditation in 2011.[15]

The meeting in 2002 offered participants "An Academic Retreat: Inventing Catholic Pastoral Traditions for This Decade." Terence Tilley's presentation on "Inventing Catholic Tradition" was followed by a panel discussion including Tilley, as well as Bishop Patrick Zurek and Bonnie Abadie of the Diocese of San Antonio, the site of the meeting that year.[16] After a series of outside presenters, addressing the changing signs of the times, the 2016 meeting marked a return to this earlier format with presentations by Brett Hoover and Marian Díaz on "Ministry Formation for a Multicultural Church," along with workshops by local presenters, again in San Antonio. A new meeting format was used for the 2018 meeting. After a vetting process, selected attendees presented prepared papers on the state of practical theology and ministry education, distributed beforehand and discussed in small groups.

As years went along, planners brought in outside presenters who brought much-needed information and challenges. H. Richard McCord of the Secretariat for Family, Laity, Women and Youth of the National Conference of Catholic Bishops (NCCB) was the first, who in 1992 presented findings of the soon-to-be-published study by the National Pastoral Life Center (NPLC), *New Parish Ministers: Laity and Religious on Parish Staffs.*[17] In subsequent years, experts were invited to address various topics deemed relevant. For example, "participants received a cultural immersion through presentations by staff of the Mexican American Cultural Center (MACC) and a field trip to sites in San Antonio" in 1998.[18] In 2006, Robert Kinast led participants in "Theological Reflection on Our Experiences as Ministry Educators." And most annual meetings in this past decade were resourced by outside presenters with a range of expertise.[19] These titles and topics represent a sample of the many concerns studied in various ways by AGPIM attendees through the years in an attempt to stay informed on critical issues and new developments relevant to lay ministry formation.

AGPIM CONDUCTS RESEARCH CONCERNING MINISTRY AND MINISTRY EDUCATION

Conducting research to better understand the new phenomenon of the postconciliar graduate education of laity for church ministry was a major focus of energy and attention. The collection of survey data prior to the first meeting in 1987 and establishment at that meeting of a research committee set the stage for what was to follow.

The most extensive research effort was a multiyear project in the early 1990s, funded by a $159,000 grant from the Lilly Endowment. The three-part project was to

(1) Gather data on lay ministry formation programs,
(2) Study the students in those programs, and
(3) Host a national ministry conference.

All three project components were successfully completed through the labors of task forces devoted to each. Fulfilling (1) was the resource prepared by Charles Topper and others, *A Survey of Graduate Programs in Ministry 1992–1993* (1993). Fulfilling (2) was Barbara J. Fleischer's *Ministers of the Future: A Study of Graduate Ministry Students in Catholic Colleges and Universities* (1993). And fulfilling (3) was the 1993 conference in San Antonio, "Ministry Educators in Conversation: What Kind of Future?"[20]

Another major funding request to the Lilly Endowment in the first years of the twenty-first century proved unsuccessful.[21] However, AGPIM's research activities were ongoing regardless, with regular surveys on programs and students. In 1995, attendees "supported the continuation of the research" and called for the survey format "to be revised and updated every five years. Tom Walters and Geri Telepak will work on the revision and submit a proposed timeline. Monies were set aside for continuation of the research."[22] Five years later, participants approved a motion "to redo both AGPIM studies," demonstrating an ongoing interest in maintaining current data.[23] Meeting minutes also reflect concern to correlate AGPIM program survey results with the data on ministry formation programs collected annually by the Center for

Applied Research in the Apostolate (CARA), a challenging task as survey questions differed.[24]

On some occasions, survey results gathered by others were reported at the annual meeting. For example, in addition to McCord's report on the 1992 NPLC Life Center data, in 1997 Ana Villamil presented the results of the survey associated with the Bishops' Conference "ecclesial lay ministry project" funded by the Lilly Endowment. In 2002, Amy Hoey reported the findings of a "Spiritual Formation Survey."[25]

It was also customary for several years to collect prior to annual meetings, data relevant to the topic of that year's meeting. For example, a survey gathered information about "theological formation" with "questions focused specifically on aspects of *Co-Workers*," in preparation for a 2007 meeting on "Intellectual Transformation for Ministry."[26] In such ways as these, research continued with some consistency through the first twenty or twenty-five years, reflecting AGPIM's conviction that sound planning must be well informed by factual and up-to-date information.

AGPIM CULTIVATES CONNECTIONS WITH OTHER ORGANIZATIONS ENGAGED IN RELATED WORK

At the end of the 1992 meeting, McCord "thanked the group for allowing him to participate" and contribute, the first person not representing an AGPIM member to do so. The group in turn "expressed their appreciation for his input," and it was then "suggested that on occasion we have other guests as liaisons with other related organizations."[27] Within a few years, from that simple beginning arose the regular practice of devoting meeting time to reports from and conversation with representatives of other organizations. In 1997, for example, this included the National Catholic Educational Association, the United States Catholic Conference, the National Federation for Catholic Youth Ministry (NFCYM), and the National Association for Lay Ministry (NALM).[28] In 2000, AGPIM reached out to several organizations, in particular the Association of Catholic Colleges and Universities (ACCU), which responded by inviting AGPIM to make a presentation at the ACCU's meeting in 2001.[29] In 2006, the Emerging Models of Pastoral Leadership Project, an initiative of six ministry associations funded by the Lilly Endowment, made a presentation on its national study of pastoral leadership.

In recent years, three connections stand out. The first is the Association of Jesuit Colleges and Universities (AJCU), which holds its annual gathering in tandem with AGPIM (same place and overlapping dates, with AJCU members participating in both meetings). The second is the National Association of Catholic Chaplains (NACC), whose executive director, David A. Lichter, has regularly attended AGPIM meetings to keep participants well informed about the ministry of chaplaincy as a potential vocation for AGPIM institutions' students. And third, staff members of the USCCB were regular attendees.

Of these three organizational connections, the longest and arguably most consequential has been with U.S. Bishops' Conference staff engaged in promoting lay ministry, including H. Richard McCord, Ana Villamil, Amy Hoey, Harry Dudley, and Marc DelMonico, with meeting attendance beginning in 1992 and continuing most years from 1997 to the present. Of particular note is a pivotal ten years beginning in the later 1990s: information shared from the bishops' staff and consultation offered by AGPIM participants contributed to development of the document that became *Co-Workers in the Vineyard of the Lord: A Resource for Guiding the Development of Lay Ecclesial Ministry*.[30] Attention to the interpretation and implementation of the document continued for several years after its 2005 publication. AGPIM was further engaged in the reception of *Co-Workers* as one of many cosponsors of the 2007 National Symposium on Lay Ecclesial Ministry, organized and hosted by Saint John's School of Theology and Seminary in Collegeville, Minnesota.[31]

These examples show AGPIM's intentional steps to work on "affiliation/conversation with other organizations,"[32] out of a recognition that many organizations have a general interest or active role to play in supporting the development of lay ecclesial ministry, and a conviction that communication and coordination among such organizations can serve the efficiency and quality of their respective and collective efforts.

FROM TIME TO TIME, AGPIM CONSIDERS ADVOCACY AND HOW TO VENTURE TOWARD IT

Whether and how to be an advocacy organization for issues pertaining to the education or careers of lay ecclesial ministers or for the merits of practical or pastoral theology as an educational paradigm has periodically been one of AGPIM's concerns, though never a defining characteristic. In the first five years, participants worked to develop a self-definition of the Association, and the "Mission Statement" formulated in 1990 stated that "on occasion, [AGPIM] provides an advocacy voice addressing larger contextual issues for ministry."[33] One such issue raised in the first meeting was the challenge laypersons face both in funding their own graduate education for ministry and in living on what they earn in a ministerial workplace.[34] Advocacy regarding such financial concerns was affirmed as part of AGPIM's mission in its 1992 position statement.

Such was the intention, yet future minutes do not indicate any sustained advocacy planning or efforts or report any advocacy results on this issue. This is not surprising as AGPIM then had a collective presence and voice only at annual gatherings, supplemented since the mid-1990s with its website. The same is true today. AGPIM executive committee members volunteer in that capacity while simultaneously serving as full-time faculty or administrators at their own academic institutions. They customarily meet as a committee only once outside the annual meeting, otherwise working via email and conference calls, and their main task is not advocacy but planning and coordinating the annual meeting. Potential for advocacy, then, depends on meeting attendees taking individual action during the year, but experience shows they find their regular responsibilities at home necessarily take precedence over pursuing AGPIM agendas.

Thus, AGPIM's advocacy has never gained real traction on finances or other topics, whether with bishops or academic colleagues. The main exception is the consultation and input provided to USCCB staff during the development of *Co-Workers*, already noted, when AGPIM urged the bishops not simply to assume the familiar model of clerical formation (seminary) adequate for forming laity for ministry, but rather to take account of their characteristically lay circumstances.[35] In a sense, however, this represents the exception that proves the rule. The 2002 executive committee at its summer meeting posed the question, "To what extent are we [participating] in AGPIM for networking and fellowship vs. lobbying/advocacy?"[36] The question may surface from time to time, but the answer, to judge by AGPIM's actions, is clearly more the former than the latter.

PERIODICALLY, AGPIM RECONSIDERS ITS IDENTITY AND PURPOSE

The process of self-definition began early in AGPIM's history. Based on survey data and discussion topics at prior meetings, those gathered in 1990 decided to prepare statements addressing three areas of concern. Task groups worked on each statement, bringing drafts to the whole assembly for discussion, leading to further revisions—an ongoing process over the course of three annual meetings. The resulting position statement was approved February 23, 1992.[37]

The first section offered a working definition of "practical or pastoral theology."[38] In comparison with, but also distinct from, the educational aims and methods of theology degree programs, AGPIM colleagues saw themselves forging "a new theological paradigm" in the academy.[39] Shaped by the needs of students seeking "graduate education for ministry," this new method was necessarily both theological and practical, and integrally both at once, each dimension contributing to the other, the practical not diluting but enriching the theological, the theological not peripheral but integral to the practical.

These priorities are reflected in AGPIM's definition of practical theology.[40] Beyond the emphasis on the conversation between the Christian tradition and contemporary experience cited in the definition, AGPIM understands practical theology as inherently a social enterprise. "Pastoral or practical theology takes place in a community of faith, implies a spirituality that is both personal and liturgical, and is directed toward individual and social transformation in Christ."[41] This communal aspect of the definition of practical theology thus speaks to the identity of AGPIM and the theological method that helps to determine it.

Second, Catholic graduate schools were not the only site of ministry formation for laity; many dioceses as well, and a few independent agencies, were developing their own certificate ministry formation programs. Aware of the attraction of such programs (as less costly and time-intensive for participants), AGPIM's Position Statement asserted the value and benefits of graduate academic education for those with leadership responsibility in ministry, citing these reasons:

1. Graduate programs in ministry provide a level of preparation that society rightly expects of professionals in all fields.
2. Graduate programs in ministry, with their access to the resources of higher education, provide an especially fitting context for ministry preparation.
3. Graduate programs foster in-depth development of students for professional growth in ministry and provide for the long-term health and mission of the larger ecclesial community.
4. These graduate programs in ministry meet or exceed standards developed by appropriate national accrediting agencies.

In the final section, AGPIM sought to advocate for better financial compensation for laity serving in ministry by stating its conviction that

1. Members of the Church have a right to be served by qualified ministers (CL, 57, 63).
2. Qualified ministers have a right to just compensation and procedures in return for a responsible exercise of ministry (Canon 231.2 and "Economic Justice for All," 351).
3. The Catholic Church, for various historical and cultural reasons, is in a situation where these rights are often not realized in practice.

4. Financial constraints and systemic complexities make changes difficult. However, failure to remedy this situation has long-term destructive effects on Catholic life.
5. The mission of AGPIM includes advocating and facilitating systemic change in this situation.

A quarter century after first formulating this three-part statement, its contents arguably remain relevant for ongoing circumstances: explaining the nature and legitimacy of pastoral or practical theology in the academy; urging the value of graduate academic education for ministry in a Church still willing to accommodate alternate standards for ministers; and advocating for a living or family wage for all in lay ecclesial ministry.

Twice in past years, AGPIM participants conducted a SWOT analysis, identifying organizational strengths, weaknesses, opportunities, and threats. The first occasion was in the mid-1990s, to aid in discerning and assessing the place of competencies in graduate ministerial education. The second occupied the Association from 2002 to 2004, informing a strategic planning process at a time some saw as "a major change generationally" in the Church, the academy, and the Association, forty years after Vatican II began and fifteen years after AGPIM's founding.[42] The 2002 meeting generated nineteen pages of SWOT data. That summer the data was synthesized by the executive committee into a one-page summary, and subsequently reformulated into ten possible "strategic themes" that were distributed beforehand to those attending the 2003 meeting.[43] Their votes (scale of 1 to 10) yielded these top three priorities:[44]

1. Promote dialogue, support, and collaboration among member schools;
2. Sustain dialogue and collaboration between member schools and Roman Catholic ecclesial leaders; and
3. Sustain conversations and collaboration regarding the spiritual formation of pastoral ministers.

That 2003 meeting consisted of a two-day "Strategic Planning and Theological Reflection" exercise, led by Gene A. Scapanski

16

(then dean of the School of Continuing Studies, University of St. Thomas, St. Paul, Minnesota), to process the information and plan for the future. Implementation of the three priorities seems to have focused mainly on the first two: on the first by means of activities such as those described in the first three sections of this chapter, and the second by means of ongoing connection and consultation with USCCB staff at AGPIM annual meetings.

CONCLUSION

The annual gatherings of AGPIM institution faculty and administrators have served them well over the years, providing the occasion to cultivate relationships with colleagues from academic programs around the country, explore issues of common concern, share information about programs and practices, and increase their knowledge and sharpen their skills to serve the students they form for ministry. The occasion of AGPIM's thirtieth anniversary prompted efforts to take stock of the Association's history and achievements and plot its future direction and priorities. In a brief exercise in reading the signs of the times, this essay concludes by considering the context of that future, using the five categories identified in our analysis of the 1987 AGPIM meeting and adding one more: faculty.

1. **Students**: What kinds of ecclesial ministers does the Church need today and are AGPIM programs forming them? What kinds of students are now enrolling in graduate ministry programs and how are AGPIM programs serving them? While today's young adult lay Catholics with a heart for ministry may agree on certain fundamentals, they have also heard and are following distinct vocational calls. As an indicator, a recent study of college campus ministers named one goal they all share, then counseled recognition of differences among the students they serve: "The formation and transformation of the student through an encounter with Jesus is the goal of many, if not all, campus ministers. It is important to recognize that

some students find conversion in devotional practices, while others experience conversion through service."[45]

This observation also describes the range of young adults drawn to ministry today: some transformed by experiences of service, looking to highlight "service/charitable work" and "social justice/advocacy" in their ministry; others transformed by devotional practices, looking in their ministry to promote "personal holiness and a personal, 'vertical' relationship with God."[46] The contrast can be overdrawn but "these differences in ministerial type or pastoral style" are nonetheless real. While these styles may sometimes be viewed as in "competition," the challenge for AGPIM institutions is to avoid that trap and instead help both kinds of students feel genuinely welcome.[47] They can do this by affirming equally their respective vocational calls and supporting their ministerial aims, while helping each appreciate the legitimacy of the other. Ways need to be sought to actively recognize and explore how "the strengths of each pastoral style fill the gaps of the other style."[48] What rethinking might this invite among AGPIM-institution administrators and faculty?

2. **Faculty**: Recognizing legitimacy in these distinct pastoral styles calls for intentionally cultivated appreciative attitudes and breadth of perspective on the part of faculty, from the most senior, who came of age in the era of Vatican II and are now nearing retirement, to the most junior generation Y and millennial scholars newly commencing their academic careers. Melanie Morey cautioned about a trait she has observed in some theologians and their *ars docendi*: "We have the tendency," she said in an interview, "to pass on our complaints about the tradition more forcefully than we pass on the tradition."[49] She urged, if and where this applies, that faculty instead be willing to let students know something of their own journey of faith, sharing "who they are as people of faith—who are,

in fact, integrating faith and reason in their own personal intellectual lives."[50]

How clearly do AGPIM students learn from watching their instructors that they need to cultivate and maintain both "the methodological rigor which is part and parcel of the business of scholarship," as well as an active "inner participation in the organic structure of the Church" with "that faith which is prayer, contemplation and life"?[51] How readily do faculty—as part of their professional role—model and communicate to students the way they themselves make the "spiritual effort to grow in virtue and holiness" that is proper to theologians?[52]

3. **Curriculum**: *Co-Workers in the Vineyard of the Lord* outlined a comprehensive curriculum for lay ecclesial ministers with detailed guidelines for human, spiritual, intellectual, and pastoral formation. It may be time to review that curriculum after fifteen years of usage, with discerning attention to the needs of the Church, society, and ministry students today. Also relevant here are the current ministerial standards, competencies, and indicators of the Alliance for the Certification of Lay Ecclesial Ministers, the Catholic Campus Ministry Association, and the NACC.[53] Is this a project for an AGPIM research team?

4. **Finances**: The first AGPIM gathering in 1987 discussed the challenge laypersons confront in financing their graduate education for ministry, and in 2015, McCord again identified this as a continuing problem, in particular now for young prospective lay ecclesial ministers already carrying significant undergraduate educational debt while anticipating modest salaries in ministry.[54] Academic institutions may offer some graduate assistantships or tuition discounts, some dioceses have limited funds for matching grants, some parishes have generous pastors, but a reliable system of support is neither in place nor in development. This remains an ongoing issue in search of an effective solution.

5. **External Relations**: Two broad theological movements took shape after the Council, commonly named for the publications associated with each—a "Concilium" movement emphasizing progressive development of conciliar reforms, and a "Communio" movement emphasizing the continuity of those reforms with tradition. The Church has room for both approaches, even if various theologians more comfortably associate with one or the other. Are there similarly two broad philosophies of theological and ministerial education—one we might name a "Land O'Lakes" philosophy emphasizing theological study pursued with academic freedom from direct ecclesial control, the other an *Ex Corde Ecclesiae* philosophy emphasizing academic freedom in fidelity to Church teaching and authority? Both values are defensible[55] and, I contend, compatible, but different Catholic theological and ministerial formation programs may identify more with one or the other. Questions for discernment then arise. Which approach will better serve the pastoral needs of the Church today, meet the formational desires of ministry students, and fulfill the hiring criteria of the priests and bishops who will employ those students? Is there potential and even need for a third way that embraces both philosophies without compromising either, embodying the strengths of both and unleashing their latent synergy? Are AGPIM schools and programs able and willing to forge that third way?

6. **Internal relations**: Whether professional education in general or graduate ministry formation in particular are any better understood and valued in the academy and in departments of theology and religious studies than in 1987, AGPIM's working definition of "practical or pastoral theology" formulated in 1992 is a valuable point of reference worth revisiting and developing. Examining the elements of that definition phrase by phrase, probing their foundations, unpacking and developing their implications, filling

in discerned lacunae, and doing so with the spirit and aspirational goals articulated in this concluding section will be a helpful exercise. It will allow AGPIM to review that definition's adequacy and update its formulation, renewing its relevance and usefulness for today and the future. It will inspire AGPIM faculty and administrators to recommit to its vision, invigorating their teaching, research, advising, and curriculum development. The resulting program clarity, pedagogical method, and student formation will demonstrate in both church and academy the value of the "theological paradigm" of pastoral or practical theology thus conceived and practiced.

I hope these concluding reflections and suggestions may prove to be useful. Most if not all can be pursued in the context of AGPIM's 2019 strategic plan and its four priorities: promoting research and publication; fostering strategic partnerships and relationships; strengthening AGPIM as an association; and advancing the vision and mission of *Co-Workers*.

The Center for Applied Research in the Apostolate has called lay ecclesial ministry "A Backbone of Today's U.S. Church," affirming the need for "the best possible academic preparation and personal formation" for those serving in that ministry.[56] AGPIM institutions have played a key role in promoting the quality of such academic programs for more than thirty years. It is imperative they continue to do so with an adaptive, creative, faith-filled response to a renewed reading of the signs of the times.

NOTES

1. From the AGPIM website, https://www.graduatepro gramsinministry.org/ (accessed July 1, 2019). Note that this body is an association of graduate *programs*. AGPIM members are academic programs and institutions. This essay refers to the persons from those institutions who attend the meetings as "attendees," "participants," or "colleagues," not as AGPIM "members."

2. This history draws on minutes of annual meetings where available, as well as on the following sources: The AGPIM Executive

Committee invited former president and longtime participant Thomas P. Walters to write a brief history of the Association, and in 2017 he completed "Association of Graduate Programs in Ministry: Celebrating 30 Years." A work informed by his own perspectives and that of many who participated in the Association over the years, it is a valuable resource for the study of AGPIM's history. So also is "Harvesting Living Memories," the paper presented at the 2018 meeting by Eilish Ryan, who has attended every meeting from 1987 up to the present. Marti Jewell's "An Unexpected Confluence: AGPIM, Accreditation, and Ministry Standards," also presented at the 2018 meeting, is a chapter in this volume. A "Brief History" of AGPIM meetings from 1987 to 2010 can be found in the member's section of the Association's website. For the 2017 meeting, I prepared a presentation reviewing the prior thirty meetings titled "Association of Graduate Programs in Ministry Celebrating 30 Years, 1987–2017."

3. CG 6 ("volunteers") and 7 ("growing numbers").

4. CG 7.

5. Eilish Ryan, "Harvesting Living Memories," unpublished conference paper (2018 AGPIM meeting), 2.

6. AGPIM, *1987 Final Report*, 7.

7. AGPIM, *1987 Final Report*, 14.

8. In the words of Gary Pokorny, then at St. Francis Seminary in Milwaukee, "AGPIM was the community within which I first discovered others who shared similar concerns, experience and perspective." Ryan, "Harvesting," 6.

9. Barbara J. Fleischer applied to AGPIM Margaret J. Wheatley's concept of community of practice. Ryan, "Harvesting," 12. See, e.g., Wheatley, *Finding Our Way: Leadership for an Uncertain Time* (San Francisco: Barrett-Koehler Publishers, 2005), at 171–78.

10. *1987 Final Report*, 1 (emphasis in original).

11. Ryan's paper cites many former participants expressing this sentiment. Joseph Merkt, e.g., described "the warm greeting, the cordial relating, the honest and open sharing" that moved him deeply; Ryan, "Harvesting," 7. Of AGPIM meetings in the 1990s Maureen O'Brien wrote, "I recall honesty and sometimes differences being aired in struggling to come to consensus on the meaning and sources for practical/pastoral theology. Always, though, mutual support and common purpose were the guiding

sensibilities"; Ryan, "Harvesting," 8. See also Ryan, "Harvesting," 11, and Walters, "Celebrating 30 Years," 10–11.

12. Maureen O'Brien described the organization's concerns in the early years: "The focus was on coming to common understandings of what constituted foundational curricula for graduate ministry education, financial support for lay graduate students, the nature of practical/pastoral theology, and compiling information as an association regarding our common efforts"; Walters, "Celebrating 30 Years," 4.

13. 1990 "Minutes," 1.

14. 1995 "Minutes," 2–3. Marti Jewell explains the background and significance of the "debate" on the use of competencies this year between Merkt and Lee, respectively pro and con; see in this volume "An Unexpected Confluence," p. 42–43. See also Ryan, "Harvesting," 9. The first mention in AGPIM minutes of competency standards for ministry dates from 1987, at 2 (the third bullet point under 2.1.2).

15. See NCS, at https://lemcertification.org/page/LEM Standards. Merkt continued to consult with AGPIM regarding the ongoing work of developing the common competencies; see, e.g., 2001 "Minutes," 2–3. For an account of the development of the competency standards, see Joseph T. Merkt, ed., *Common Formation Goals for Ministry* (NALM, NFCYM, NCCL, 2000).

16. "A Brief History," 5. Tilley had recently published *Inventing Catholic Tradition* (Maryknoll, NY: Orbis, 2000).

17. By Philip J. Murnion with David DeLambo (NPLC, 1992).

18. "A Brief History," 4.

19. 2010, six guest panelists, "Reimagining the Vineyard: Ministry and Education for Today and Tomorrow"; 2011, Edward P. Hahnenberg, "The Ecology of Calling: The Role of Community in Vocation and Discernment," following publication of his *Awakening Vocation: A Theology of Christian Call* (Collegeville, MN: Liturgical Press, 2010); 2012, Richard Rohr, "Landscape of Leadership: Formation for Transformation"; 2013, Robert J. Schreiter, "A New Creation: Ministry as Reconciliation"; 2014, Kathleen A. Cahalan, "Integration in Theological Education"; 2015, Thomas Rosica, Sebastian Gomes and Teresita Gonzales, "'The Francis Effect,' the Church, and Ministry Education"; 2017, Edward Foley, "Context, Reflection, and Integration in Ministerial Education Today"; 2019,

Anna Floerke Scheid, "Public Theology in the Service of Dialogue amidst Polarization."

20. Walters, "Celebrating 30 Years," 5n8; minutes of the meetings from 1989 to 1994; "Brief History," 2–3.

21. See minutes of the meetings in 2000 (2), 2001 (1–2), and 2002 (5).

22. 1995 "Minutes," 1.

23. 2000 "Minutes," 2.

24. See, e.g., the 2007 "Minutes," 1.

25. 1997 "Minutes," 1 (Villamil); 2002 "Minutes," 4 (Hoey).

26. 2007 "Minutes," 1; cf. *Co-Workers*, 42–46. More broadly, "A Brief History" (7) reports participants that year "discussed survey findings focusing on the current and future preparation of Catholic lay ministers, particularly related to admissions criteria, theological literacy, applied learning models, and core curriculum."

27. 1992 "Minutes," 13.

28. 1997 "Minutes," 9–10.

29. The 2000 "Minutes," 2, record a call for "proactive efforts to be AGPIM voice with CTSA and other organizations." In 2001, AGPIM's president, Maureen O'Brien, reported that, "as directed by the membership last year, a letter was sent to Monika Hellwig at ACCU, with copies to CTSA, CTS, and the Canon Law Society. Monika Hellwig replied for ACCU, inviting AGPIM officers to lead a breakout session at their January meeting. Maureen and [past president] Bernard Lee did so and distributed AGPIM information"; 2001 "Minutes," 3.

30. Ryan writes that "Amy Hoey, Project Coordinator for the USCCB's subcommittee on Lay Ministry from 1996–2006, remarked that she was 'grateful for the honest, faithful spirit of the dialogues' at AGPIM during the years of the development of *Co-Workers*"; "Harvesting," 12.

31. This event was developed "in cooperation with the USCCB Secretariat for Family, Laity, Women and Youth, the USCCB Committee on Hispanic Affairs, and fifteen co-sponsoring and collaborating organizations"; see the Symposium web site at https://www.csbsju.edu/sot/lifelong-learning/lay-ecclesial-ministry/2007-national-symposium-on-lay-ecclesial-ministry.

32. 2001 "Minutes," 3.

33. 1990 "Minutes," 5.

34. E.g., one school reported turning away thirty to forty applicants "because of an inability to pay tuition costs" (AGPIM, *1987 Final Report*, 6), and a small group addressing financial challenges discussed the dilemma of prospective students deterred from graduate education for ministry "because of high tuition costs and low pay-back job opportunities" (AGPIM, *1987 Final Report*, 8). In 1990, attendees agreed AGPIM needed to be an "advocate for just wages for pastoral ministers" (1990 "Minutes," 2), and adopted a resolution "to consult with colleagues at home regarding advocacy for justice for lay ministers" (AGPIM, *1990 Minutes*, 5). It is of interest to note that in 2015 Richard McCord still identified finances as a continuing problem, in particular for young lay ecclesial ministers who may carry significant educational debt while earning low salaries in ministry; for the comment and his recommendation, see McCord's address, "*Co-Workers in the Vineyard of the Lord*—Ten Years Later: What Do We Have to Celebrate?" given in reception of St. John's "Wisdom and Service Award" and available at https://www.csbsju.edu/Documents/SOT/Events/Co-Workers/Rick%20McCord%20Keynote--May%202015.pdf (accessed September 3, 2018), 6.

35. The AGPIM executive committee "Minutes" of 2002, 4, reflect concern that the bishops "are simply working out of [the] clerical culture that they know," and that without AGPIM advocacy they "will replicate that Priestly Formation document for LEMs."

36. August 2002 Executive Committee "Minutes," 5.

37. 1992 "Minutes," 15 (an addendum to the minutes; the vote approving the statement is recorded on page 11).

38. Recall Bernard Lee's 1990 presentation on "the method of praxis" stated above.

39. Aware of the disregard in which professional education could be held, AGPIM colleagues wanted here a "clear statement" for use "within the academy" to affirm "the validity of practical theology," demonstrating it was not "'soft theology'"; 1991 "Minutes," 3.

40. AGPIM, Meeting Minutes, 1992. This definition is quoted in full in the introduction to this volume.

41. AGPIM, Meeting Minutes, 1992.

42. August 2002 Executive Committee "Minutes," 4 ("a major change generationally").

43. August 2002 Executive Committee "Minutes," 6–7 (summary). Greg Sobolewski, letter of January 31, 2003 ("strategic themes").

44. "AGPIM's Themes for Strategic Planning 2003," dated January 20, 2003. Themes four through ten received scores from 5.33 to 8.33.

45. "A National Study on Catholic Campus Ministry 2017: A Report Prepared for the United States Conference of Catholic Bishops Secretariat of Catholic Education," by Brian Stark and Maureen K. Day (Washington, DC: USCCB, 2018), 15. Available at http://www.usccb.org/beliefs-and-teachings/how-we-teach/ catholic-education/campus-ministry/upload/A-National-Study -on-Catholic-Campus-Ministry.pdf.

46. Stark and Day, "*Study on Catholic Campus Ministry*," 10.

47. Stark and Day, "*Study on Catholic Campus Ministry*," 9.

48. Stark and Day, "*Study on Catholic Campus Ministry*," 9.

49. Richard Byrne, "A Researcher Sees 'Room in the Middle,'" *Chronicle of Higher Education* 54, no. 31 (April 11, 2008): A12. (Morey coauthored, with John J. Piderit, *Catholic Higher Education: A Culture in Crisis* [New York: Oxford University Press, 2006].) Regarding tradition and young adults, is there any merit in this alternative, more recent, journalistic perspective? "As the Catholic Church continues to work to keep people in and attract people to the faith, it would do well to remember that the pull of tradition can be an attractive one, even or perhaps especially for the millennial generation, which is famously interested in old things, from record collecting to jarring pickles. If evangelical and 'next generation' worship have been, in part, about making church cool, ironically, there is nothing cooler than a first edition, and the Catholic Church is about as vintage as you can get." Anna Keating, "Why Evangelical Megachurches Are Embracing (Some) Catholic Traditions," *America* online, May 2, 2019, at https:// www.americamagazine.org/faith/2019/05/02/why-evangelical -megachurches-are-embracing-some-catholic-traditions (accessed May 5, 2019).

50. Byrne, "A Researcher Sees 'Room in the Middle,'" A12.

51. Joseph Ratzinger, "On the 'Instruction Concerning the Ecclesial Vocation of the Theologian,'" in his *The Nature and Mission of Theology* (San Francisco: Ignatius Press, 1995), 101–20, at 105.

52. Congregation for the Doctrine of the Faith, *Instruction on the Ecclesial Vocation of the Theologian* (1990), no. 9.

53. For the Alliance, see the web address in note 15. For the CCMA, see https://www.ccmanetwork.org/natstandards. For the NACC, see https://www.nacc.org/certification/.

54. See McCord, *"Co-Workers in the Vineyard of the Lord*—Ten Years Later," 6.

55. E.g., see John I. Jenkins, "Land O'Lakes 50 Years On," *America* 217, no. 2 (July 24, 2017): 28–35. Jenkins, the current president of the University of Notre Dame, offers a reading of the 1967 document that situates its often-cited claim of "true autonomy and academic freedom in the face of authority of whatever kind, lay or clerical, external to the academic community itself" (30) in the context of the full statement whose provisions as a whole, says Jenkins, describe "a university whose Catholicism is pervasively present at the heart of its central activities" (32). See also Neil Ormerod, "Mission Driven and Identity Shaped: *Ex Corde Ecclesiae* Revisited," *Irish Theological Quarterly* 78, no. 4 (2013): 325–37, arguing "that the broader vision of *Ex corde ecclesiae*, in terms of identity, mission, and culture, remains relevant and is still a challenge for Catholic universities" (325, from the article's abstract).

56. "Lay Ecclesial Ministry: A Backbone of Today's U.S. Church," *The CARA Report* 23, no. 1 (Summer 2017): 1 and 11, at 1.

Chapter Two

AN UNEXPECTED CONFLUENCE

AGPIM and the Development of Accreditation and Ministry Standards

Marti R. Jewell

We have learned, though perhaps are no wiser for that learning, that the number of people enrolling in seminaries and graduate theological programs increases, often significantly, following a war. Such was the case after World War I, when, in quick succession, three entities supporting ministry education came into existence, all eventually involved with the accreditation of theological programs in Catholic colleges and universities. The year 1917 saw the advent of the National Catholic War Council, later to become the United States Conference of Catholic Bishops (USCCB), founded to address issues of immigration, education, lay organizations, and social action in the aftermath of World War I. Next came the Association of Theological Schools (ATS), founded in 1918 under the title of the American Association of Graduate Schools. Its members hoped to bring overwhelmed and struggling theological schools into conversation.[1]

A year later, in 1919, the precursors of national and regional accrediting agencies began collecting data on academic programs. Each of these entities became involved with accreditation and ministry standards as they addressed the need to provide well-formed persons for ministry. Throughout the twentieth century they worked with seminaries and colleges in developing programs in response to this ebb and flow of need for persons in ministry, a need dictated by unexpected forces.

By the 1980s, the Catholic Church saw one such response in the arrival of nonordained persons—lay and religious— ministering in Catholic parishes, persons who needed formal ministerial education. Catholic colleges took up the call to offer lay ministry programs, although some professors and clergy opposed the idea of laity studying theology.[2] The idea of preparing students for ministry, but not ordination, challenged long-held assumptions about pedagogy, ecclesiology, and ministry, even as these new practitioners began enrolling in everything from master of divinity degrees to diocesan certificate programs. Education, however, was not the only challenge. These same practitioners had begun forming national lay ministry organizations that felt called to develop standards for the professionalization of ministry. Colleges had to deal with these ministry standards at the same time as they needed to find a way for these programs to meet the standards of regional accrediting agencies. To address this growing reality, professors from Catholic colleges and universities began meeting in 1987, forming the Association for Graduate Programs in Ministry (AGPIM).[3] Everything was in place for the tumultuous, creative events in the 1990s, when we see the confluence of three significant, synchronous developments that together would affect the future of theological education and ministry formation. Three very different groups crossed paths: accreditors, ministry practitioners, and academics. Academics struggled to understand best practices for theological and pastoral curricula, turning to and developing the new discipline of practical or pastoral theology.

Needing to meet new demands for accreditation, Catholic seminaries and college theology programs turned to the Association of Theological Schools (ATS). Seminaries began combining with Catholic colleges to get the needed accreditation, which meant that they also had to meet the standards of regional accrediting bodies. Looking for ways to increase their ability to conduct peer reviews, accrediting bodies were developing new standards looking to the new field of outcomes-based competencies for guidance.

As for the practitioners, with the need for professionalization in their work increasing, lay ministers began developing competency-based ministry standards, in collaboration with the U.S. Bishops' accrediting body, all in a changing parish context. The Notre Dame Study of Catholic Parish Life, published in the late 1980s, was the first national study of parishes and noted great change in parish life.[4] At the same time, the National Pastoral Life Center began studying the growing phenomenon of lay ministry in parishes. In 1992, the Center's director, Philip Murnion, along with sociologist David DeLambo published a study noting a virtual revolution in how ministry functions in the United States, with laity gaining positions of influence and leadership in parish ministry.[5] In 1995, these three initiatives came together as AGPIM members were treated to a debate, by all accounts memorable, on theological education and the use of ministry standards in graduate programs in ministry. Decisions made because of this debate would prove crucial for the development of national lay ministry standards, and consequently critical for education and accreditation.

This chapter will look at three questions: (1) to whom are graduate ministry programs accountable—accreditation; (2) to what do they hold themselves accountable—competency-based standards; and (3) how do they provide competency-based theological education—practical theology. To understand the evolution of these questions, we will look at the historical development of these three areas and the significant role the Association for Graduate Programs in Ministry played in this development. As we shall see, today's competency-based ministry education and practical theology are the result of the courage, foresight, questions, and decisions made by early AGPIM members. But to get there, we must begin with the development of the three initiatives.

ACCREDITATION

The practice of accreditation, put in motion after World War I, was developed by the United States Catholic Conference (USCC), ATS, and regional accrediting bodies. As these bodies developed through the early twentieth century, they would once again be impacted by war, this time World War II. During the war, the U.S. military establishment needed many certified military chaplains who could both minister and lead on the battlefield. Considering this high demand, the effort to ensure individual certification of chaplains became unmanageable. The military decided it would be sufficient to demonstrate graduation from an accredited Clinical Pastoral Education (CPE) program, rather than proving individual certification.[6] This decision posed a problem for Catholics serving in the military. Catholic seminaries did not have CPE programs and were not regionally accredited. The only accredited CPE programs were in Protestant seminaries. U.S. Bishops found themselves facing some difficult decisions. To ensure the presence of Catholic chaplains, would they outsource training to Protestant seminaries? Did they need to find ways for Catholic seminaries to become accredited? Something had to happen. The need for Catholic chaplains had to be met.

In order to receive accreditation, Catholic seminaries would have to join the larger academic order.[7] Consequently, bishops looking for ways to provide Catholic CPE programs created the National Association of Catholic Chaplains (NACC) in 1965.[8] Designed to oversee both the certification of chaplains and the accreditation of CPE programs, this association was housed in the National Conference of Catholic Bishops/United States Catholic Conference (NCCB/USCC) under the oversight of a board of examiners, all bishops. Recognized in 1969 by the U.S. Department of Education (USDOE), the USCC had become an official certifying agency.[9] Soon twenty Roman Catholic organizations had established CPE programs, first through the Catholic health care system, followed by CPE programs in Catholic seminaries, all accredited by the Board of Examiners. This arrangement worked well until, once again, the U.S. government intervened with a decision that proved challenging to the Bishops' ability to maintain an accrediting agency. The USDOE decided that if a chaplain was sued for malpractice, not only was the chaplain liable, so too were the program he graduated from *and* the program's accrediting agency. What had seemed a viable solution for accreditation and certification, now had the potential of becoming a serious financial and legal problem. To both retain recognition by the USDOE and resolve liability issues, the Bishops moved to create a separately incorporated legal entity, which would exist outside of the Bishops' conference. The USCC's secretary general, Thomas Kelly, OP, first orchestrated the movement of NACC out of the Bishops' conference.

In 1986, after intense negotiating between the NACC Board of Trustees and the Board of Examiners, Kelly led the effort to create a legally separate entity, the United States Catholic Conference/Commission on Certification and Accreditation (USCC/CCA). Recognized as the official agent of the Bishops for the certification of persons in specialized ministries and accreditation of training programs, the new Commission was housed in St. Louis with the Catholic Hospital Association. They received USDOE recognition as an accrediting agency in 1987, the same year AGPIM was founded. As part of recognition, the USDOE required seating practitioners, as well as bishops, on the Commission's certifying bodies and boards. In meeting this requirement, the Catholic Conference decided that only one bishop would sit on the board of the new commission, leaving the other seats open to lay and ordained practitioners. The lay ministers nominated to these bodies recognized the importance of accreditation and certification and saw the need to develop their own standards. They then pushed the Commission to look at developing standards for nonordained ministry and diocesan lay ministry certificate programs. And in 1993, national lay ministry organizations began bringing ministry certification standards to the Commission, standards that would become critical for the accreditation of graduate programs in ministry.

The Bishops were accrediting CPE programs, but what about accreditation for graduate ministry degrees? Prior to 1980, Catholic seminaries held accreditation from pontifical institutes, primarily from the Catholic University of America. Otherwise isolated from academia, they were unable to meet the requirements for accreditation, and so looked to another certifying body for theological education, the Association of Theological Schools (ATS). Although ATS had thus far only worked with Protestant schools, they welcomed the interest and membership of Catholic seminaries, a membership that required schools and seminaries to meet ATS accreditation requirements.

This, of course, meant that Catholic and Protestant seminaries would be working together, which was not a problem until Catholic member schools underwent papal seminary visitations in the mid-1980s. After visiting each Catholic seminary in the United States, Vatican congregations made a series of demands regarding curricula. Interference with academic freedom, a high value for all graduate schools, became a significant concern for ATS members. To deal with a potential conflict, and in order to ensure full authority to set its own standards, ATS decided its standards would base accreditation of programs on how each program met the *standards set by the denomination* of the seminary or university. The task of deciding what constituted academic freedom would belong to the denomination alone. This decision led to a review and redevelopment of the ATS standards in the early 1990s, conducted by a committee made up of practitioners and academics, chaired by Dr. Katarina Schuth, OSF. This ensured accreditation where these standards were met, but was it enough? What about regional accreditation?

Some seminaries, in an attempt to acquire accreditation, had begun merging with universities such as Seton Hall, St. John's (Collegeville, MN), and St. Paul's—all schools needing regional accreditation. For the first time, lay and ordained ministry candidates studied side by side, earning similar degrees and meeting similar academic standards. These universities, however, to be regionally accredited, needed standards for their graduate programs. ATS had made sure its revised standards aligned with those of the regional accrediting bodies, which had worked successfully for Protestant theology schools and would now be of use to Catholic schools.[10] But who was setting and reviewing denomination-specific standards for Catholic schools? The fact that Catholic programs being accredited by ATS, the CCA, *and* regional accrediting agencies needed denomination-specific standards made the standards conversation critically important to AGPIM schools who were looking for help in working with accrediting bodies.[11]

NATIONAL COMPETENCY-BASED MINISTRY STANDARDS

Quietly and without fanfare, alongside these developments in accreditation, lay ministers began forming national ministry organizations. The National Conference of Diocesan Directors (NCCD), begun in 1967, later to become the National Conference of Catechetical Leaders (NCCL), focused on the developing role of religious education ministers. The National Association for Lay Ministry (NALM) started as a gathering of diocesan lay ministry formation practitioners in 1976. And the National Federation for Catholic Youth Ministry (NFCYM) formed in 1981, after its parent organization, the National Catholic Youth Organization Federation, better known as CYO, was moved out of the Bishops' conference, ostensibly for financial reasons. Privately however, the USCC staff, under the leadership of General Secretary Kelly arranged this carefully calculated displacement to wrest control of lay ministry from a faction of bishops who actively opposed this burgeoning movement. Thus assured of their independence, these national organizations were now in a position to provide the practitioners required for the board of directors of the newly formed CCA. Since at this time standards only existed for chaplaincy programs, it was to these three national organizations the Commission turned.

When pastoral ministers received the call to begin drafting standards in the early 1990s, they had no idea what was to come.[12] In 1982, the NCCD Board conducted a survey of U.S. dioceses and discovered that many had developed content standards for catechist formation, especially in Scripture and theology, but no formation methodology. Following consultation with its members, NCCD published its first set of ministry competencies for directors of religious education in 1985, competencies that assumed graduate level education. In 1993, the CCA invited NCCD to develop certification standards (sets of competencies) for parish directors of religious education for approval by the CCA. After a decade of consultations with its own members and with the Commission, NCCD (now called NCCL) received approval for its standards in 1996. Youth ministry leaders in NFCYM created a subcommittee on leadership development and, working with the CCA, developed a list of competencies for youth ministers. In 1990, after extensive consultation with its membership, NFCYM became the first national lay ministry organization to have its competencies approved by the Commission.

That same year NALM began drafting its competencies. A regional group of NALM members, having been instructed by Dr. Margaret Early, SSSF, on the use of competency-based outcomes and assessments, began teasing out the knowledge and skills needed by pastoral associates and parish life coordinators.[13] Two of the drafters, Dr. Ruth Eileen Dwyer, SP, and Dr. Joseph Merkt, both among the cofounders of AGPIM, would soon play pivotal roles in the development of standards. The task was daunting but, armed with little more than the early drafts of the NFCYM competencies, they began to develop a list, one competency at a time, along with indicators of what those would look like in practice. Their competencies were approved by the CCA in 1995. In this same year, the U.S. Bishops promulgated *Called and Gifted for the Third Millennium,* which acknowledged lay ministry and called the Church to commit the resources needed for the development of laity for professional church ministry.[14] The CCA began accrediting diocesan ministry formation programs, and before the end of the decade the U.S. Bishops would acknowledge the use and significance of standards in their 1999 document, *Lay Ecclesial Ministry: The State of the Question.* The authors of this document stated, "The attempt to create competency certification standards...for lay ministers in parish-level positions is still relatively new....The movement and energy are almost entirely 'bottom up' phenomena. As is the case with other aspects of lay ministry, this is an example of a field gradually structuring itself....As such, this is a major movement of self-definition and accountability."[15] First one, then three, then five national organizations developed standards for their particular ministries. The National Association of Pastoral Musicians and the Federation of Diocesan Liturgical Commissions had joined the conversation. The lists of common or shared competencies, compiled by Dr. Merkt, morphed into an arrangement of five sets of core and specialized standards: personal, pastoral, spiritual, intellectual, and professional. The three national organizations came together to create these standards, which would represent the particularities of different ministries. This collaboration proved contentious and hard-fought, but the belief that standards were necessary for lay ecclesial ministry, which at this point had no direction from the Bishops, was enough to keep drafters at the table.

In 2003, with the approval of the CCA, the three ministry organizations published the first joint set of national certification standards for lay ministry. The 2011 revision dropped the professional standard, retaining the pastoral, spiritual, intellectual, and pastoral in order to align with standards for priestly and diaconal formation, which are based in four dimensions of formation.

The unexpected partner and catalyst in the development of standards? AGPIM! The growing field of lay ministry needed well-educated persons to take on new roles in parishes and dioceses, and turned to Catholic colleges to provide graduates in theological education. By now the revised Code of Canon Law had given laity the ability to study the sacred sciences (CIC 218) and required that all ministers be properly formed. In 1987, the year of the Synod on the Laity, a number of these professors met in Denver to share thoughts and challenges. Energized by the exchange, they decided to meet annually. Their agenda: addressing questions related to curricula for graduate programs in lay ministry and the emerging call for outcomes-based programming with its implications for both accreditation and academic freedom. Members of the newly formed AGPIM were standing on the brink of paradigmatic shifts in both ministry and theological education. Parishes having solely ordained ministers were giving way to ministry by laity, as well as by clergy, while theological education moved from solely research-based curricula to pastoral programs needed for training ministry professionals. Even the Vatican joined this conversation by issuing a 1992 apostolic exhortation on the formation of priests, *Pastores Dabo Vobis,* challenging seminaries to rethink their educational models.[16]

So, while ministry practitioners were writing competencies as a gold standard for ministry, academics were looking for ways to express and live out the newly developing paradigm of ministry education. Not used to academic or accreditation language, practitioners had made the fortuitous decision to write competencies in a knowledge and indicator format that, it turns out, aligned well with the movement toward the outcomes-based approach required by regional accrediting agencies. But how to incorporate the new competencies? Even the CCA, used to working with standards, was confused by sets of competencies, which contained no processes or procedures for their implementation.

Driven by the necessity to get the standards needed for accreditation, AGPIM schools set the goal for their graduate programs in ministry to meet or exceed standards set by ATS and nationally recognized accrediting bodies. To learn more about ministry standards, AGPIM invited the director of the CCA and representatives of the national lay ministry organizations to speak at their meetings. Those first presentations surfaced large questions about the use of competencies and their consequences for universities, for relationships with dioceses, and for the question that always loomed large: Would they provide an opportunity for the bishops who approved them to impede academic freedom? AGPIM created a committee to study these concerns. In a 1993 membership letter, Drs. Bernard Lee, Barbara Fleischer, and Charles Topper wrote, "AGPIM recognizes that while the familiar structures of ministry and leadership in the United States are being transformed or, in some instances disappearing, there is no coordination at the national level of the many entities engaging in the education and formation of lay ministers and leaders moving into the structure."[17] These disparate movements were unfolding without any strategic planning, coordination, or collaboration, but with an amazing synchronicity. Could AGPIM provide this coordination? Having been introduced to the lay ministry competencies by representatives of the national organizations, AGPIM's executive committee asked Dr. Joseph Merkt, also a member of NALM, to make a presentation on the current challenges of professionalization in ministry. Naming issues affecting AGPIM schools, such as standards, accreditation, assessments, and liability, Merkt reminded members that both ATS and regional accrediting bodies were moving toward outcomes-based education, and urged AGPIM to work with the national organizations in developing needed competency-based standards.

One of the questions confronting members was this: If AGPIM schools worked with the newly approved competencies, would they have to reconsider theological methodology? More than this, members wanted to know if standards would compromise systematic theology itself and were concerned about control of their programs. As for the standards themselves, competencies were being approved with no assessment or behavioral indicators on which to base assessments. Institutional questions surfaced. Would competency standards affect teaching in a traditional theology classroom? Need to be divided between academic and pastoral courses? Hurt pedagogical creativity? Curtail freedom to explore knowledge for its own sake? Academic freedom itself? Meeting standards set by others was associated with unwelcome "outsider" requirements, such as those imposed by regional accreditation agencies.

Then there was the question about entanglement with the local bishop. AGPIM's concern about inappropriate bishop involvement went so deep that they had rejected an offer from the National Catholic Education Association to become one of its departments. These concerns were not unfounded. The question of bishop involvement had not previously arisen, as theological education previously done in Catholic seminaries was thought to be an ecclesial task.[18] Seminaries formed priests.[19] They had a unique relationship with bishops. But the Vatican visitations in the 1980s had surfaced significant implications for the conversation on academic freedom, as attested to by ATS, and now universities came to share these concerns as they began preparing laypeople for ministry.

Catholic colleges in the United States had a carefully held autonomy, thanks to the visions of their founders, as well as U.S. legal requirements protecting academic freedom. As we have seen, ATS very carefully threaded this needle for their relationship with Catholic seminaries. Catholic universities looked to *Ex Corde Ecclesiae*, Pope John Paul II's "Apostolic Constitution on Catholic Universities."[20] Promulgated in 1990 and resting on Canon 218 of the 1983 Code of Canon Law, *Ex Corde* clearly stated that every Catholic university, and every scholar in these universities (including theologians), was guaranteed academic freedom "so long as the rights of the individual person and of the community are preserved within the confines of the truth and the common good."[21] How should AGPIM respond? They had not missed the unexpected opportunities surfacing. Standards could provide curriculum planning guidance and assistance with regional accreditation. This was an opportunity for academics to begin to identify their role in the conversation, both internally and nationally. Members had a sense that this might serve as a bridge between academia and the world of ministry.

After lengthy discussion, AGPIM decided to use their next meeting to work toward an agreement on whether or not they would approve the standards and their role in developing competent graduates. Drs. Bernard Lee and Joseph Merkt, apparently at odds on the topic, would lead the conversation. Dr. Lee was against any imposed standardization of ministry formation. Dr. Merkt believed standards, rather than limiting, could be foundational in the preparation of lay ministers. The stage was set for the "debate" between Merkt and Lee, but there was yet another player in this "perfect storm" moment. Accreditation and standards not only had to reconcile with each other. They also had to be viewed in light of the developing conversation about theological education for ministry and the growing tension between those teaching theology as a scientific discipline and those teaching theology for professional pastoral practice.

THEOLOGICAL EDUCATION FOR MINISTRY

From its inception, AGPIM had been a significant player in developing theological and pedagogical paradigms, which address the pastoral life of the Church. According to Maureen O'Brien, an early president of AGPIM, "In the early years, the focus was on coming to common understandings of what constituted foundational curricula for graduate ministry education...and the nature of practical or pastoral theology.[22] The 1992 mission statement recognized practical theology as the discipline having the best potential for their ministry degrees, and they began to explore the emerging discipline.

AGPIM professors were excited about the possibilities for theological scholarship coming from Vatican II with its recognition that there is a pastoral discourse in which "pastoral" meant both resting on doctrinal principles *and* seeking to express the relation of the Church to the people of today.[23] The understanding of a well-prepared minister was no longer that of the one who knows theology, but rather as the one who knows how to work with people...*theologically*. Realizing classical theological education was not working for the preparation of professional ministers, ministry programs began parsing the difference between seminary-style training and university curricula. But what might this be saying about the relationship between the high scientific standards in theology and its pastoral aim? At stake was the very heart of the pastoral nature of theology (PDV 55).[24]

These discussions were taking place in a world that had begun to see U.S. seminaries as isolated from academia, with theological education effectively sealed off from general educational developments.[25] Needing to reframe curriculum in light of accreditation requirements, some seminaries and universities, especially those operated by religious orders, adopted professional degrees such as the master of divinity in place of the *Ratio Studiorum* (a manualist approach) in an effort to improve their academic quality and integrity.[26] But were these changes effective? To assist AGPIM schools with this question, the Lilly Endowment awarded the fledgling association a grant to conduct research on the educational goal, as well as on the perceived knowledge and skills of incoming and graduating students in member institutions. Published in 1994, the study reported that pastorally centered graduate programs, and not traditional theology-centered programs, were becoming more the norm for professional ministerial preparation.[27] The years that followed saw the rigorous development of practical theology as a discipline. While this movement is complex, its development and how the new standards impacted this discipline bear mention here.

One of those addressing these concerns, theologian Edward Foley, wrote about learning to integrate *phronesis* (professional intelligence) and prudence (practical wisdom).[28] In the early

Church, training for ministry, such as it was, had the goal of producing wise and virtuous men who could act in any situation. In the patristic era people were still chosen for "gentlemanly" qualities, but by AD 375 a preference for those better educated had surfaced.[29] The goal was nurturing educated people, as well as wise. There was little ministerial education through the Middle Ages until finally called for by the Council of Trent, at which time it became framed by the Thomistic or Scholastic manuals.

Enter the now famously named "Athens-Berlin Debate."[30] Theologian David Kelsey, in exploring the changing nature of ministry formation, described the "Athens" model of ministry formation as one of developing a wisdom figure who could then interpret the world through a theological lens.[31] Also called *paidia*, this model placed importance on forming a virtuous and ethical person, who would then be able to provide leadership. In use since the first century, this model would proffer St. Ambrose of Milan, long praised for his wise and pastoral leadership, as a good example. The "Berlin" model, the clerical paradigm emerging in the early nineteenth century, called for an intellectual grasp of theology that could be applied to ministry. Here ministerial formation gave way to theological education, moving from the cultivation of wisdom to developing reason, logic, and science. It was not until the twentieth century that these were combined into a professional education model, which provided both the liberal and pastoral arts, one that challenged theological educators who believed the classical liberal arts education could not be measured.[32]

By the late twentieth century, this conversation had become one of pedagogy and outcomes. According to Farley, "If theology's primary meaning is scholarly knowledge and its preoccupation with text interpretation and doctrinal exposition, the result will be to ignore religion's actual practices."[33] Rather, he believed, "theology concerns the wisdom by which one brings the resources of a religious education to bear on the world."[34] Clearly Farley is calling for something more, but how would this dovetail with the use of standards? AGPIM, following this line of thinking, recognized the emergence of practical theology as a new theological discipline. It set out its vision of this discipline as a mutually interpretive, critical and transforming conversation between the Christian tradition and contemporary experience. Historical, hermeneutical, and sociocultural analyses are integral to this method of theology, which is understood to take place in a community of faith. It implies a spirituality that is both personal and liturgical, and is directed toward individual and social transformation in Christ.[35]

But now they were faced with a new challenge. How would the introduction of ministry standards influence their rigorous commitment to practical theology? Well, that was quite a conversation!

THE DEBATE

The stage was set for AGPIM's 1995 meeting. Drs. Joseph Merkt and Bernard Lee were to present opposing sides of the issue of using competency-based standards in the classroom. The well-known Dr. Lee held strongly to a more traditional teaching approach that favored the professor as mentor. Dr. Merkt had the unenviable task of introducing a significant change in how ministry classrooms would be structured. When he first introduced competencies to AGPIM members, Lee had strongly opposed them—not from a theoretical or theological standpoint—but from a pedagogical one.

At that time, Lee was deeply influenced by a recently published book, *Back to the Rough Ground*.[36] The author, Joseph Dunne, an educator of future teachers, was disturbed by a new movement in the field of education toward a behavioral-standards model. Today we call this outcomes-based education. Working from an intuition that something was going to be lost in using this new pedagogy, Dunne investigated the nature of preparing a person for a profession by going back to the basics. After a deep exploration of five philosophers and housing his findings in Aristotelian language, he concluded that students need *techne*: the knowledge and skills for their profession. But even if they could reproduce these with mastery, that would not, in and of itself, make them good at their profession. They also needed *phronesis,* what we would call the art of ministry: the ability to know when and how to do ministry and the right context in which to use this knowledge; the recognition that much ministry is relational, calling for high emotional intelligence; and the development of good practice based on the authenticity of the minister (Dunne's "teacher").[37] His conclusion? Teaching knowledge is not enough. Learning a systematic body of knowledge is necessary but the understanding and judgment of the practitioner is critical to ensuring success.[38] This is the mindset Dr. Lee brought to the conversation, speaking for those who felt the use of the standards would cause a more mechanical pedagogy, rather than the Athens apprenticeship model: forming the artist.

Speaking for proponents of competency-based learning, Dr. Merkt countered that the standards were not about methodology, but rather presupposed that students would be formed by the spiritual and theological standards, and receive mentoring for the practical pieces. Starting from insights garnered while working with practitioners, Merkt asked whether or not ministry formation is more like the formation of an apprentice by a master artist or more the formation of a "technical person," who is taught in a trade school, where education includes both the theoretical knowledge needed for the discipline and the practical skills to make the mechanics of ministry work. This was the Athens-Berlin debate, writ for lay ministry students. Neither side had fully embraced the emerging practical theology model, but both faced the same practical challenges: working in a changing landscape, while concerned about academic freedom and the impact of bishop-approved standards. In the end, decisions made at this meeting proved to be critical to the ongoing development of national ministry standards, graduate ministry programs, and their accreditation.

THE REST OF THE STORY

Following the debate, AGPIM decided the standards had merit and that it could play a moderating role in the national conversation. Members wanted to be clear that in encouraging their further development, the standards would need to be understood in the light of practical theology. AGPIM then made a decision pivotal to the development of ministry standards. It tasked Merkt, with the assistance of Dr. Margaret Cooper, with conducting an intensive reading of the nearly two thousand individual ministry competencies developed by the national organizations, categorizing them, and organizing them into groups of common and specialized competencies. This work took well over a year to complete. Once the newly designated "common competencies" were collated, AGPIM asked Lee and Merkt to form a subcommittee that would look at these "common" competencies, critique them, and then make recommendations to the national organizations. It was this recognition of common or shared competencies that opened the door to what was to follow.

Next, AGPIM sent representatives to a gathering of national organizations called together to look at the new set of common competencies. Those present included NALM, NFCYM, NCCL, NACC, and permanent deacons from the USCCB, joined by the CCA. Discussing the now-familiar issues, attendees expressed hope that having standards would provide a tool against the movement toward a narrow orthodoxy and recognized the importance of assessment. The concerns discussed included ethical use of standards, legalism, and clericalism; the need to be sensitive to academic realities; concern about assessments turning poetic and prophetic elements into technical and adversarial roles; and episcopal resistance. At the conclusion of this meeting, the three national ministry associations agreed to publish jointly the newly devised common competencies, the work to be edited by Merkt and Cooper, and requested AGPIM's seal of approval. *Common Formation Goals for Ministry*, consisting of competencies identified by NALM, NFCYM, and NCCL, was published in 2000. In the introduction, the editors spoke of ministry as an art, which honored the values of personal growth and ministerial identity, theological education, and development of professional skills.[39]

An AGPIM subcommittee, in reviewing the work of Merkt and Cooper, concluded that member schools would be well served by AGPIM approving the common competencies, which could assist schools in receiving regional and ATS accreditation, and would reflect AGPIM's commitment to practical theology. Acknowledging the importance of respecting the ownership of the standards by the national organizations, AGPIM endorsed the development of lay ministry standards.

At the same time these conversations were happening, the Bishops' Office on Laity, Marriage, Family Life, and Youth set up a subcommittee to study the growing reality of lay ministry. In 1995, it hosted an invitational meeting on the preparation of lay ministers, inviting representatives from AGPIM. In 1998, AGPIM published the following statement: "Accrediting agencies are expecting graduate programs to have clearly defined competency-based outcomes for their ministry studies curricula. The ability of an individual school to draw on nationally recognized standards could be of help in their negotiation with the accrediting agencies."[40] In 1999, the Bishops endorsed the Laity Subcommittee's document, *The State of the Question*, which recognized the importance of standards. AGPIM produced a white paper in 2000. And in 2003, the CCA approved the *National Certification Standards for Lay Ecclesial Ministers*, which outlined five ministerial standards for all lay ministers based on the core competencies and providing a solid framework for developing or reviewing education and formation programs.

This grassroots effort opened the door to the Bishops conducting a ten-year nationwide consultation on formation for lay ministry, directed by Amy Hoey, RSM. This study concluded in 2005 with the USCCB's promulgation of *Co-Workers in the Vineyard of the Lord: A Guide for Formation*. As the consultation proceeded, significant questions surfaced about the nature of lay ecclesial ministry and what would be proper for their education and formation. The document weighed in on the question of the nationalization of standards, relying heavily on the CCA-approved national ministry standards and stating, "There is no intention to establish national standards or a single uniform policy, but rather to present goals and guidance."[41] Within six years, the 2011 *Revised National Certification Standards* stated, "Certification standards give evidence of a profession's focus and activities and the values to which it is committed; designate the knowledge, skills, and attitudes it deems desirable or necessary for effective functioning as a practitioner of the profession; and may be used as educational criteria in a process of formation and assessment criteria in a process of certification."[42]

Today, AGPIM members remain active in this conversation, advising those tasked with the next required revision of the standards. The national ministry organizations have created the *Alliance for Certification of Lay Ecclesial Ministry*,[43] a national certification program for lay ecclesial ministers. After reviewing the role of the CCA, the USCCB determined there was no longer a need for a separately incorporated accrediting agency and closed the Commission in 2011. In its place, the USCCB created the Subcommittee on Certification for Ecclesial Ministry and Service, housed in the Bishops' education committee. The USCCB now solely approves certification standards and procedures for certification. It no longer accredits programs. And thus far, bishops have not curtailed academic freedom because of the standards.

CONCLUSION

In compiling this short but intense history of the development of lay ministry standards and their use for theological education and practical theology, what surfaced is the existence of a community of people—academics, practitioners, and accreditors—who care very much about the preparation of persons for ministry. Some may know each other or about each other, but mostly they have worked on their own, each doing what they can to aid this endeavor. Perhaps in the end this is the greatest learning. We owe a great debt of gratitude to the many men and women whose dedication and commitment paved the way for a competent and qualified lay ministry. Rather than putting up boundaries and barriers, we would all do well to discover who else is in this community and work together with all, which leads to a second learning. There are unexpected partners and allies if we are willing to look for them. Impetus for forward movement may come from somewhere totally unanticipated.

AGPIM can be proud of its significant, pivotal, and largely unknown role in the development of competency-based ministry standards. Member schools now have standards that can be used for regional and ATS accreditation, and many colleges and universities have aligned their programs with the standards. AGPIM members have proven their ability to be a national liaison in the world of lay ministry and lay ministry formation.

The conversation, however, is far from over. We have seen the demise of many diocesan lay ministry programs, as well as graduate programs in ministry, even as the number of lay ecclesial ministers serving U.S. parishes continues to soar, now nearing fifty thousand. There continue to be those who seem to hold an assumption that lay ecclesial ministry is administrative rather than pastoral, diminishing the vocational and leadership roles of laity, and undermining the right of the faithful to educated ministers. There is continued animosity, at least in some universities, between those teaching scientific theology and those offering pastoral ministry degrees. *Co-Workers* is now more than a decade old, and even though bishop-approved competency-based standards are up for reaccreditation, they have been assigned to the Bishops' educational committee, rather than to the vocations committee, which handles formation programs for priests and permanent deacons.

As the Church evolves into the twenty-first century, with all that that implies, we must continue to look for ways in which ministers, both lay and ordained, can best meet the needs of the contemporary church. This history was written from the perspective of AGPIM. Other histories will be written from the vantage point of the national organizations or the USCCB. Whatever the perspective, we need to take a step back and recognize there were synchronous events that came together to create a new and much-needed approach to ministry education. What we have collectively created is outcomes-based education with competency-based curricula, rooted in practical theology as the needed discipline for ministry preparation. Each of us brings something unique and important to the table. However, we are better together than we are apart. And when the confluence surfaces, and we are willing to discover what happens when it does, then we can begin to focus on what matters most—forming persons for ministry who will, in the words of theologian Ilia Delio, "let go of the past and engage the future, because the future is upon us."[44]

NOTES

1. Glenn T. Miller, *A Community of Conversation: A Retrospective of the Association of Theological Schools and Ninety Years of North American Theological Education* (Pittsburgh: The Association of Theological Schools, 2008), 2.

2. Miller, *Community of Conversation*, 26.

3. AGPIM members are Catholic colleges and universities that offer degrees in ministry or pastoral theology to lay students.

4. Joseph Gremillion et. al., *Notre Dame Study of Catholic Life* (University of Notre Dame, 1989).

5. Philip J. Murnion, *New Parish Ministers: Laity and Religious on Parish Staffs* (New York: National Pastoral Life Center, 1992), 11.

6. Miller, *Community of Conversation*, 7.

7. Miller, *Community of Conversation*, 10.

8. Because this chapter is based on oral history from interviews, meeting minutes, and association histories, there were occasionally some minor disagreements on dates and sequence of events. What follows are the author's best estimate of these facts based on multiple sources.

9. "40th Anniversary, (2005) NACC History: 1965–2005," accessed October 15, 2017, https://www.nacc.org/about-nacc/history/40th-anniversary-2005/.

10. For more on this, see Miller, *A Community of Conversation.*

11. AGPIM Meeting Minutes, 1998.

12. Countless numbers of people nationwide were involved in the development of standards and accreditation, and their subsequent revisions. I am especially grateful to the following for taking time to be interviewed for this history: Katarina Schuth, OSF, for ATS; Charlotte McCorquodale for NFCYM; Jean Marie Weber for NCCL and the CCA; and Joseph Merkt for AGPIM. I am contributing my own memories for NALM.

13. Parish life coordinators were understood to be those who are assigned to administer a parish under Canon 517.2.

14. USCCB, *Called and Gifted for the Third Millennium* (Washington, DC: USCC, 1995).

15. USCC, *Lay Ecclesial Ministry: The State of the Questions: A Report of the Subcommittee on Lay Ministry* (Washington, DC: USCC, 1999), 35.

16. John Paul II, Apostolic Exhortation, "On the Formation of Priests in the Circumstances of the Present Day," *Pastores Dabo Vobis*, 1992, nos. 58, 61, accessed August 14, 2018, http://w2.vatican.va/content/john-paul-ii/en/apost_exhortations/documents/hf_jp-ii_exh_25031992_pastores-dabo-vobis.html.

17. AGPIM membership letter, 1993.

18. Robert J. Wister, "Theological Education in Seminaries," in *Theological Education in the Catholic Tradition: Contemporary Challenges* (New York: Crossroads, 1997), 158.

19. Wister, "Theological Education in Seminaries," 158.

20. John Paul II, Apostolic Constitution of the Supreme Pontiff, John Paul II, on Catholic Universities, *Ex Corde Ecclessiae*, 1990.

21. *Ex Corde*, nos. 12, 29.

22. Maureen O'Brien, quoted by Eilish Ryan in "Celebrating Thirty Years," membership meeting, February 2018.

23. Kathleen A. Cahalan, "Roman Catholic Pastoral Theology," in *Opening the Field of Practical Theology*, ed. Kathleen A. Cahalan and Gordon S. Mikoski (Lanham, MD: Rowen & Littlefield, 2014), 220.

24. *Pastores Dabo Vobis*, no. 55.

25. Cahalan, "Roman Catholic Pastoral Theology," 218; Phillip Gleason, "Catholic Higher Education as Historical Context for Theological Education," in *Theological Education in the Catholic Tradition: Contemporary Challenges*, ed. Patrick W. Carey and Earl C. Muller (New York: Crossroads Publishing Company, 1997), 24.

26. Cahalan, *Opening the Field*, 221. See GS, preface n1.

27. Bernard J. Lee, Barbara Fleischer, and Charles Topper, "A Same and Different Future: A Study of Graduate Ministry in Education in Catholic Institutions of Higher Learning in the United States," Executive Summary, Funded by the Lilly Endowment granted to the Loyola Institute for Ministry, for the Association of Graduate Programs in Ministry (1994), 12.

28. Edward Foley, "Practical Theology: Oxymoron or Method for Ministerial Studies," paper presented at the AGPIM 2017 meeting.

29. Bernard Cooke, "Ministry Formation: Historical Precedents," in *Ministry Educators in Conversation: What Kind of Future?*, Proceedings of the Invitational Conference, San Antonio, TX (1993), 4.

30. See David Kelsey, *Between Athens and Berlin* (Grand Rapids: Eerdmans Publishing, 1993).

31. Craig L. Neesan, "Mission and Theological Education—Berlin to Athens, and Tanquebar: A North American Perspective," *Mission Studies* 27 (2010): 177.

32. Daniel O. Aleshire, "The Emerging Model of Theological Formation," *Theological Education* 51, no. 2 (2018): 35; Phillip Gleason, *Catholic Higher Education*, 25.

33. Edward Farley, "Four Pedagogical Mistakes: A Mea Culpa," *Teaching Theology and Religion* 8, no. 4 (2005): 200.

34. Christian Century Staff, "Influential Writer on Theological Education Dies at 85," *Christian Century*, January 21, 2015, accessed August 13, 2018, https://www.christiancentury.org/article/2015-01/influential-writer-theological-education-dies-85.

35. AGPIM Meeting Minutes, 1992. The full definition developed by AGPIM can be found in the introduction to this volume.

36. Joseph Dunne, *Back to the Rough Ground: "Phronesis" and "Techne" in Modern Philosophy and in Aristotle* (Notre Dame, IN: University of Notre Dame Press, 1993).

37. Dunne, *Back to the Rough Ground*, 367.

38. Dunne, *Back to the Rough Ground*, 358.

39. Common Formation Goals for Ministry, ed. Joseph Merkt, STD (self-published by NALM, NCCL, and NFCYM, 2000), 3.

40. AGPIM Meeting Minutes, 1998.

41. *Co-Workers*, 34.

42. NCS 2011; 1.

43. See "Alliance for Certification of Lay Ecclesial Ministry."

44. Ilia Delio, *The Emergent Christ* (Maryknoll, NY: Orbis Books, 2011), 113.

Chapter Three

REVISITING *CO-WORKERS IN THE VINEYARD OF THE LORD*

A Proposal for Theological Development

William H. Johnston

The U.S. Catholic Conference of Bishops' document *Co-Workers in the Vineyard of the Lord: A Resource for Guiding the Development of Lay Ecclesial Ministry* has been called "the most mature and coherent ecclesiastical document ever produced on a theology of ministry."[1] Yet certain aspects of its theology chapter say less than one might expect regarding lay ecclesial ministers themselves, with emphasis instead on the role and agency of the ordained, thus yielding a certain imbalance. To address this shortcoming and contribute to ongoing theological reflection on both lay and ordained ecclesial ministry, this essay selects two such aspects: the document's teaching on "ordered charisms" and on ministerial relationships, and proposes by way of example a development of each topic that gives greater attention to the role and agency of lay ecclesial ministers vis-à-vis that of the ordained, affirming both but in a more balanced way.

A wide range of postconciliar magisterial and theological literature could resource this effort. In this essay, for each example, I will draw principally on a single selected passage from a document of Vatican II—from *Apostolicam Actuositatem* (AA) to address ordered charisms, and from *Lumen Gentium* (LG) to address ministerial relationships. This latter discussion will then lead to a consideration of the ministerial workplace as an arena for the exercise of spiritual works of mercy, offering a pastoral way forward when ministerial relationships go awry. Concluding remarks suggest a spirituality to cultivate as a basis for actual effective progress in these areas.

My hope in the four sections of the essay is to build on and invite further reflection concerning the theology, spirituality, and pastoral implementation of *Co-Workers*. This groundbreaking document continues to serve the Church by drawing attention to, endeavoring to make theological sense of, and guiding the way forward, during what has been called "one of the most significant periods of ministerial transformation in the history of the Church"—the ministerial transformation that is lay ecclesial ministry.[2]

ORDERED CHARISMS

Co-Workers describes charisms as "gifts or graces of the Spirit that have benefit, direct or indirect, for the community."[3] They are gifts given to be used for others, the Spirit bestowing them, as the Council taught, "among the faithful of every rank...[making] them fit and ready to undertake the various tasks and offices which contribute toward the renewal and building up of the Church" (LG 12).

The Council also taught that the apostolate and charisms of laity can be exercised anywhere, designating the "secular" realm as distinctive for lay activity yet affirming as well their role in church ministry.[4] *Co-Workers*, accordingly, acknowledges the distinctive orientation of lay activity to "the world" while affirming that laity are also, by "baptismal incorporation into the Body of Christ,...equipped with gifts and graces to build up the Church from within" (p. 12). *Co-Workers* here recognizes a broad range of roles by which laypersons serve the ecclesial community (pp. 9–10), but the document was written to focus specifically on those relative few who serve as "lay ecclesial ministers"[5] in response to a charism or charisms "bestowed by the Spirit" (p. 26).

As the Church is by nature "an organic and ordered communion" (*Co-Workers*, 20), what makes the use of lay ecclesial ministers' charisms well-ordered in and for the communion and mission of the Church? *Co-Workers* calls for lay charisms within the Church to be exercised "in cooperation with the hierarchy and under its direction" (p. 12). Accordingly, the document's defining characteristics of lay ecclesial ministry include "*close mutual collaboration* with the pastoral ministry of bishops, priests, and deacons" and "*authorization* of the hierarchy to serve publicly in the Church" (*Co-Workers*, 10, emphasis in original). Both notes recur throughout the document—the lateral note of collaboration, that lay ecclesial ministers work with the ordained (*Co-Workers*, 5, 10, 12, 24, 25, 26, 48, 54, 56, 60), and the vertical note of authorization, that lay ecclesial ministers work under, or at least only at the contingent behest of, the ordained (*Co-Workers*, 5, 10, 11, twice on 12, twice on 23, and 54–60, a dedicated chapter on authorization).

With "authorization of the hierarchy," agency resides with the ordained.[6] Yet, even when a more shared agency might be expected, as in the lateral dynamic of collaboration, at times *Co-Workers* attributes lead agency to the ordained, as when indicating it is the hierarchy who "draw certain laypersons into a close mutual collaboration with [their] pastoral ministry" (*Co-Workers*, 5), or that lay ecclesial ministers "look to their priests for leadership in developing collaboration that is mutually life-giving and respectful" (*Co-Workers*, 24). There is also a preponderant attention to the role of the ordained in the sections on their relationships with lay ecclesial ministers (*Co-Workers*, 21–25). "The Bishop and Lay Ecclesial Ministers," for example (*Co-Workers*, 21–23), devotes five paragraphs to bishops and two sentences to lay ecclesial ministers. Those five paragraphs are essentially a mini-catechesis on the nature and authority of the episcopacy. Only the final paragraph and a half address how bishops relate to lay ecclesial ministers, a relationship characterized as episcopal agency typically delegated to and exercised by diocesan priests. There is not a word in the section on how lay ecclesial ministers relate to bishops.

Perhaps this predominant clerical emphasis in a document devoted to lay ecclesial ministry is attributable to timing and context. *Co-Workers* was published within a decade of the 1997 Vatican document *Ecclesiae de Mysterio,* the "Instruction on Certain Questions Regarding the Collaboration of the Non-ordained Faithful in the Sacred Ministry of Priests," written to clarify and affirm the role of the ordained in response to perceived ambiguities about or threats to that role.[7] More proximately, *Co-Workers* was developed in the immediate aftermath of the U.S. clergy sex abuse crisis of 2002, certainly a low ebb in the tide of Catholics' respect for their clergy. Whether from these or other factors, the document seems to reflect the bishops' concern to (re)assert a dimension of the Church's nature and structure they saw to be in particular need of upholding, namely, the hierarchical nature of the Church and the pastoral mission and authority of the ordained. This dimension of the Church was rethought, reaffirmed, and set forth in the teaching of Vatican II, as in the third chapter of *Lumen Gentium,* and is not in question here; my suggestion is that to such passages we juxtapose other conciliar texts, which have relevance and bring added perspective to our topic.[8]

The first of these texts is from the fourth chapter of *Lumen Gentium,* on the laity, and represents a notable theological development of then current teaching. For the half-century before the Council, the active role of laity was articulated in the theology of "Catholic Action," which viewed laypersons as participating in the apostolate of the hierarchy, by delegation of the hierarchy. Vatican II significantly reconfigured this teaching in two ways: (1) by affirming that laity participate in the *Church's* mission and apostolate, (2) to which they are deputed "by the Lord himself" (LG 33). This very point was explicitly repeated the following year in *Apostolicam Actuositatem* (AA 3). Rereading today what that passage says about the apostolate and charisms of laity provides theological warrant for supplementing and balancing what we find in *Co-Workers.*

In that passage, the Council states that from their union with Christ, and through the sacraments of baptism and confirmation, laity possess a "duty and right" to an active share in the Church's apostolate.[9] These are powerful words. To say "duty" means laity are called and bound to bear their part in the apostolate even if personally disinclined; to say "right" means they have a call and claim to do this even if opposed by others. While no one can claim a duty or right to any particular form or position of ecclesial ministry on one's own, both terms strongly affirm lay agency generally, on the solid foundation of "their union with Christ their head." But the theological, canonical, and practical implications of this conciliar affirmation for the context of lay ecclesial ministry have yet to be sufficiently thought through and acted on.[10] For example, once a layperson has been hired into a position of lay ecclesial ministry, duly authorized by the hierarchy and "given responsibilities for ecclesial ministry by competent church authority" (*Co-Workers*, 54), how then does the "right and duty to the apostolate" they have from the Lord (AA 3) become operative and exercised in that church ministry context? How, so to speak, do the now overlapping authorizations—one by the hierarchy, one by the Lord—play out in that layperson's ecclesial ministry in a way that honors the will of the Lord, the role of the hierarchy, the rights of that layperson, and good order in the Church? The document then states, "The Holy Spirit sanctifies the people of God through the ministry and the sacraments and, for the exercise of the apostolate, gives the faithful special gifts besides" (AA 3; see 1 Cor 12:7). Note that it is from the Holy Spirit personally that the laity receive these gifts, later called "charisms," indicating they are given by the Spirit with the intent they be used by those who receive them for the benefit of those to be served. Indeed, the text affirms laity have a "right and duty" to use them, repeating for emphasis those key terms that again designate respectively lay empowerment and lay responsibility. Failure to recognize these charisms, when genuine, or to allow their exercise would be to impede the work of the Spirit in the Church.

What follows next are a series of phrases each adding a layer and depth of meaning to the document's teaching on the operation and ordering of charisms in the exercise of the laity's apostolate. We can usefully reread this passage on laity generally to consider its implications for lay ecclesial ministry today. Let us notice four phrases.[11]

The Council asserts that laypersons have the right and duty to exercise charisms (1) "in the Church and in the world for the good of humanity and the development of the Church." This chiastic phrase indicates the provenance of the lay apostolate as both world and church, correcting a view that would not only direct but also limit lay activity to the former. Further, laity are not only gifted with charisms directly by the Spirit; the text states they can use those charisms in the same manner they were given, that is, (2) "in the freedom of the Holy Spirit who 'chooses where to blow' (John 3:8)." The affirmation is striking: laity can exercise their charisms with the same divine freedom of action with which those charisms were given—a freedom as beyond human control as the wind. These two phrases powerfully highlight lay giftedness and agency, and merit theological reflection to discern what implications follow for ordering the charisms of lay ecclesial ministers and respecting the giftedness and agency they bring to their ministry.

Yet after these phrases, which on their own suggest a virtually unchecked scope and force for the right and duty of laity in exercising their charisms freely, there follow two further phrases that contextualize this same right and duty. Laity are to discern and exercise their charisms not only on the basis of their own spiritual intuition, sense of calling, and personal judgment, but also (3) "in communion with the sisters and brothers in Christ" (AA 3), thus recognizing the integral and essential role of the faith community. In a very real sense these are not matters that belong to an individual alone but with both theological and sociological necessity involve and depend on others in the ecclesial community. This communal dimension, this giving due weight to the voice of others, is to function for both individual and community not as a limitation but as an aid, guide, service, and safeguard to vocational discernment, good order, and fruitful ministry.

The text then gives to this ecclesial dimension of discernment and exercise of charisms one further specification: it is to be done with their sisters and brothers in Christ and (4) "with the pastors especially [*maxime*]." To them it belongs, says the text, "to pass judgment on the authenticity and good use" of these charisms—again, intended not as a limitation but as a service for the individual and community. This role of pastors is then provided its own biblical warrant and directive (as though to complement the "blows where it chooses" of John 3:8, cited earlier): the purpose of rendering judgment is "not [to] quench the Spirit...but [to] test everything; hold fast to what is good" (1 Thess 5:19, 21).

The responsibility inherent in judging can of course be well or poorly understood and exercised. A pastor could misinterpret the passage to maximize his part in a way that minimizes that of others, or even be tempted to a lording-over others in ministry (see Mark 10:33–45). Augustine's realization of the situation that this judging responsibility put him in was more perceptive, and the Council cites his words as instructive for pastors: "When I am frightened [in Latin *terret*, literally "terrified"] by what I am to you, then I am consoled by what I am with you. To you I am the bishop, with you I am a Christian. The first is an office, the second a grace; the first a danger, the second salvation" (LG 32).

Why terrified? Why a danger? Because given his ecclesial role, he must judge the authenticity and use of charisms that others claim, but in judging he may misjudge and thus stand in the way of a deputation Christ has given one of his faithful, or deny the use of a genuine charism bestowed by the Spirit, effectively "quenching the Spirit," which the Word of God expressly warns him not to do.[12] In fulfilling his role, a pastor unaware of or unafraid and dismissive of the possibility of error is not yet sufficiently mindful of the burden he bears or its peril. Needed instead is a due mindfulness, not to paralyze his ministry with debilitating fear but rather to inspire a salutary fear that calls him to prayer, instills a servant's spirit, and leads him to rely gratefully on regular collaboration with the community of Christ's faithful in exercising the authority he has been given. For while judging of God's action in a person's life can be a fearsome responsibility, it is made less so when brothers and sisters in Christ share the burden with their advice and counsel.

These elements of the Council's vision of how charisms given to laity are ordered in the Church invite further development of *Co-Workers'* understanding of the charism of lay ecclesial ministry. Such concepts as right, duty, deputation by the Lord, charism, freedom of the Spirit, and involvement of the community add a dimension of lay agency and empowerment vis-à-vis the pastoral and leadership role of the ordained, which is still affirmed by the Council as ultimately entailing the proper if perilous responsibility of judging. These reflections do not negate but aim to broaden and balance *Co-Workers'* more limited description and rationale for authorizing lay ecclesial ministry and discerning and ordering the charisms of lay ecclesial ministers.

Co-Workers' perspective on ordering the charisms of laity, turning to another relevant conciliar text, can similarly enrich its description of ministerial relationships between lay and ordained ecclesial ministers.

MINISTERIAL RELATIONSHIPS

How should ministerial relationships work in the life of the Church? For the purposes of this essay, let us focus by way of example on *Co-Workers'* treatment of the relationship of lay ecclesial ministers with priests, with whom they often relate in the ministerial workplace.

Nearly the entire section on pages 23 and 24 in *Co-Workers* is devoted to explaining the priest's role and his relationships with the bishop, with Christ, and with "the community of disciples" in general. Nothing is said of his relationship with lay ecclesial ministers. The section's single sentence mentioning lay ecclesial ministers indicates they "look to their priests for leadership in developing collaboration that is mutually life-giving and respectful" (*Co-Workers*, 24). The implication that this is something priests are to provide is a point well-taken in naming an element of their ordained ministerial agency, but the section lacks anything regarding mutual relationships with lay ecclesial ministers or their lay ministerial agency.

The first paragraph (LG 37.1) speaks of lay rights and agency, including the right both to receive from pastors "the Church's spiritual treasury" (chiefly, word and sacraments) and to communicate to them their "needs and desires" freely and confidently. The text then affirms that "to the extent of their knowledge, competence or authority, the laity are entitled [*facultatem... habent*], and indeed sometimes duty-bound [*officium*], to express their opinion on matters which concern the good of the Church," a sentence particularly apt for lay ecclesial ministers, calling for and authorizing their voice in ecclesial affairs. Note that laity have this faculty (and at times duty) of manifesting their thoughts on church affairs not by another's delegation, but because they have (and in the measure that they have) relevant "knowledge, competence or authority," which lay ecclesial ministers often acquire through years of education and experience. This communication is to be done through established channels or procedures, and exercising the three virtues of "truth," not surprisingly, but also "courage and prudence," both relevant for lay ecclesial ministers if the informed "opinion" (*sententiam*) they have to speak to an employer may not be welcomed.[13]

Their communication is also to be done "with reverence and charity" toward the ordained because "by reason of their office [they] represent the person of Christ." How this theological point translates into attitudes and practices depends on which christological themes are highlighted. Viewing Christ as both head of the Church and the one who came not to be served but to serve yields a dialectical theology of ordained ministry combining leadership and service—authorizing leadership characterized by service, calling service toward the responsibility, opportunities, and burdens of leadership. These christological themes and their consequent ministerial theology can inform and shape how priests view their identity and conduct their ministry as representatives of Christ the Head and Shepherd, exercising leadership so as to serve; this can in turn inspire lay ecclesial ministers' respect for priests whose leadership truly serves those in their pastoral care.[14]

If the first paragraph of LG 37 authorizes lay agency, the second (LG 37.2) turns the table and speaks of obedience. Laity are to "promptly accept in Christian obedience what is decided by the pastors who, as teachers and rulers in the Church, represent Christ," whose example of obedience (see Phil 2:8; Heb 5:8) laity thus follow. The word here translated "accept" (*amplectantur*) might better be rendered "embrace," "hold fast," "welcome," or "esteem." It conveys a warmth and ready willingness in the obedience, suggesting an underlying attitude of love and trust—first toward Jesus, then accordingly and derivatively toward his "representatives" in the Church, for whom laity should also pray as those "placed over them," who will in turn have to "render an account of our souls" (referencing Heb 13:17). This paragraph of LG 37.2 and its relational dynamics are best understood assuming that ecclesial authority is exercised, in the words of Romano Guardini, as an "authority of service," which is met by a responding obedience that seeks to be "in harmony with the Church" and "an earthly image of that mystery in which the obedience of the Son is equal to the will of the Father."[15]

If the second paragraph of LG 37 puts laity, so to speak, at the mercy of clergy, the third paragraph (LG 37.3) prescribes how clergy are to relate with laity—applied to our context, with lay ecclesial ministers.[16] Here it states that pastors are to "recognize and promote the dignity and responsibility of the laity in the church," which would suggest support whenever possible for lay ecclesial ministry, not its minimization or elimination. Pastors are also to "willingly use their prudent advice," which presumes willingly seeking it. They are to "confidently assign offices to them in the service of the church," doing this in a way that leaves laity "freedom and scope for activity" and encourages their undertaking works "on their own initiative." In short, in practical, proactive, and open-ended ways, the ordained are to promote lay responsibility and agency in ecclesial ministry. They are also to consider with "paternal love" and "attentively in Christ" (Jesus, as it were, looking over their shoulder) the "initial moves, suggestions and desires" laity propose, with a footnote referencing 1 Thessalonians 5:19 and 1 John 4:1.

In the interplay and interweaving of themes throughout LG 37, this third paragraph complements the second and presents an image of laity willingly (in "obedience") recognizing their dignity and embracing their responsibility to serve the Church's apostolate, advising clergy with new ideas and recommendations, exercising a wide-ranging freedom of action in the Church, taking steps on their own initiative, all with the respect and support of the ordained, who also have the responsibility to exercise a discernment of spirits alluded to in the biblical references of a footnote.

The final paragraph (LG 37.4) indicates benefits that follow from this "familiar relationship between the laity and the pastors." Laity are strengthened in the sense of their own responsibility, more fervently inspired, and readier to associate with the works and ecclesial ministry of the ordained—factors all of which support the development of lay ecclesial ministry. Pastors, helped in these ways by a more active and ecclesially engaged laity, "are enabled to judge more clearly and more appropriately in spiritual and in temporal matters," echoing the prior discussion of AA 3. The paragraph concludes by orienting all the relational dynamics sketched in LG 37 to the Church's mission effectiveness.[17]

We might render the message of this passage with a two-part prescription: "embrace the difference, embrace the deference."[18] Throughout the passage both are affirmed—the difference between ordained and lay and the deference each owes the other. The deference is grounded in a baptismal dignity and vocation both share equally, with mutual respect and affirmation its expression. The difference is grounded in the fact that "the ordained [are] empowered in a unique and essential way by the Sacrament of Holy Orders" (*Co-Workers*, 20), which "configures the recipient to Christ the Head" and brings about a "particular relationship of service" on behalf of the community (*Co-Workers*, 21). The underlying theological concept here is "sacred power" (*sacra potestas*)—that by virtue of ordination, as the Council said, "the ministerial priest" acts, with effect, "by the sacred power that he has"[19] (*Catechism of the Catholic Church* 1551, with references to Mark 10:43–45 and 1 Peter 5:3).[20]

Such is the ideal. It can come to pass when those with the personal character, chosen intention, and positional mandate to become the servants of others' good in the name of the Church have the power to do so; then, the Church's communion and mission, full human development, and the common good can flourish. But this happy confluence of circumstances is not always realized. What if a ministerial workplace experiences not mutual respect and effective collaboration but "conflict situations between lay ecclesial ministers and the ordained" (*Co-Workers*, 23)? What if, for example, that power (*sacra potestas*) is handled ineptly or even intentionally misused, a lay ecclesial minister encountering in a pastor the flaws detailed by the *Catechism*—"human weaknesses, the spirit of domination, error, even sin"—to the point where these "harm the apostolic fruitfulness of the Church" in the place that pastor and lay ecclesial minister serve (CCC 1550)? If this describes the actions or character traits of an ordained minister exercising his power as employer and supervisor, what can a lay ecclesial minister do? What protections does she or he have?

Co-Workers mentions certain human resource "ideas" (*Co-Workers*, 61–62), but without requiring them. That the entire document is nonbinding is made clear from its start and is thus implicit throughout; it is made explicit again at the beginning of the section on "The Ministerial Workplace."[21] In that section we read that a bishop's guidance of lay ecclesial ministry in his diocese can include "supporting the resolution" of conflict situations (*Co-Workers*, 23). The text also notes that "grievance procedures provide an objective process for addressing good faith claims by those who think they have been unfairly treated" (*Co-Workers*, 64). In practice, such measures may or may not be enacted; if employed, they may or may not be effective, and may in either case be unable actually to protect the long-term interests of a lay ecclesial minister desiring to serve the Church and earn a livelihood in that way in that diocese.

In short, when ministerial relationships are problematic in this way, protections for lay ecclesial ministers are tenuous to nonexistent. But even when existing measures, such as the magisterial weight and moral suasion of conciliar texts (including AA 3 and LG 37) and information on business best practices (including grievance procedures in *Co-Workers*, 64), fall short and fail to preserve right relationships and fair dealing among lay and ordained ecclesial ministers, the situation is not irredeemable. The Christian tradition has other resources with potential to bring good even out of such disorder. Consider what positive potential for grace might emerge through the practice of the spiritual works of mercy.

SPIRITUAL WORKS OF MERCY

A first step might be *to instruct the ignorant.* "Ignorant" is not a term of insult but simply indicates not-knowing, a lack of information; instructing the ignorant means informing the uninformed, communicating knowledge (sometimes self-knowledge) to one who happens to lack it. Perhaps a priest's flaw is never to have learned, or from insufficient ongoing formation to have forgotten, his responsibility not just to provide priestly services and exercise pastoral authority but also to call forth and actively promote the apostolate and gifts of those in his charge, including staff. He could be informed of this responsibility, with reference to relevant sources. Or, perhaps his short temper alienates and silences staff and parishioners alike. As Sidney Callahan explains in her extended treatment of the spiritual works of mercy, "If we love persons, we are forced in charity to tell them truthfully how we respond to them," because otherwise they may never know, to their detriment.[22] If our communication with them is not honest, "sooner or later they pay for the fact that others did not love them enough to tell them what they needed to know or to force them to confront the real consequences of what they do."[23] It is an act of mercy to speak the truth that can instruct the ignorant.

More seriously, circumstances may call one *to admonish the sinner*, though this may appear difficult or even "repellant" in a culture that prizes being nonjudgmental and tolerant,[24] and given the command not to judge (Matt 7:1–5). But as Callahan writes, "If we don't care enough, or have courage enough, to admonish one another's sins, we fail in love," for ultimately this work of mercy "is an effort to liberate another through Christ's saving power of love."[25] Admonishing is not condemning, attacking, intruding, or condescending, but is more a matter of reminding a brother or sister in Christ of what they already know in conscience but by choice turned from or by habit have forgotten.[26] It is a helping hand stretched out to aid another to return to their first love (Rev 2:4–5a). When the person to be admonished has power over the one admonishing, as pastors do over lay ecclesial ministers, the task becomes at once more difficult and more necessary as others may, because of the risks, avoid it.[27] Here we see the relevance of the Council's three virtues of truth, courage, and prudence (LG 37.1), for truthfulness in charity is the basis of this difficult practice; prudence shows how to begin, with "private, tactful" steps; and if those fail, courage comes into play, with John the Baptist as a model for wading "into deeper, riskier waters."[28]

If such efforts lead to negative consequences from one's supervisor, one may find oneself needing *to bear wrongs patiently*. In an era when oppressed persons rightly resist the wrongs imposed on them, this work of mercy can seem wrongheaded, an unfair and counterproductive counsel of surrender to injustice. Callahan recasts the virtue: "To bear wrongs patiently is an active, enabling form of love and power. It is having the firmness to hold ourselves and others up, through strain, stress, and evil times, without causing more suffering and evil."[29] Rather than succumbing to the wrongs of a dysfunctional ministerial workplace, this work of mercy can instill various virtues: strength to carry on with good ministry despite workplace stresses, good cheer to lift spirits of others in that workplace, hope to look for positive change, and patience to work for it over the long haul. For we know that "one must bear wrongs patiently while at the same time admonishing, resisting, and working to right the wrongs."[30]

Whether one's efforts to practice these spiritual works of mercy succeed or fail, it always remains appropriate *to pray for the living and the dead,* including one's present and former supervisors and colleagues in ministry. Along with the good this may do, in God's providence, for those for whom we pray, it does good also to us who pray for their good, opening our hearts to "seek God's will for them, as well as for ourselves," coming to recognize, respect, and love them "as fellow creatures beloved by God."[31] If they have harmed us, prayer for them "will eventually quiet our fury and dissolve our resentment" as the love of God we ask for them is exercised in us as well. Prayer in this way may move us toward "reconciliation and realignment in the subjective relationship we have with others" whose behavior in the ministerial workplace has wronged us.

CONCLUDING REFLECTIONS

This essay began by noting an imbalance in aspects of the theology chapter of *Co-Workers,* and then proposed developments to foster a well-balanced theology. A final concern here is that we not engage in the merely "deskbound theology" Pope Francis critiqued for neglecting its role in the mission of the Church, or in proposing "utopian solutions" that may be theologically sound and elegant, but nonetheless abstract, out of touch, and unworkable in practice.[32] At some point, then, appropriately specific and down-to-earth recommendations would be in order.

At the same time, I find practical wisdom in advice St. John

Paul II offered in his 2001 apostolic letter, *Novo Millennio Ineunte*, advice we can apply to our concerns. In a section of that letter challenging the Church to grow as "*the home and the school of communion*," he counseled that before making concrete "practical plans" comes the need to cultivate what he called "*a spirituality of communion*."[33] He judged that plans, structures, and procedures designed to foster communion would only be effective if the persons using them were themselves genuinely converted and committed to communion. Otherwise, "external structures" would accomplish little, functioning more as "mechanisms without a soul" or even as "'masks' of communion rather than its means of expression and growth." First, "a spirituality of communion indicates above all the heart's contemplation of the mystery of the Trinity dwelling in us, and whose light we must also be able to see shining on the face of the brothers and sisters around us." This spiritual awareness aims to foster a deep and even sacred respect for the other as a person in whom the Trinity dwells. Further, pondering mutual relations among the trinitarian divine persons as a model for ecclesial ministerial relations in a given place can invite each person there to a gift of self and spirit of love able to foster a dynamic ministerial communion powering collaborative service to the Church's people and mission in that place.

Third, "a spirituality of communion implies also the ability to see what is positive in others, to welcome it and prize it as a gift from God: not only as a gift for the brother or sister who has received it directly, but also as a 'gift for me.'" This perspective can strengthen both the affirmation of priests for the "charismatic gifts" of the lay ecclesial ministers with whom they serve, as well as the appreciation of lay ecclesial ministers for the "hierarchic...gifts" of priests (LG 4).

The outcome of these four reflections can be a genuine conversion and deepening commitment of heart and mind among lay and ordained ecclesial ministers alike, calling forth mutual support and creating conditions conducive to a greater balance in the ordering of charisms and in ministerial relationships in the Church.

Perhaps it was with such goods in view that John Paul II recommended the spirituality of communion become "the guiding principle of education...wherever ministers of the altar, consecrated persons, and pastoral workers are trained." For all, it can be a constitutive element of their spiritual formation—its theological basis studied in intellectual formation, its influence cultivated in human formation, its implications fleshed out in pastoral formation. Such well-grounded and well-rounded formational efforts hold great potential to further the balanced development and ongoing implementation of *Co-Workers in the Vineyard of the Lord,* benefitting the Church's lay and ordained ministers directly, and ultimately all whom they serve.

NOTES

1. Richard R. Gaillardetz, "The Theological Reception of *Co-Workers in the Vineyard of the Lord,*" in *Lay Ecclesial Ministry: Pathways to the Future,* ed. Zeni Fox (Lanham, MD: Rowan & Littlefield, 2010), 21.

2. Edward P. Hahnenberg, "Theology of Lay Ecclesial Ministry: Future Trajectories," in Fox, 71.

3. *Co-Workers,* 18.

4. See LG 31 and 33. Also AA 9: "The lay apostolate, in all its many aspects, is exercised both in the church and in the world"; sections attending especially to the lay apostolate in the Church include AA 10, 24, and 25.

5. For the document's description of what constitutes lay ecclesial ministry and who is a lay ecclesial minister, see *Co-Workers,* 10–12.

6. We give attention to "agency" as a significant dimension of human dignity in the framework of the divine economy of salvation: "For God grants his creatures not only their existence, but also the dignity of acting on their own, of being causes and principles for each other, and thus of cooperating in the accomplishment of his plan" (CCC, 306). This chapter proposes that whether and how lay ecclesial ministers exercise agency can serve as an indicator of the recognition, ordering, and development of this new form of ministry in the life of the Church.

7. For brief but helpful background and context regarding the document (in response to widespread critique), see John L. Allen Jr., *All the Pope's Men: The Inside Story of How the Vatican Really Thinks* (New York: Doubleday, 2004), 90–94.

8. On "juxtaposition" in conciliar documents, see Henk Witte, "Reform with the Help of Juxtapositions: A Challenge to the Interpretation of the Documents of Vatican II," *The Jurist* 71 (2011): 20–34.

9. AA 3. Council quotations in this and the following eight paragraphs are from AA 3.

10. Canonist Elissa Rinere has noted that "although the Council taught about these gifts [i.e., charisms pertaining to lay ministry], as well as about the rights and responsibilities that come with them, there has been little practical application of these teachings"; Rinere, "Canon Law and Emerging Understandings of Ministry," in *Ordering the Baptismal Priesthood: Theologies of Lay and Ordained Ministry*, ed. Susan K. Wood (Collegeville, MN: Liturgical Press, 2003), 77. To move the process forward, canonist Lynda Robitaille has offered "A Canonical Wish List for the Authorization of Lay Ecclesial Ministers," in *In the Name of the Church: Vocation and Authorization of Lay Ecclesial Ministry*, ed. William J. Cahoy (Collegeville, MN: Liturgical Press, 2012), 117–40; Robitaille's endnotes provide extensive and helpful bibliography, at 134–40.

11. For another discussion of this same passage, see William H. Johnston, "Lay Ecclesial Ministry in Theological and Relational Context: A Study of Ministry Formation Documents," in *Catholic Identity and the Laity*, The Annual Publication of the College Theology Society 2008, vol. 54, ed. Tim Muldoon (Maryknoll, NY: Orbis Books, 2009), 229–33. More briefly, see Richard R. Gaillardetz, "Vatican II's Noncompetitive Theology of the Church," *Louvain Studies* 37, no. 1 (2013): 22.

12. The misjudging may work the other way as well, if he accepts as genuine a person's claim to a charism and its exercise in the community when it is not that but instead, for example, that person's felt need for status or power.

13. That is, *per instituta ad hoc ab Ecclesia stabilita*. Stelten's entry for *institutum* lists "precept, custom, regulation; purpose, plan; mode of life; institution, institute"; Leo F. Stelten, *Dictionary of Ecclesiastical Latin* (Peabody, MA: Hendrickson Publishers, 1995), 135. In the Flannery translation of the Council documents we find here "institutions"; in the Abbott translation, "agencies."

What established structures or procedures might have been meant in 1964? What might apply today? Pastoral and finance councils? The ordinary "best practices" of staff meetings, program planning proposals, monthly reports, or annual performance reviews? Peter Hünermann, in his way echoing Rinere (see n. 11 above), critiques this section (LG 37.1) for granting laity rights but leaving the honoring of those rights wholly to the clergy's good will, without the support of actual legal regulations; see his "Theologischer Kommentar zur dogmatischen Konstitution über die Kirche *Lumen gentium*," in *Herders Theologischer Kommentar zum Zweiten Vatikanischen Konzil,* Band 2 (Freiburg im Breisgau: Herder, 2004), 479–80.

14. Consider the way St. John Paul II relates and draws ministerial consequences for the ordained from these two aspects of Christ's role: "Jesus Christ is head of the Church his Body. He is the 'head' in the new and unique sense of being a 'servant,' according to his own words: 'The Son of Man came not to be served but to serve, and to give his life as a ransom for many' (Mark 10:45). Jesus' service attains its fullest expression in his death on the cross, that is, in his total gift of self in humility and love [citing Phil 2:7–8]....The authority of Jesus Christ as head coincides then with his service, with his gift, with his total, humble and loving dedication on behalf of the Church" (*Pastores Dabo Vobis* 21). On this basis the reciprocal relations described in LG 37 can develop. To represent Christ as described here, priests will exercise leadership marked by humility and love, wholly dedicated to serving the people and mission of the Church, in love and service to Christ; priestly ministry of this kind will prompt in return people's gratitude and respect.

15. Excerpts from Romano Guardini's reflections, contemporaneous with *Lumen Gentium*, on authority, service, and obedience in the Church. The full passage reads, "This authority is not one of domination, so that the individual is subject to her, but the Church is the great servant of the individuals, and becomes by this service that which she really is. Her authority is the authority of service, and the acceptance of this authority, obedience, is the reception of the message of salvation and cannot be rendered superfluous by the maturity of the receiver. On the contrary, as the believer ripens to greater maturity he carries out more freely

and consciously his obedience in reception and in action, so that the sacred relation of mission and proclamation on one side and of hearing and accepting on the other may be perfectly carried out. The Christian who truly understands himself knows that he is in harmony with the Church, so that the authority of the proclamation may be ever more purely and fully realized—an earthly image of that mystery in which the obedience of the Son is equal to the will of the Father." Romano Guardini, *The Church of the Lord*, trans. Stella Lange (Chicago: Henry Regnery Company, 1966), 105–6.

16. The verbs in LG 37.3 are largely in the subjunctive mood. If intended or taken as jussive subjunctives, the section is, as proposed here, prescriptive; if the subjunctives are optative, the indicated clergy behavior is encouraged, not required. Hünermann takes it in the latter sense, seeing moreover bishops assuming a "princely" pose wholly out of touch with the freedoms of contemporary society, offensively patronizing laity; see "Theologisch Kommentar," 480–81.

17. The foregoing also correlates well with Pope Francis's understanding of synodality in the Church. For example: "A synodal Church is a Church which listens, which realizes that listening 'is more than simply hearing' [*Evangelii gaudium* 171]. It is a mutual listening in which everyone has something to learn. The faithful people, the college of bishops, the Bishop of Rome: all listening to each other, and all listening to the Holy Spirit, the 'Spirit of truth' (John 14:17), in order to know what he 'says to the churches' (Rev 2:7)"; Francis, Address at the Ceremony Commemorating the 50th Anniversary of the Institution of the Synod of Bishops, available at http://w2.vatican.va/content/francesco/en/speeches/2015/october/documents/papa-francesco_20151017_50-anniversario-sinodo.html (accessed July 21, 2018).

18. I borrow the "difference/deference" language from the keynote address of Stephen Bevans at the 2014 NALM annual conference; Bevans referenced John C. Sivalon, *God's Mission and Postmodern Culture: The Gift of Uncertainty* (Maryknoll, NY: Orbis Books, 2012), 46–49, as the source he drew on and adapted.

19. LG 10; also LG 18 and 27, PO 2, and elsewhere. See CCC 874–75 (citing LG 18), 1538, 1551.

20. See the well-nuanced treatment of power in Jack Risley, "The Minister: Lay and Ordained," in *The Theology of Priesthood*, ed.

Donald J. Goergen and Ann Garrido (Collegeville, MN: Liturgical Press, 2000), 119–37; the section "Presider/Coordinator" (134–35) echoes various themes of LG 37. At greater length, though with more mixed success, see the essays in *Power in the Church*, Concilium: Religion in the Eighties, ed. James Provost and Knut Walf (Edinburgh: T&T Clark, 1988).

21. *Co-Workers'* introduction states the document "does not propose norms or establish particular law" (*Co-Workers*, 6). While "The Ministerial Workplace" section concludes (*Co-Workers*, 65) by noting the benefits of the human resource practices it lists, it begins by making clear those ideas "are to be evaluated by individual dioceses in light of their own circumstances. These comments are not intended to be prescriptive or normative" (*Co-Workers*, 61).

22. Sidney Callahan, *With All Our Heart and Mind: The Spiritual Works of Mercy in a Psychological Age* (New York: Crossroad, 1988, 1989), 53. My thanks to Robert Marko of Aquinas College (Grand Rapids) for the reference to Callahan's study, which informs this section of the paper.

23. Callahan, *With All Our Heart*, 53.

24. Callahan, *With All Our Heart*, 21.

25. Callahan, *With All Our Heart*, 37 ("if we don't care") and 36 ("is an effort to liberate"); see also 30–31.

26. See Callahan, *With All Our Heart*, 28, 37.

27. See Callahan, *With All Our Heart*, 33.

28. Callahan, *With All Our Heart*, 33.

29. Callahan, *With All Our Heart*, 125.

30. Callahan, *With All Our Heart*, 129. Compare: "To go on picket lines, was to perform spiritual works of mercy. It was to dramatize by a supplicatory procession the needs of the worker, the injustice perpetuated against him. To bear wrongs patiently, yes, but not to let the bosses continue the sin of exploiting you. To forgive the injury, yes, but to try to do away with the injury"; Dorothy Day, "The Scandal of the Works of Mercy," *Commonweal* 51, no. 4 (November 4, 1949): 100. While public picketing with hand-held signs is still a tool of political action, what other means today might serve the same end—using what truthful words or images, communicated how often, on what social media platforms?

31. Callahan, *With All Our Heart and Mind*, 175, for this and other quotations in this paragraph.

32. Francis, *Evangelii Gaudium*, no. 133 ("deskbound theology"). Luigi Sartori, "The Structure of Juridical and Charismatic Power in the Christian Community," in *Charisms in the Church*, Concilium, no. 109, ed. Christian Duquoc and Casiano Floristan (New York: A Crossroad Book, The Seabury Press, 1978), 57 ("utopian solutions").

33. John Paul II, *Novo Millennio Ineunte*, no. 43 (emphasis in original), in the context of NMI 42–45, a section titled "Witnesses to Love." Unless otherwise noted, quotations in the rest of this essay are from NMI 43.

Chapter Four

LAY ECCLESIAL MINISTRY AND THE *SENSUS FIDEI*

Giving Voice to the Faithful

Howard Ebert

Both the *sensus fidei* and lay ecclesial ministry are realities that challenge a rigid division between the laity and the clergy, between the learning Church and the teaching Church. While the *sensus fidei* and lay ecclesial ministry have received greater emphasis in light of Vatican II's ecclesiology, recent discussions of both terms are often filled with ambiguities, contested claims, and fluctuations regarding their respective meaning, validity, and significance. This confusion springs from numerous factors, including changing ecclesial models, lack of universal definitions, and varying practices within the worldwide Church. In addition to these obstacles, current discussions of these two terms often neglect the relational and social dynamics embedded in ecclesial life. Utilizing the basic insights of the French sociologist and theorist Pierre Bourdieu, this chapter argues that lay ecclesial ministers—by virtue of their "marginal" place along the clergy-laity border—can play a crucial role in the identification, discernment, and articulation of the *sensus fidei*.

The first two sections of this chapter briefly examine recent theological understandings of the *sensus fidei* and lay ecclesial ministry, respectively. The examination in both cases focuses on the social dynamics intrinsically present in these realities. Both sections also note that because this social reality is unacknowledged or underdeveloped, impoverished theologies develop. Applying the basic components of Pierre Bourdieu's sociological analysis to address the underdeveloped social nature of these ecclesial realities, the third section argues that lay ecclesial ministry can and should play a pivotal role in providing an avenue for nurturing, discerning, and expressing the *sensus fidei*.

SENSUS FIDEI AND *SENSUS FIDELIUM*

God graces the entire body of believers with a "sense of the faith" (*sensus fidei*) that enables the Church as a whole to discern truth from error, and thus remain faithful to the revelation of God in Christ. This notion has a long history in the Christian tradition. It received new attention in the nineteenth century through the work of John Henry Newman and others. And it was unambiguously affirmed at Vatican II, which taught,

> The whole body of the faithful who have received an anointing which comes from the holy one (see 1 John 2:20, 27) cannot be mistaken in belief. It shows this characteristic through the entire people's supernatural sense of the faith [*supernaturali sensu fidei totius populi*], when, "from the bishops to the last of the faithful," it manifests a universal consensus in matters of faith and morals.[1]

The Council's unambiguous affirmation did not resolve all ambiguities surrounding this category. For example, what kind of knowledge is this "supernatural sense"? How are we to understand a supernatural sense that is both individual and communal? And, given the inevitable differences among individuals and groups within the community, where is the common "sense of the faith" of the Church as a whole to be found?

This confusion prompted the International Theological Commission (ITC) to provide a clarification of terms in its 2014 document *Sensus Fidei in the Life of the Church*. Referring to the two-fold nature of the "sense of the faith," the document states,

> On the one hand, the *sensus fidei* refers to the personal capacity of the believer, within the communion of the Church, to discern the truth of faith. On the other hand, the *sensus fidei* refers to a communal and ecclesial reality: the instinct of faith of the Church herself, by which she recognizes her Lord and proclaims his word.[2]

The document refers to the former (the personal capacity of the believer) as the *sensus fidei fidelis* ("sense of the faith of the faithful one") and the latter (the communal, ecclesial reality) as *sensus fidei fidelium* ("sense of the faith of the faithful"). The abbreviated form *sensus fidei* is commonly used to reference the individual reality, *sensus fidelium* is used to reference the communal reality. However, to add to the confusion, depending on context, the phrase *sensus fidei* can apply to either the individual believer or the church community—as the quotation above illustrates.

As a kind of supernatural instinct, the *sensus fidei* broadens the notion of truth beyond the narrow boundaries of rationalism and the neatly defined propositional statements to include the affective, the intuitive, and the relational. The ITC document states,

> The *sensus fidei fidelis* arises, first and foremost, from the connaturality that the virtue of faith establishes between the believing subject and the authentic object of faith, namely the truth of God revealed in Christ Jesus. Generally speaking, connaturality refers to a situation in which an entity A has a relationship with another entity B so intimate that A shares in the natural dispositions of B as if they were its own. Connaturality permits a particular and profound form of knowledge....It is a knowledge by empathy, or a knowledge of the heart.[3]

The distinctive character of this emergent expression of faith challenges any reduction of knowledge to Enlightenment rationalism and offers a wider, multidimensional presentation of faith. Reflecting on the work of Latino theologian Orlando Espín, Edward Hahnenberg states, "The type of intuitive knowledge involved in the believer's sense of faith (*sensus fidei fidelis*) is not the detached rationality of modernity. Rather it is a thoroughly relational knowledge that comes by way of actual engaged living (*experiencia*) within the network of relationships that find their primary expression in popular religion."[4] The truth derived from the *sensus fidei* is more inclusive than propositional statements or cognitive beliefs. This recognition of the expansive nature of the truths embedded in the sense of the faithful has implications for where one looks and what one finds. Examination of popular religion becomes a necessary element in discerning religious truths.[5] One attends to the practices—devotions, rituals, songs—of ordinary believers. One comes to recognize in this examination that, in the past, faith had often been too narrowly defined and restricted.

Richard Gaillardetz contends that this recognition raises crucial ecclesiological issues:

> What, for example, is the proper relationship between the wisdom of God's people (*sensus fidelium*) and church doctrine? The insight and wisdom of ordinary believers often eludes propositional form, embedded as it is in the concrete narratives and daily practices of Christian discipleship. There is a temptation to consider this non-propositional form as inchoate doctrine, as if Christian wisdom cannot achieve its maturity until it has been received by the bishops and given normative expression as doctrine. But is this always the case?[6]

Gaillardetz responds negatively to this question, noting that doctrine should not be seen as the only and ultimate formulation of Christian belief. The distinctive transcognitive nature of *sensus fidei* raises the question of the "status" of it in relationship and weight relative to doctrinal formulations, bringing into the open questions about relationship, authority, and power.

For example, Gaillardetz argues that privileging the *sensus fidei* as a genuine site of the Church "expressing" its belief challenges any rigid line of demarcation between lay and clergy as reflected in the traditional distinction between the teaching Church (*ecclesia docens*) and the learning Church (*ecclesia discens*). In this binary view, ordinary believers were seen as passive recipients of knowledge dispensed by the clergy, hierarchically ranked, who were defined as the sole teachers of the faith. Gaillardetz observes that this bifurcation is, to an extent, a modern invention:

> At least since the French Revolution, consideration of the ecclesial dynamics of listening and learning have been eclipsed by ever more expansive considerations of the dynamics of ecclesial teaching. These dynamics presupposed what Lonergan referred to as a "classical cognitivist" framework in which God communicates a divine message through doctrines that are taught by the magisterium and passively received by the Christian faithful....This framework paid much more attention to the distinctive assistance of the Holy Spirit given to the bishops than it did to the work of the Spirit in the life of the whole people of God.[7]

In such a view, "the faith" was seen more as a given, presented to the individual for her passive reception. The dynamic interchange between individuals, community, and Church leaders was completely ignored.

As Gaillardetz and other contemporary theologians note, Vatican II's recovery of the *sensus fidei* challenges this sharp division. This challenge is built on the recognition that those who belong to the community of believers are not passive agents, but graced-by-God persons who have distinctive gifts to contribute to the Church. An authentic interpretation of the *sensus fidei* acknowledges that there is a two-way street (i.e., mutuality) between the community of faith and that community's authoritative teachers. The 2014 ITC document states,

> The whole Church, laity and hierarchy together, bears responsibility for and mediates in history the revelation

which is contained in the holy Scriptures and in the apostolic Tradition. The Second Vatican Council stated that the latter form "a single sacred deposit of the word of God" which is "entrusted to the Church," that is, "the entire holy people, united to its pastors." The Council clearly taught that the faithful are not merely passive recipients of what the hierarchy teaches and theologians explain; rather, they are living and active subjects within the Church. In this context, it underscored the vital role played by all believers in the articulation and development of the faith: "the Tradition that comes from the apostles makes progress in the Church, with the help of the Holy Spirit."[8]

Thus, the ITC document affirms the potential contribution of the individual *sensus fidei* to the communal *sensus fidelium*; however, it leaves the dynamics of this relationship undeveloped.

Hahnenberg observes the failure of the ITC document to relate the individual and the communal:

> Despite repeated reminders that the *sensus fidei* is always an ecclesial reality, the document's treatment of the *sensus* in relation to the virtue of faith is surprisingly individualized and interiorized. Beginning its systematic analysis with the believer's *sensus fidei* (chapter 2), the document struggles to move on to the *sensus fidelium* (chapter 3)....When the document turns to the question of discernment in chapter 4, it lists several subjective dispositions that indicate a believer's authentic participation in the sense of the faith. While these dispositions are thoroughly ecclesial, embedding the believer in the life of the Church and teaching of the magisterium, they nevertheless presuppose that the discernment is the act of the individual.[9]

How does the *sensus fidei* relate to the *sensus fidelium*? If one recognizes the grace-laden nature of both, as Vatican II appears to do, then one must see the two realities in a mutually conditioning relationship. That is, *sensus fidelium* informs *sensus fidei* and the *sensus fidei* embodies, informs, and reforms the *sensus fidelium*. In order for this dynamic to occur, there needs to be mediating agents that bridge the individual and the collective sense of the faith. The neglect of attention to the essentially mutual interaction between the individual and the community glosses over a deep and significant fact: there can never be a clear separation between an individual's faith and one's communal context. One learns the faith from, and in, community. Faith is saturated with communal experience.

At the same time, the ambiguity can lead to ignoring the realities of authority and power at work in various relationships within the Church. This neglect, intentional or not, is detrimental to discerning an authentic expression of the *sensus fidelium* since it is constituted by the interaction, in part, between the faithful and the hierarchy. If the role of authority and power are left unexamined, unproductive and unhealthy dynamics between individual and communal realities are left unchallenged. Hahnenberg states the dilemma: "The smooth movement from the mind of the individual to the 'mind' of the Church can easily gloss over the conflicts and power structures endemic to social existence, and minimize the complexity of crossing cultural horizons."[10] A central contention of this chapter is that one simply cannot appreciate either the potential or the challenges of the "sense of the faith" of the whole people of God without attending to the realities of power and authority. These realities play a crucial role in recognizing the possibility of the lay ecclesial minister serving as a spokesperson for the *sensus fidelium*.

Emerging from the life of ordinary believers, the *sensus fidelium* is also seen as an important component for the Church's self-understanding and realization. This affirmation carries with it a more expansive understanding of truth and its conveyance. It also raises questions of how the sense of the faithful is to be nurtured so that it can become ever more part of the Church's lived reality. Before these questions can be addressed, we first examine the phenomenon of lay ecclesial ministry in the hope that, by better understanding the lay ecclesial minister's location on the ecclesial "boundary" between clergy and laity, we might better appreciate their role in "crossing over" from the community's "sense of the faith" to the magisterium's authentic articulation of that faith.

LAY ECCLESIAL MINISTRY IN THE LIFE OF THE CHURCH

The examination of the *sensus fidei* in the previous section reveals that the ambiguity surrounding the use of the term not only causes confusion, but also obscures its intrinsically relational nature. Such obscuring masks deeper questions of authority and power. It is instructive that one finds the same dynamics at work in the naming of lay ecclesial ministry.

In their 1980 statement, *Called and Gifted: The American Catholic Laity,* the U.S. Bishops noted a new reality in their midst, "lay persons who have prepared for professional ministry in the Church."[11] They called these laypersons "ecclesial ministers" and welcomed them as a gift. Fifteen years later, the bishops issued a second pastoral statement on the laity, *Called and Gifted for the Third Millennium.* There they described "ecclesial lay ministers" as "professionally prepared lay men and women offering their talents and charism in the service of the Church."[12] In their most comprehensive statement to date, *Co-Workers in the Vineyard of the Lord,* published in 2005, "ecclesial lay ministers" became "lay ecclesial ministry." The acceptance of this term occurred after years of struggling with what designation would be appropriate in naming the reality of laypersons' work in and for the Church. The struggle over terminology reflects the collision of two distinct ecclesial views. On the one hand, those who see the "inner work of the Church" to be the purview of the clergy maintain that the term *ministry* be reserved for the work of the ordained. In fact, as Thomas F. O'Meara notes, it was only in 1994 that Pope John Paul II "grudgingly allowed the biblical word 'ministry' to be applied to the 'lay faithful.'"[13] The term *ecclesial* has also been challenged, on the grounds that the primary responsibility of the laity is to serve not in the Church, but "in the world."

On the other hand, proponents of the term base their advocacy on Vatican II's affirmation that in baptism all the faithful share in the common priesthood of Christ. This common priesthood carries with it responsibilities both inside and outside of the Church. Advocates argue that ministry is in fact taking place and, given its pervasiveness and efficacy in building up the Body of Christ, it needs to be officially recognized as such. *Co-Workers* offers this recognition, acknowledging that "lay ecclesial ministry has emerged and taken shape in our country through the working of the Holy Spirit."[14]

This affirmation by the U.S. Bishops is significant for several reasons. First, acceptance of the term *lay ecclesial ministry* brings formal, institutional validation to this form of ministry. The validation legitimates and creates an institutional space, formal power, and support. Second, as Richard McCord observes, *Co-Workers* contributes to "*naming, claiming,* and *sustaining* lay ecclesial ministry as a valid and necessary dimension of church ministry today."[15] In formally declaring the significance of lay involvement in the workings of the Church, the document calls for significant educational, financial, and institutional resources to encourage and support the further development of lay ministry.

Co-Workers provides a framework for education in applying the same "pillars" of formation required for the formation of priests and deacons: human, spiritual, intellectual, and pastoral. The development of the competency-based NCS is another example of how the bishops, working with three national ministry associations, offer curricular guidance and substance to formation programs. Financially, the Church on a national level has funded studies and resources for lay ministry. On a local level, some dioceses have supported individuals preparing for lay ministry through scholarships. Diocesan offices have worked collaboratively with schools of higher education to offer formation programs. Efforts toward more formal authorization have centered around certification, commissioning, or reception of an academic degree.

Theologically, *Co-Workers* develops its understanding of ministry considering Vatican II, and subsequent magisterial statements, including Pope John Paul II's *Christifideles Laici* (1989). Gaillardetz identifies six significant theological principles developed in *Co-Workers*: (1) the priority of the baptismal call of *Christifideles*; (2) ministry as more than discipleship; (3) ministry within an ecclesiology of communion; (4) collaboration, not competition; (5) ministry within a theology of mission; and (6) vocational discernment.[16] Elsewhere, Gaillardetz observes, "A solid case can be made that *Co-workers* is the most mature and coherent ecclesiastical document ever produced on a theology of ministry."[17] What is remarkable about this claim is that the ministerial reality—as lay—that exists on the margins of ecclesial authority has become the stimulus for the development of the most comprehensive and theologically sophisticated statement on ministry produced by that authority.

While the focus of this chapter is on the potential role of the lay ecclesial minister in developing a deeper sense and articulation of the *sensus fidei*, one must be cognizant of the current juridical parameters that dictate the responsibilities of and restrictions on this ministry. These parameters reflect the power structures in which current configurations of lay ecclesial ministry exist. Sharon Euart observes that the 1983 Code of Canon Law offers a wide range of opportunities for the lay faithful to carry out the mission of the Church.[18] In line with Vatican II's call for the baptized to participate in the prophetic, priestly, and kingly work of Christ, the Code lays out opportunities for laypersons in the teaching office (*munus docendi*), sanctifying office (*munus sanctificandi*), and governing office (*munus regendi*). For example, in teaching, the laity may offer ecclesial advice to pastors, catechize, and do missionary work; in sanctifying, nonclerics can lector, cantor, distribute communion, and preside over prayer services; in governing, laypersons can serve as chancellors and notaries, and in other important leadership roles. By no means exhaustive, this list is a clear indicator that, in canonical understanding, a layperson's role can be defined in expansive ways in service to ecclesial life.

In the United States, *lay ecclesial ministry* is a generic term that covers a wide range of responsibilities named in canon law. The reality includes various roles in Catholic parishes, dioceses, and other organizations, including directors of religious education, youth ministers, pastoral associates, school principals, chaplains, and many more. While the elasticity of the term is helpful on one level, it introduces challenges on another. The lack of clear role identity contributes to an unequal reception of the term *lay ecclesial ministry*. The anxiety that lay ecclesial ministry may lead to the "clericalization of the laity," competing with religious and the ordained, has led many bishops to avoid using the language of lay ecclesial ministry or to minimize its recognition by having no type of authorization ritual. Zeni Fox comments,

Although *Co-Workers* outlines characteristics of those who could be designated as lay ecclesial ministers and the roles that might be called lay ecclesial ministry, the document also states that it is for each bishop to apply the term in his own diocese. This has led to considerable confusion about the boundaries of lay ecclesial ministry....If *Co-Workers* is to have the desired impact on both the formation of those laypersons who serve in leadership roles in the community and the collaboration of all in ministerial leadership, greater clarity regarding who is a lay ecclesial minister is certainly needed.[19]

The uneven reception of lay ecclesial ministry is another expression of how power and authority in the Church is understood by different ecclesial leaders.

Though formally acknowledged, lay ecclesial ministry holds an ambiguous position within a hierarchically structured church. As a Spirit-driven—that is, charismatic—reality, which the bishops acknowledge, lay ecclesial ministry exists in a highly fluid state. This fluidity is determined, in part, by the lay ecclesial minister's social location within the institution. Emerging at the ecclesiastical margins, lay ecclesial ministry is forging a new reality at the interface of clerical and lay "states" as traditionally defined.[20] Lay ecclesial ministry is at the boundary, carving out space and challenging traditionally rigid divisions between clergy and laity.[21] In this space, lay ecclesial ministry poses new questions, opportunities, and challenges. Writing from a systems theory perspective, Fox states that with the emergence of lay ecclesial ministry, the Church is at a new point of self-awareness:

> One could say that in the Church system, Catholics are in a time of birth of a new form of ministerial leadership and death of a rigid clerical/lay divide. (Note that it is the rigid divide that is posited as dying.) There is potential in this moment for healing old hurts and for a new awareness of God's presence with us on the journey, ever shepherding his people. Already, the incorporation of laypeople into roles of liturgy (lectors, cantors, etc.) signals that we are not simply clergy and laity, two

separate groups with two entirely separate functions and places, but a diversity of ministers, carrying forward the mission of Jesus. We are reminded that God, ever active, is present in and through all persons in the community, in all places in the world.[22]

Edward Hahnenberg echoes Fox's contention that lay ecclesial ministry heralds a new moment in the Church:

> The emergence of lay ecclesial ministry since the Council stands out as one of the top four or five ministerial shifts of the past two thousand years. It ought to be compared to the changes in the church brought on by the rise of communal forms of monasticism in the fifth century, the birth of the mendicant orders in the thirteenth century, the creative constitution of apostolic orders in the fifteenth century, or the explosion of women's religious communities in the seventeenth century.[23]

He goes on to note that "lay ecclesial ministry represents a call to a new way of *doing ministry,* but it also represents a new way of *being a minister.*"[24] It is precisely this new way of being a minister, existing as it does in a new social location within the Church, that invites a new consideration of the *sensus fidei.*

BRIDGING THE GAP: *SENSUS FIDEI* AND LAY ECCLESIAL MINISTRY

Given its status as a nondiscursive spiritual instinct, the *sensus fidei* presents a problem for a religious tradition that claims that this "sense" takes on a collective aspect—a *sensus fidelium*—that "comes from the holy one" and thus "cannot be mistaken in belief."[25] The problem is this: How is this implicit, intuitive, preconceptual supernatural instinct identified and articulated? What concrete structures foster, discern, and convey the faithful's lived reality of the faith? The lay ecclesial minister has the potential resources and ecclesial location to play an important mediating role between the community's *sensus fidei* and the official articulation of that "sense of the faith." Several preliminary observations are in order.

First, it is not surprising that a Church that operates within a structure of rigid hierarchical boundaries would lack structures to carry on communication that flows in both directions over the clergy/laity divide. It is true that after Vatican II some institutional structures (such as regional bishop conferences, synods, and parish councils) developed, offering the promise of greater dialogue.[26] Still, it is a widely acknowledged fact that there is still a paucity of structures that would enable believers to make genuine contributions to the wider Church. The lack of such "mediating structures" reflects the Church's inadequate understanding of the social and dynamic nature of the *sensus fidelium.*

Second, we need to recognize that identifying the *sensus fidei* requires more than a survey or a majority vote. Deep, textured examination is necessary in order to provide a "thick description," a layered interpretation that will reflect the complexity and comprehensive nature of lived faith.

Third, the *sensus fidei*—as the primary embodiment of the faith, defined broadly—cannot be disconnected from the social relationships among believers, regardless of their status within the Church. Indeed, lay ecclesial ministers, by virtue of their distinctive social location, play a key role in articulating the sense of the faith of the faithful among whom they serve. They are at the boundary between clergy and laity. In this marginal, liminal space, the lay ecclesial minister receives formal ecclesial recognition, while at the same time remaining clearly lay. In this marginal space there is still a power differential, but that differential is less pronounced than the simple dichotomy of clergy/laity. Of course, this marginal state carries its own uncertainty, ambiguity, and risk. Yet this position also carries an element of latitude and freedom. As part of an emergent, Spirit-driven, evolving reality, lay ecclesial ministers are writing their own history.

Given the lay ecclesial minister's potential to serve as a facilitator and spokesperson for the *sensus fidei*, intentional, sustained study of the social dynamics embedded in this role is desperately needed. Practical theology, with its appropriation of insights from the social sciences, is an essential method for examining the social reality that is at work in the interactions between the lay minister and the group. Sociology, in particular, offers critical insight into the relationship between individuals and institutions. This relationship is at the heart of discerning the *sensus fidei*. Understanding the dynamics of this relationship is essential both to developing a theologically sound and socially nuanced view of the *sensus fidei*, and to implementing structures for nurturing it and incorporating it into the public life of the Church.

The work of the French sociologist Pierre Bourdieu (1930–2002) offers some helpful categories for the kind of sustained study needed. Bourdieu developed an approach to the social world that attends to thick descriptions of experience, the interplay between individual and group, and the dynamics of power. Given their shared concerns, practical theologians have found Bourdieu's framework very helpful.

Take, for example, Bourdieu's concept of *habitus*. For Bourdieu, *habitus* describes a socialization process in which an individual internalizes objective structures:

> [Subjects] are active and knowing agents endowed with a *practical sense*, that is, an acquired system of preferences, of principles, of vision and division (what is usually called taste), and also a system of durable cognitive structures (which are essentially the product of the internalization of objective structures) and of schemes of action which orient the perception of the situation and the appropriate response. The *habitus* is this kind of practical sense for what is to be done in a given situation—what is called in sport a "feel" for the game.[27]

In other words, the individual not only learns the rules of the game but internalizes them. By emphasizing the mutual interplay of the two, *habitus* helps overcome the dichotomy between objective social structures and subjective internal agency. The dynamism by which social structures are internalized and, in turn, reproduced, describes a process of socialization that involves every aspect of the individual's life: cognitive, affective, and behavioral. In its holistic approach and ability to overcome the divide between communal context and the individual subject, *habitus* offers a fruitful way of imagining the individual and communal intuition that is the *sensus fidei*. What else is the sense of the faith than the individual believer's internalization of the ecclesial community's wisdom and practices—a process that gives the faithful one a "practical sense" of the Church's faith?

Habitus is the appropriation of what is "given" by the social environment. Bourdieu describes this social environment as constituted by several overlapping "fields." He describes a field as "the locus of the accumulated social energy which the agents and institutions help to reproduce through the struggles in which they try to appropriate it and into which they put what they have acquired from it in previous struggles."[28] Inherent in the dynamics of a field are power relations. Bourdieu views a field as a space in which power relations and power differentials are at work. There is a variety of fields with their own distinctive power forms, including economic, educational, political, and religious forms—each with its own *habitus*.

Applying Bourdieu's theoretical framework to the religious field yields critical insights into the social dynamics that are at work between the individual believer and the community of faith. A person's *sensus fidei* (understood as a *habitus* that is cognitive, affective, and behavioral) is formed within a religious community (understood as a field), which consists not only of conceptual content but also, and more importantly, of social relationships. These relationships are constituted within fields marked by power differentials and subtle forms of violence. Terry Rey notes,

> [For Bourdieu, the religious field, like any other field of activity] must be first examined in terms of its relationship to the broader, all-encompassing "field of power"; a blueprint of its internal structure must be produced; and the nature and functions of its actors' *habitus* must be taken carefully into account. Along the way, furthermore, one must be diligent to identify any and all forms of symbolic violence manifest in the field, because symbolic violence is the paramount source of distinctions between individuals and groups in society. And only where there is distinction can there be domination.[29]

Bourdieu's attention to the power differential as a foundational element in understanding social interaction is one of his central assertions:

> Any analysis of the logic of the interactions that may develop between agents in direct confrontation with one another must be subordinated to the construction of the structure of the objective relations between the positions these agents occupy in the religious field, a structure that determines both the form their inter-actions may assume and the representations they may have of these interactions.[30]

It is significant that most work on the *sensus fidei* focuses attention on the beliefs and practices of either individuals or the univer-sal Church, not attending at all to the social positions and power relations of the various constituents.[31]

When Bourdieu turns his attention to the relationship between clergy and laity in the realm of religion, it is not surpris-ing that his analysis focuses on power:

> The constitution of the religious field goes hand-in-hand with the objective dispossession of those who are excluded from it and who thereby find themselves constituted as the *laity* (or the *profane,* in the double meaning of the word) dispossessed of *religious capital* (as accumulated symbolic labor) and recognizing the legitimacy of that dispossession from the mere fact that they misrecognize it as such.[32]

Struggle in the religious field is between the Church (*église*) and its priests, on the one hand, and the prophet (*heresiarch*), on the other. Furthermore, Bourdieu identifies distortions that religious language serves to neglect or suppress. He argues that most, if not all, religious language obfuscates the true power dynamic—what he calls "misrecognition." For example, the word *pilgrimage* masks the fact that this religious travel is really tourism, where certain parties gain economic benefit (i.e., capital)—just as priests are "called" to a higher office, when, in fact, they have been granted social and economic capital through promotion. This "double game" uses euphemisms to cover up structures of domination.

Bourdieu's recognition of the role of power dynamics within the religious field raises critical questions for discerning the *sensus fidei*—particularly considering the lack of mediating structures for expressing and incorporating this sense of the faith into a larger ecclesial context. If one takes his analysis seriously, one must attend to the social relationships that serve as a matrix and as the engine for religious practices. This attention generates new, and often disturbing, questions for those in power. Does the division between clergy and laity already tip ecclesial discourse in such a way as to prevent genuine listening and communal discernment? Did the debate about the use of the term *lay ecclesial minister*, and similar titles, such as *chaplain* and *coordinator*, reflect a struggle over who holds power?[33] Given the bifurcation between laity and clergy, and its distorting impact, who really can speak for the *sensus fidei?*

Bourdieu's understanding of the constitutive role of power and its unequal distribution between the laity and clergy would seem to doom the lay ecclesial minister—precisely as lay—to irrelevance. Yet, in the formal recognition of lay ecclesial ministry, the model of an all-or-nothing distribution of power begins to crack. Bourdieu saw that in the religious field the role of the prophet is crucial for change. The prophet occupies a position where power is gained "outside" the institutional structure. Bourdieu argues that the prophet derives power, in part, from those with whom she is communicating. He contends that prophecy "is only effective if its message resonates with the understandings and interests of the laity."[34] Only if such a social context exists can the prophetic voice be heard. This "derived power" is based on how well the prophet can express the experiences and aspirations in a way that resonates with the community. Though Bourdieu is not a theologian, his focus on the role of the prophet aligns with key theological principles that mark current conversations of lay ecclesial ministry and the *sensus fidei*. Power and authority are derived from how well the minister can express and connect with the experience of the individual and community.

It is the contention of this chapter that lay ecclesial ministry, given its distinctive social location at the boundary between laity and clergy, is uniquely positioned to help the Church break down rigid boundaries and give rise to a new set of practices for Christian living today. For lay ecclesial ministers to assist in "birthing" this new Church, much work needs to be done. This work includes expansion of current theologies of ministry; analyses of the dynamics of social interaction; facilitation of genuine dialogue; and revision of the education and formation of lay ecclesial ministers. Practically, lay ecclesial ministry must be fostered and sustained. The recommendations outlined in *Co-Workers* must be implemented and extended.

New forms of lay ecclesial ministry must be supported. Within ministerial formation, greater attention must be paid to the skills of facilitating genuine conversations, deliberations, and discernment. Hahnenberg recognizes that lay ecclesial ministers must be equipped with these new skills: "We need a theology of community organizing, a theology of the charism of coordination. By virtue of their leadership roles, lay ecclesial ministers are not just ministers in relationship with others, they are ministers with a special responsibility for fostering ministerial relationships among others."[35] The development of these skills requires programmatic changes in the education of lay ecclesial ministers. These are significant changes and require widespread, sustained effort. In addition to the ecclesial resources identified in *Co-Workers*, the work of organizations such as the AGPIM and NALM is needed. AGPIM, with its years of collaborative work among a wide range of schools dedicated to ministry formation, is positioned to play a central role in curricular development and promoting programs dedicated to fashioning lay ecclesial ministers as agents of the *sensus fidei*. In the concrete, local contexts within which they work, lay ecclesial ministers serve as a critical mediator, a bridge, between the sense of the faith of the faithful and those who articulate that faith in authentic and authoritative ways.

CONCLUSION

This chapter argues that lay ecclesial ministers play a critical role in nurturing and articulating the *sensus fidei*. Their social location at the borders of the clergy/laity divide is a basis for challenging rigid dichotomies and generating new understandings of the Church and its faith. Bourdieu's work is helpful in recognizing the social dynamics and the role of power in constructing beliefs and practices. Forming the lay ecclesial minister to be a spokesperson for the sense of the faithful requires the efforts of many within the Church—especially those practical theologians who study ordinary believers and educate future ministers.

NOTES

1. LG 12.

2. International Theological Commission, *Sensus Fidei in the Life of the Church* (2014), 3, http://www.vatican.va/roman_curia/congregations/cfaith/cti_documents/rc_cti_20140610_sensus-fidei_en.html.

3. ITC, *Sensus Fidei*, 50.

4. Edward P. Hahnenberg, "Learning to Discern the *Sensus Fidelium Latinamente*: A Dialogue with Orlando Espín," in *Learning from* All *the Faithful: A Contemporary Theology of the* Sensus Fidei, ed. Bradford E. Hinze and Peter C. Phan (Eugene, OR: Pickwick, 2016), 270. See Orlando Espín, *The Faith of the People: Theological Reflections on Popular Catholicism* (Maryknoll, NY: Orbis, 1997).

5. See Robert A. Orsi, *Between Heaven and Earth: The Religious Worlds People Make and the Scholars Who Study Them* (Princeton, NJ: Princeton University Press, 2005) and *History and Presence* (Cambridge, MA: Belknap Press, 2016).

6. Richard R. Gaillardetz, "Power and Authority in the Church: Emerging Issues," in *A Church with Open Doors: Catholic Ecclesiology for the Third Millennium*, ed. Richard R. Gaillardetz and Edward P. Hahnenberg (Collegeville, MN: Liturgical Press, 2015), 95.

7. Gaillardetz, "Power and Authority in the Church," 93–94.

8. ITC, *Sensus Fidei in the Life of the Church*, 67.

9. Hahnenberg, "Learning to Discern the *Sensus Fidelium Latinamente*," 265. Utilizing relationship, rather than ontological states, as fundamental to an understanding of ministry has profound implications. See Edward P. Hahnenberg, *Ministries: A Relational Approach* (New York: Crossroad, 2003).

10. Hahnenberg, "Learning to Discern the *Sensus Fidelium Latinamente*," 265.

11. CG 372.

12. CG3 16.

13. Thomas F. O'Meara, "Being a Ministering Church: Insights from History," in *Lay Ecclesial Ministry: Pathways to the Future*, ed. Zeni Fox (Lanham, MD: Rowan & Littlefield, 2010), 61.

14. *Co-Workers*, 14.

15. H. Richard McCord Jr., "*Co-Workers in the Vineyard of the Lord*: A Pastoral Perspective on Its Reception," Fox, 6 (italics in original).

16. Richard R. Gaillardetz, "The Theological Reception of *Co-Workers in the Vineyard of the Lord*," Fox, 21–29.

17. Gaillardetz, "Theological Reception of *Co-Workers*," 21.

18. Sharon A. Euart, "Lay Ecclesial Ministry and Parish Leadership Options: Canonical Reflections in Light of *Co-Workers in the Vineyard*," in Fox, 104.

19. Zeni Fox, "Strengthening Ministerial Leadership: Perspectives from Systems Theory," in Fox, 203–4.

20. For an important text on the relationship between marginality and interpretations, see Terry A. Veling, *Living in the Margins: Intentional Communities and the Art of Interpretation* (New York: Crossroad, 1996).

21. Historically, religious orders (sisters, brothers, etc.) were also working at the boundaries.

22. Fox, "Strengthening Ministerial Leadership," 208.

23. Edward P. Hahnenberg, "Theology of Lay Ecclesial Ministry: Future Trajectories," in Fox, 71.

24. Hahnenberg, "Theology of Lay Ecclesial Ministry," 75 (italics in original).

25. LG 12.

26. See Bradford E. Hinze, *Practices of Dialogue in the Roman Catholic Church: Aims and Obstacles, Lessons and Laments* (New York: Continuum, 2006).

27. Pierre Bourdieu, *Practical Reason* (Stanford, CA: Stanford University Press, 1998), 25.

28. Pierre Bourdieu, *The Field of Cultural Production* (Columbia University Press, 1993), 78–79.

29. Terry Rey, *Bourdieu on Religion: Imposing Faith and Legitimacy* (New York: Routledge, 2014), 55.

30. Pierre Bourdieu, "Legitimation and Structured Interests in Weber's Sociology of Religion," in *Max Weber, Rationality, and Modernity*, ed. Sam Whimster and Scott Lash (London: Allen and Unwin, 1987), 121 (italics in the original).

31. It is significant to note that one of the criticisms leveled against Baggett's deep-textured analysis of the *sensus fidei*, an analysis in which he used Bourdieu's concepts of *habitus* and field, is his lack of attention to power differentials in the Church. See Robert Cortegiano, "The Use of Sociology in the Study of *Sensus Fidelium*: An Evaluation of the Contribution of Jerome Baggett," in Hinze and Phan, *Learning from All the Faithful*, 113.

32. Pierre Bourdieu, "Genesis and Structure of the Religious Field," *Comparative Social Research* 13 (1991): 9 (italics in original).

33. See Congregation for Clergy et al., "Instruction on Certain Questions Regarding the Collaboration of the Non-ordained Faithful in the Sacred Ministry of Priests," practical provisions, art. 1, http://www.vatican.va/roman_curia/congregations/cclergy/documents/rc_con_interdic_doc_15081997_en.html.

34. Rey, *Bourdieu on Religion*, 123.

35. Hahnenberg, "Theology of Lay Ecclesial Ministry, 79.

PART TWO

THE PRACTICES OF MINISTERIAL FORMATION

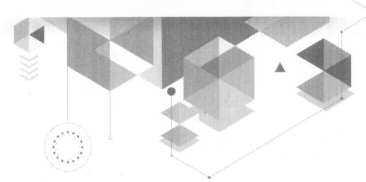

Chapter Five

YOU TOO GO OUT INTO THE VINEYARD

Ministerial Formation in a Culturally Diverse Church

Hosffman Ospino

Catholics in the United States welcomed the twenty-first century in the midst of major cultural transitions. Secularism (nearly a quarter of the U.S. population claim not to associate with a religion or a religious institution) and defection (almost forty million people in the United States are former Catholics) are good contenders to top the list of sociocultural concerns that keep Catholics awake at night, and each deserves much attention when reflecting about ministerial formation.[1] However, I contend that cultural diversity is likely the most significant factor redefining the U.S. Catholic experience today. While millions do not self-identify as Catholic anymore, and the winds of secularism blow perhaps stronger than ever before in our society, Catholicism continues to grow in the United States.

Three dynamics stand behind the continued growth of U.S. Catholicism: immigration, family reunification, and high birthrates among young Catholics. Of interest, however, is that most people fueling the growth of U.S. Catholicism are not Euro-American, white, or European. Most trace their roots primarily to Latin America and the Caribbean, Asia and Africa. For instance, Hispanics are responsible for 71 percent of the growth of Catholicism since 1960.[2] The "new" Catholic faces tend to be significantly younger (e.g., median age of Hispanics is twenty-nine; median age of Asians is thirty-four) compared to Euro-American, white Catholics (median age fifty-five).

The formation of Catholic pastoral leaders in the rest of the twenty-first century demands institutions, curricula, and pedagogies committed to prepare women and men intentionally to serve amid cultural diversity. Some Catholic universities, seminaries, and pastoral institutes are pioneering interesting models of ministerial formation (e.g., Hispanic Serving Institutions); others are making slow changes. Yet, it is fair to say that most Catholic institutions of ministerial formation and the organizations associated with them still have a long way to go to embrace the culturally diverse nature of present-day U.S. Catholicism. Many have not managed to transition from a U.S. Catholic experience that was primarily white, Euro-American a few decades ago—and primarily at the service of that population—to one highly diverse in terms of culture, race, and ethnicity. Some seem not to fully understand what it means to be Catholic amid cultural diversity; others choose to resist it or ignore it; and far too many remain tepid in their commitments.

I suggest that the following two factors permeate attitudes of resistance, inability, and tepidness: (1) lack of cultural, racial, and ethnic diversity among faculty and administrators in Catholic efforts of ministerial formation; and (2) lack of a simple, yet prophetic vision that looks at cultural diversity as an opportunity to be embraced, not a problem to be solved. This chapter offers some constructive notes to address both factors.

SETTING THE VISION

CONTENDING WITH
CULTURAL DIVERSITY...AGAIN

Compare the following three statements:

"The Church [Italians] found here was far remote from
what they had been accustomed to at home. The immediate result was, as [Oscar] Handlin says, 'a struggle,
parish by parish, between the old Catholics and the
new...that involved the nationality of the priest, the
language to be used, the Saints' days to be observed,
and even the name of the church....And there was the
greatest grievance of all, for by the 1890s, the hierarchy was almost entirely of Irish descent.'"[3]

"The Chicano has a different view and different insights
into the interpretation of law, liturgy, and moral theology, and these have been suppressed. And when
one's values are suppressed, a person has two choices:
cultural suicide or rejection of the institution. Both
phenomena are normal for [Spanish-speaking per-
sons] in the United States toward [their] church."[4]

"We also realize the ways that racism has permeated
the life of the Church and persists to a degree even
today....Not long ago, in many Catholic parishes,
people of color were relegated to segregated seating, and required to receive the Holy Eucharist after
white parishioners. All too often, leaders of the
Church have remained silent about the horrific violence and other racial injustices perpetuated against
African Americans and others."[5]

These texts capture poignantly the long, sometimes repeti-
tive journey of Catholics in the United States wrestling with questions of culture, language, race, and ethnicity within their own
institution. All three texts point to relationships among Catholics.

What makes the three texts fascinating is not just the content, or the fact that cultural, racial, and ethnic diversity are often sources of tension in faith communities, but the time periods to which they refer: late nineteenth century, mid-twentieth century, and early twenty-first century, respectively.

Many contemporary conversations about cultural diversity in Catholic faith communities and institutions of ministerial formation throughout the United States are far from being "new." Anyone who has ventured to study the history of U.S. Catholicism can see many of today's conversations as déjà vu.[6] Yes, we have been there. Yes, we have wrestled with difference and diversity before. Have we learned anything from the process?

The hope is that U.S. Catholics have learned a few good lessons after centuries of presence in the U.S. territory—engaging in constant processes of trial and error, retaining some cultural traditions and letting others go, embracing the "American way" of doing things while being critical of it when it appears to be incompatible with Catholicism.[7] Yet, we need to be honest. Many Catholics, including those who work in ministry and are engaged in theological education for ministry, often fail to know our own Catholic history. Many simply choose to ignore the past and live in the present as if things have always been this way.

I am somewhat bewildered when I meet classes of graduate students in ministerial and theological programs, or address large groups of pastoral leaders at conferences, and discover how little many know about questions of cultural diversity in the Church, yesterday and today. Every now and then, pastoral leaders tend to assume that to minister in a culturally diverse Church, "good will" and some form of "uncritical abandonment to God's divine providence" are good enough. I do believe in good will as well as in God's divine providence, yet I also believe that grace builds upon nature and we must do our homework. We must roll up our sleeves, learn our histories, study reality as it confronts us, analyze shifting sociocultural dynamics, denounce prejudice, and adjust processes of ministerial formation as needed in order to respond to the challenges of serving in a diverse Church.

It is not rare to encounter Catholic pastoral leaders who are convinced that the first roots of Catholicism in the United States were established during the nineteenth century with the arrival of English, Irish, German, and Italian Catholics. Such a view tends to ignore or underappreciate previous Catholic migration waves and the history of Catholics living in large parts of what today is the U.S. territory, particularly Hispanic and French Catholics during colonial times.[8] Affirming such cultural roots is important if one wants to understand better the Hispanic presence that is transforming U.S. Catholicism in our day.

Many Catholics still speak of racism as if this corrosive and degrading social cancer—a grave sin, to use theological language—were a dynamic affecting "other people."[9] As Catholics, we can excel at turning the conversation about racism into abstract talk, devoid of real-life connections. Such strategies can lead into the slippery slope of assuming that we do not need to talk about racism in our communities or ministerial formation programs. Racism is much more than the attitude of some people "not being nice to others," or something that Uncle Joe and Aunt Mary do because that is who they are and one cannot change certain people's ways. Racism, at least as primarily experienced in the United States, has to do with explicit discrimination, denial of rights, and violence, expressed in various ways, against people of dark skin color to benefit groups of people with lighter skin color.[10] No serious conversation about ministerial formation in a culturally diverse Church should ignore such reality.

Our U.S. Catholic history is not innocent. Racism and exclusion unfortunately have accompanied the remarkable growth of many of our communities. For a long time, Black, Hispanic, Asian, and Native American children were excluded systemically from educational institutions, including Catholic schools, because of the color of their skin and their cultures.[11] Black and Hispanic Catholics were not welcomed in most Catholic churches serving primarily white, Euro-American Catholics until only a few decades ago. Still in our day, some Catholic communities struggle with racial and cultural diversity. Many of the so-called traditionally Black parishes and Hispanic parishes emerged mainly in response to racial exclusion and marginalization.

This is our history. Yes, it is déjà vu, and recognizing déjà vu is good. The unfolding of history gives Catholics in the United States another opportunity to contend with cultural diversity—and to do it better than it was done in the past. We certainly do not come into this conversation as blank slates. We have a history that is part of us; it is a history that we must own. Ministerial formation programs that ignore that overarching history and the particular histories of the various cultural communities that constitute the Church in this country put their credibility at risk.

As we enter the second decade of the twenty-first century, a rich expression of cultural diversity defines U.S. Catholicism. In broad strokes, about 47 percent of U.S. Catholics self-identify as Euro-American/white, 43 percent as Hispanic, 5 percent as Asian/Pacific Islander, 4 percent as African American/Black, and slightly less than 1 percent as Native American. Nearly 60 percent of all Catholics younger than eighteen are Hispanic. We can already anticipate the type of U.S. Catholic experience that will shape the rest of this century. Are we preparing our pastoral leaders to serve the Church of today and tomorrow?

REVISITING THE QUESTION OF A "THEOLOGY OF CULTURE"

Catholic theological reflections about ministry have been profoundly enriched during the last half century by a renewed focus on culture.[12] Much of this focus owes its impetus to the positive anthropology and cosmology that imbued the documents that emerged from Vatican II (1962–65), particularly the Pastoral Constitution on the Church in the Modern Word, *Gaudium et Spes*. But *Gaudium et Spes* did not develop in a vacuum. Many of the insights about culture found in this document echo important developments in the social and human sciences available at the time. Much has been said about culture after the Council. The work of anthropologists, philosophers, and practical theologians in particular has also been instrumental, not to mention the influence of the field of cultural studies.[13]

The opening words of *Gaudium et Spes* reveal the audacity of those gathered at the Council to be challenged by historical reality as the starting point of evangelization and theological reflection: "The joys and hopes, the grief and anguish of the people of our time, especially of those who are poor or afflicted, are the joys and hopes, the grief and anguish of the followers of Christ as well."[14] These powerful words respond to the same document's conviction that to advance the work of evangelization, it is imperative to read the signs of the times: "In every age, the Church carries the responsibility of reading the signs of the times and of interpreting them in the light of the Gospel."[15]

On the one hand, we learn that evangelization does not happen in a vacuum, but always functions in response to the hopes and needs of flesh-and-blood women and men in the here and now of a particular historical and sociocultural existence. On the other hand, evangelization must be an exercise of discernment. With this framework in mind, therefore, the pastoral constitution presents us with a powerful and dynamic definition of culture, which reflects an important anthropological turn compared to previous definitions of culture:

> The word "culture" in the general sense refers to all those things which go to the refining and developing of humanity's diverse mental and physical endowments. We strive to subdue the earth by our knowledge and labor; we humanize social life both in the family and in the whole civic community through the improvement of customs and institutions; we express through our works the great spiritual experiences and aspirations of humanity through the ages; we communicate and preserve them to be an inspiration for the progress of many people, even of all humanity.[16]

This short paragraph provides three important insights. First, *Gaudium et Spes* names an obvious, yet sometimes forgotten aspect of reality: *every human person is shaped by culture and everyone belongs to a cultural tradition.* Today we take these assumptions for granted, yet the West has not always understood culture in such a broad way. At points, the term *culture* has been associated primarily with social status, educational attainment, and even blood lineage.[17] It was not unusual for dominant groups in a society to speak of minoritized communities as "cultured" groups—as if those enjoying some power or privilege were not also "cultured." Naming others as "cultured" usually emphasizes external, colorful, and exotic aspects of the cultural traditions (e.g., dress, music, food) belonging to groups considered culturally other, while ignoring and dismissing the depths of their intellectual and spiritual lives. Everyone is shaped by a particular cultural matrix. There is no such thing as a cultureless or culturally neutral person.[18]

Second, *Gaudium et Spes* is keen to affirm *human agency* in the process of building culture. In other words, culture is the result of human intentionality. Such insight is important because it demands that we recognize every person in society, regardless of his or her racial, ethnic, social, religious, and even migratory status, as a contributor to culture. Monadic interpretations of culture, represented in convictions such as "our culture cannot change" or "there is only one way to become part of this culture" are challenged by the fact that cultures change as people change. The more we empower people to be agents of cultural construction and transformation, the more people will own the responsibility to "render social life more human," as the document asserts.

Third, if human cultures are the result of human effort and intentionality, we must then acknowledge their *spiritual dimension.* Cultures are expressions of the human capacity to make meaning. Such capacity reflects who we are as spiritual beings. As Christians, we find ourselves making meaning of reality in light of our relationship with the God of Jesus Christ who calls us to communion and perfection. We do this in light of the values of the gospel. However, we make meaning by borrowing the language, symbols, artifacts, rituals, and traditions of our most immediate cultural reality. When someone adopts a new culture different from the one in which she or he was born, chances are that this person adopts its language, symbols, artifacts, rituals, and traditions, yet without necessarily forgoing those once embraced.

It is in the realm of culture that God comes to our encounter, affirming who we are as agents of our reality and as spiritual beings. Humanity receives the gift of God's revelation and interprets it in the particularity of culture. Through such engagement with humanity in the realm of culture(s), God reveals a "divine pedagogy":

> The ultimate goal of God's pedagogical project is to give life to every aspect of our human existence: "I came so that they might have life and have it more

abundantly" (John 10:10). That includes transforming the cultures in which we live as these allow the message of the gospel to take root so God's reign becomes a reality everywhere—and for everyone. As this occurs, God's pedagogy is prophetic. It shows the path and affirms the signs of life present in all cultures. Yet it also unmasks, confronts, and rejects the path and the signs of death, sin, and injustice that may be present in them.[19]

Culture, therefore, is the medium through which we encounter God, others, and the world. It is within culture that we make meaning. It is in culture that we assert our spiritual existence. However, there is no one, single culture that mediates *exclusively* the encounter with God in history and empowers people to make meaning and assert their spirituality. In fact, there are many cultures because there are many ways of being human. In principle, save for those aspects that are contrary to the gospel, every culture has the potential to mediate the encounter with God in history and empower people to make meaning and assert their spirituality. We find ourselves, therefore, facing the possibility of being human and being Christian in many ways.[20]

Culturally diverse contexts are perfect spaces to contemplate how those multiple ways of being human and of being Christian coincide. There, cultures negotiate values, live in tension, learn from one another, and challenge one another. Culturally diverse contexts allow many ecclesial particularities to flourish, with their own characteristics, each providing a glimpse of the universality of what it means to be the people of God—the Church.

During the last half century, Catholic theologians, philosophers, and other thinkers have explored theoretical models that help us name the relationship between faith and culture(s). "Inculturation" has captured the imagination of many, using the mystery of the incarnation as inspiration. Just as the Word of God becomes flesh in the realm of history, transforming it on the path to the perfection God envisioned from the beginning, the gospel enters a culture to transform it from within, affirming those elements that are true, good, and beautiful in it, and purifying those that are not.[21] This is an oversimplification, of course, but it provides us with some basic understanding of what inculturation aims to capture.

Yet, as valuable as the category of inculturation is, it does not seem the most appropriate to name and explain the complex dynamic of what happens in culturally diverse contexts. Besides assuming an often taken-for-granted, one-way relationship—that is, gospel transforms culture—and often failing to be uncritical of the fact that "the gospel" is actually mediated by unnamed cultural categories and presuppositions, inculturation seldom accounts for the complexity of multiple ways of being human and being Christian in the same context, and how those many ways interact with one another.[22]

One category that holds promise for a renewed theology of culture in the context of cultural diversity is that of "interculturality." Interculturality allows cultures to enter into dialogue as universal particularities that hold their own ground and validity yet remain open to being transformed as they engage in critical interaction with other cultures. Members of all cultures in a diverse context participate in the construction of knowledge. From a Christian perspective, the multiplicity of cultures is an opportunity to contemplate many ways in which the Church can interpret, live, and celebrate the mystery of Jesus Christ.[23]

An intercultural approach to culture, and ultimately to theological education in a culturally diverse Church, facilitates the emergence of voices and traditions belonging to cultural groups that at some historical point were marginalized because of social, political, economic, religious, or sociocultural reasons. Interculturality is essentially an empowering framework that takes the risk of naming the sins of the past with prophetic voice (e.g., racism), perhaps upsetting a given status quo, while remaining open to being surprised by what the "cultural other" can say.

Interculturality provides an interpretive framework that understands cultures as much more than monads or simple, isolated units. Cultures are complex and interdependent, often changing realities. To unravel their meaning, it is necessary to engage the methods and wisdom of multiple disciplines. Interculturality not only fosters, but also thrives in interdisciplinarity. Presupposing a much-needed intellectual—and religious—humility, interculturality requires that scholars and educators engage in dialogue with various disciplines, learning from their methods, insights, and discoveries as they analyze culture. The implications of such commitment to interdisciplinarity holds enormous potential for theological education in culturally diverse contexts, particularly in matters of curriculum development, collaboration with other schools and programs, and the embrace of pedagogical practices that affirm and sustain diversity.

In an intercultural worldview, *difference* is perceived first not as suspect and obscure, perhaps threatening, but as novel and charged with possibility—while always remaining mindful of limitations. Cultural diversity and difference, therefore, are not judged, embraced, or dismissed a priori in light of preconceived notions, subject to the ever-present biases that inevitably shape human understanding of reality. Rather, difference is engaged in *relation to* and in *relation with* other cultural realities. Interculturality is an invitation to confront dominant models of action and reflection that dismiss, consciously or unconsciously, the voices, stories, experiences, and ideas that are present in culturally diverse contexts. Interculturality engenders hope insofar as it affirms the potential of culture, as well as the agency of every human person, in their own particularity, to journey as architects of culture in the here and now of their historical existence.[24]

THEOLOGICAL EDUCATION FOR MINISTRY IN A CULTURALLY DIVERSE CHURCH

Institutions dedicated to the theological and ministerial formation of Catholic pastoral leaders in the United States must ask the following question: *What kind of pastoral leaders do our faith communities need today, in light of their spiritual needs and particular sociocultural location?* No institution or program of ministerial formation can afford to circumvent this question. Ironically, there are signs that far too many institutions and programs advance under the illusion that they can move forward without seriously addressing the question. How far can they go?

In the midst of the demographic and sociocultural transitions that are transforming U.S. Catholicism this century, institutions dedicated to the theological and ministerial formation of pastoral leaders must be aware of the following three temptations:

One is becoming self-serving. It is true that every seminary, university, independent theologate, and pastoral institute has a vision upon which it was established and a specific mission to advance. One cannot ignore, however, that the way institutions carry out their mission often changes. Some institutions may have grown too comfortable with their prominence or with practices of recruitment and formation that may have yielded abundant fruits at a different historical time. They may assume that the traditional populations enrolling in them today do so mainly because of their brand name or the reputation of their programs. They may be more concerned about rankings and standards of accreditation than making necessary adjustments and investments to serve new populations.

A second is being unable to adjust educational environments to welcome students from diverse communities that are transforming Catholicism at the grassroots. There is an air of institutional entitlement in many of our Catholic institutions dedicated to the theological and ministerial formation of pastoral leaders. Despite the rich diversity that characterizes Catholicism in parishes and dioceses, still the vast majority of faculty and administrators in these institutions are Euro-American, white, mostly male, and primarily English-speaking. Academic programs, extracurricular activities, lecture series, administrative priorities, among other dynamics, reflect primarily the concerns of Euro-American Catholics, who tend to be the "majority" group in such institutions, although not in the grassroots communities that are expected to send their leaders to be formed in them. In far too many programs, faculty and administrators of color are severely underrepresented. Many of these Catholic institutions replicate the tokenistic hiring practices (e.g., one Hispanic scholar, one

Black scholar) that continue to plague higher education in the United States.

Finally, abandoning ship is a temptation. The demographic and sociocultural transformations that are reshaping U.S. Catholicism are often accompanied by financial and administrative struggles in institutions dedicated to the theological and ministerial formation of pastoral leaders. In some parts of the country, schools are merging or closing, sometimes without measuring the impact of such decisions upon the new Catholic populations. In parts of the country where the Catholic population is booming, there is little or no investment to open similar institutions. We are failing mightily at creating structures of solidarity—something about which Catholics preach regularly—that compel stronger institutions to support others with fewer resources. We begin to see examples of ministerial formation institutions and programs that finally transferred leadership to faculty and administrators of color. However, many of these leaders are receiving "sinking ships" that force them to shoulder the blame for failures that began decades earlier or the responsibility to fix inadequate administrative and formation models—sometimes without the necessary resources to do so.

These three temptations are real, and we must be alert to them as we embrace the fact that Catholicism in the United States is a richly diverse experience. Naming the temptations is helpful because it helps us to highlight that the landscape of theological education for ministry is changing. "To prepare pastoral leaders for the changing and complex world they will encounter in the twenty-first century parish, ministry education programs must themselves adapt their models and expectations," asserts Marti R. Jewell.[25] I could not agree more.

Changes at the grassroots, especially in parishes, are also exacerbated by changes in the place of theology and religion in the world of higher education.[26] Daniel O. Aleshire, former executive director of the Association of Theological Schools (ATS), observes that we are currently witnessing the transformation of the "professional paradigm" of theological education into a paradigm that affirms personal and spiritual formation, without abandoning the commitment to intellectual and pastoral rigor.[27] This observation makes more sense in the world of Protestant theological education. In fact, Aleshire sees Catholic theological education as a model for other expressions of this enterprise in the United States.[28] Yet, his point is well taken.

Something is changing in the way we educate today's Catholic pastoral leaders. I am convinced that the professionalization of pastoral leaders emerging from the minoritized communities that are transforming U.S. Catholicism is more urgent than ever. Therefore, we should not give up on this. At the same time, we need to pay attention to models of theological and ministerial formation emerging within these communities. In particular, I bring attention to the emergence of diocesan pastoral institutes, centers of ministerial formation sponsored by ecclesial movements, and nondegree programs of leadership formation associated with seminaries and universities. More reflection about these emerging initiatives, largely the effort of nonwhite Catholics, remains a work in process.

A vision for Catholic ministerial formation in a culturally diverse Church would not be complete if I did not mention areas of growth. Allow me to mention five:

1. Every program of Catholic theological and ministerial formation must have a cultural diversity requirement. Most professional schools in other fields have such a requirement for their professionals. Catholic ministerial formation programs should not be the exception.
2. Catholic theological and ministerial formation programs in the United States must ensure that most courses—if not all—introduce students to the histories, practices, bodies of knowledge, spiritualities, and methods of theological reflection of the communities that constitute the Catholic population in this country.
3. Catholic institutions dedicated to theological and ministerial formation must redouble their efforts to

diversify their faculties and administration. Hiring processes must be checked to ensure that institutions move beyond tokenism.

4. Catholic institutions dedicated to theological and ministerial formation must develop credible and effective pathways from local noncredit programs to programs that will lead to degrees, ordination, and other forms of authorization, especially among underrepresented populations.

5. No one should be authorized to serve ministerially in the Catholic Church in the United States without clearly demonstrating the intercultural competencies necessary to work in today's diverse communities. We need better criteria to assess these competencies and integrate them into the entire process of theological and ministerial formation.[29]

PRACTICAL COMMITMENTS

Theological education in a culturally diverse Church—and a culturally diverse society—requires a growing awareness of who we are as an ecclesial community in the here and now of our historical reality. In the United States of America, we cannot effectively prepare women and men for Catholic ministry without having an informed understanding of the diverse groups that constitute our ecclesial and sociopolitical communities. However, disengaged understanding and mere awareness are not enough.

When confronted with the reality of cultural diversity, theological education for ministry demands practical commitments, which in the face of cultural bias, resistance, or institutional self-preservation, must espouse a prophetic and countercultural character. Three such commitments are essential. They are the commitment to (1) institutional diversification; (2) intercultural competency; and (3) honest assessment. Let me share a few brief thoughts on each commitment.

1. CHOOSE INSTITUTIONAL DIVERSIFICATION

A common concern among Catholic institutions of theological and ministerial formation is that of diversification of their academic communities. Such concern is often encouraged by accrediting entities such as the Association for Theological Schools (ATS). For instance, the ATS general standards for accreditation ask member schools to consider the following:

- In their institutional and educational practices, theological schools shall promote awareness of the diversity of race, ethnicity, and culture widely present in North America and shall seek to enhance participation and leadership of persons of color in theological education.[30]
- Schools shall give evidence of efforts in admissions to encourage diversity in such areas as race, ethnicity, region, denomination, gender, or disability.[31]
- Faculty should be of sufficient diversity and number to meet the multifaceted demands of teaching, learning, and research. Hiring practices should be attentive to the value of diversity in race, ethnicity, and gender.[32]
- In accordance with the school's purpose and constituencies, insofar as possible, the members of the school's own community of learning should also represent diversity in race, age, ethnic origin, and gender.[33]
- Insofar as possible, staff shall be appointed with a view toward diversity in race, ethnicity, and gender.[34]

Compliance with such standards helps institutions discern how to develop practices that lead not only to the diversification of the student body, faculty, and administrators, but also to the creation of academic environments where cultural diversity is honestly affirmed and sustained.

The commitment to diversification also echoes the long-held view in many quarters of U.S. higher education, namely, that an inclusive, empowering, and participatory education is essential for the construction of a society that embodies similar characteristics.

Educational institutions dedicated to professional training model themselves on the type of community for which they train their leaders. The urgency of such an educational vision becomes more critical when there is an explicit commitment to forming members of underrepresented communities, which, for historical, social, and even legal reasons, have not benefited from regular processes of leadership development. In some cases, such explicit commitment means reparation; in others, it calls from schools a preferential option for the poor and most vulnerable; in still others, such commitment demands explicit recognition that without certain investments (e.g., scholarships, dedicated mentoring, affinity groups) many pastoral leaders from underrepresented communities will continue to lag behind more privileged groups. All three imperatives find strong echoes in Catholic social teaching.

For Catholic seminaries, universities, independent theologates, and pastoral institutes in the United States, a commitment to institutional diversification should flow naturally from the cultural diversity that defines Catholicism in the country. When that is not the case, institutions of ministerial formation need to ask, to what level are they "in sync" with the diverse faith communities at the grassroots that they claim to serve? How culturally diverse is the population that they are welcoming into their formation programs? How much of a commitment to a culturally diverse faculty and administration do they really have? What support structures exist to cultivate and affirm cultural diversity? How do they support a vision that honors cultural diversity as a sine qua non characteristic of their entire educational praxis? These questions, as we will see below, echo a much-needed set of criteria for assessment to demonstrate progress or lack thereof in this area of ministerial formation.

2. FOSTER INTERCULTURAL COMPETENCIES

The quest for professionalization in ministry, at least in the U.S. context, goes hand in hand with the identification of desirable competencies expected of pastoral leaders. It is clear that readiness for ministerial activity demands more than just the completion of a training program, receiving a degree in theology or ministry, joining a guild dedicated to pastoral activity, or being hired to perform certain ministerial functions within a faith community or institution. We cannot forget the importance of vocation and authorization, uniquely defined within specific theological frameworks discerned within particular religious traditions.[35] However, the professional dimensions of ministerial activity, with particular care to ensuring the well-being of those entrusted to ministers, presuppose certain human, spiritual, intellectual, and pastoral competencies on the part of the ministers.[36]

Besides these general areas of competence, which define much of the curriculum in programs of ministerial formation in the Catholic world, there are also specific competencies that respond to specific needs in a particular context. One of the most important contributions to Catholic ministerial formation in the United States is the call that the Catholic bishops made through their Secretariat for Cultural Diversity in the Church in 2011 for all pastoral ministers in the country, both those in formation and those already serving, to be trained in intercultural competencies.[37] An intercultural competency is here defined as "the capacity to communicate, relate, and work across cultural boundaries. It involves developing capacity in three areas: knowledge, skills, and attitudes."[38] The bishops' initiative builds upon decades of reflection and work by leaders in the business and political world, programs of ministerial formation through which members of religious orders prepared for missionary activity, and the wisdom of leaders and thinkers from other Christian denominations preparing ministers to serve in diverse communities.

There are different ways of receiving this training—the most common being the dedicated workshop. Nonetheless, the best way to achieve the goal that all ministers are adequately prepared to serve in culturally diverse communities throughout the country is by integrating such intercultural sensibilities into every aspect of ministerial formation. Intercultural competency workshops are important because they serve largely as remedial professional development opportunities. As such, it is unfortunate that many pastoral leaders consider them optional. Given the culturally diverse nature of Catholicism in the United States, we must move from such remedial approaches to models that fully integrate intercultural competence in all aspects of human, spiritual, intellectual, and pastoral formation.

3. EMBRACE CRITERIA TO ASSESS COMMITMENT TO CULTURAL DIVERSITY

A few decades ago, in his reflection on constructing local theologies, Robert J. Schreiter acknowledged that as local Christian communities develop theological discourses, usually drawing from their most immediate resources and interpreting the larger Christian tradition through the lens of those resources, there would arise a welcomed abundance of theological perspectives, all engaged in mutual dialogue. The larger Christian community would eventually be confronted with the following question: What makes a particular theological discourse Christian? The question is as valid for local and newer discourses as it is for those that are more established. One of the most interesting contributions of Schreiter's reflection was his proposal of general criteria to determine what makes a theology "Christian." He offered five criteria: (1) the cohesiveness of Christian performance, (2) the worshiping context and Christian performance, (3) the praxis of the community and Christian performance, (4) the judgment of other churches and Christian performance, and (5) the challenge to other churches and Christian performance.[39] These five criteria, while not overly restrictive, and not pretentiously exhaustive, provide a solid starting point for assessment.

I want to take a cue from Schreiter regarding the idea of general criteria, although I do this in the context of theological education in a diverse Church. I have had the privilege of serving for several years as a member of the Committee on Race and Ethnicity (CORE) of the Association of Theological Schools in the United States and Canada (ATS). A regular question that members of the committee discuss, echoed by leaders and faculty in the institutions of theological formation that we regularly engage, is the following: How do we know that our institutions of theological and ministerial formation are authentically embracing, affirming, and sustaining cultural diversity? The question calls for general and measurable criteria that would allow institutions to assess progress or, at a minimum, to establish achievable goals toward creating academic environments committed to affirming and sustaining cultural diversity.[40] Along these lines, I would propose five general criteria:

a. *Resonance with the needs and expectations of the diverse communities that constitute the Church.* Catholic institutions of theological and ministerial formation cannot afford to ignore the questions and realities that shape the lives of the culturally diverse communities that constitute the Church in the United States. Doing so would be to risk irrelevance or to preserve structures that historically have kept minoritized groups of Catholics on the margins. In attracting candidates for ministerial formation from culturally diverse communities, including communities serving Euro-American white Catholics, ministry programs have an obligation—ecclesial and educational—to engage the needs and expectations of those communities, to engage their questions, their traditions and ideas, and to prepare *all* those enrolled in ministerial formation programs to serve them.

b. *A culturally, racially, and ethnically diverse student body.* Students are perhaps the most visible sign of the commitments embraced by a Catholic institution of theological and ministerial formation. In an ideal world, the student population in these institutions would reflect the demographic and cultural composition of the communities that constitute Catholicism in the United States. A quick look at the student body in an educational institution can say much about how that institution wrestles with questions of race and ethnicity, of the contexts from which students are recruited, and of the school's preferred student profiles. At a deeper level, the cultural diversity of the student population (or the lack thereof) calls for an assessment of admissions practices, the assignment of targeted support resources, partnerships to ensure pathways into ministerial formation, structures to mentor nontraditional students, and even criteria to evaluate the work of students whose ways of learning may differ from those traditionally cultivated in the U.S. Catholic educational system.

114

c. *Culturally, racially, and ethnically diverse faculty and administrators.* The diversification of faculty remains one of the major challenges for both Catholic institutions of higher education and Catholic institutions of theological and ministerial formation in the United States. Historically, most faculty and administrators in these institutions have been white Euro-American men. We cannot dismiss the fact that the number of students from racially and ethnically underrepresented communities in most of these institutions has been exceedingly small, sometimes nonexistent, until recently. Therefore, it is difficult to expect a commitment from these populations to teaching and serving in these institutions in the form of "giving back," as is the case with white Euro-American Catholics. The numbers of some underrepresented populations, as in the case of Hispanic and Asian Catholics, has dramatically increased in recent decades; thus we as a Church are still discerning pathways by which leaders from these populations could enter into the institutions that are forming the next generations of Catholic ministers. These historical and sociodemographic realities are exacerbated by implicit and explicit biases that prevent the diversification of faculties and administrative bodies in Catholic institutions of theological and ministerial education. Among such practices, we must name—and denounce—racism; racial/ethnic tokenism; sexism (particularly affecting women of color); unrealistic expectations for faculty and administrators of color regarding institutional and ecclesial commitments; pigeonholing faculty of color as "spokespersons" and "experts" on their particular communities, yet not considering them seriously when they address broader issues; poor retention of faculty and administrators of color; earnings disparities; lack of promotion; and so on.

d. *An environment that reveals a community at home with its culturally diverse identity.* As we discern ways to assess and support how Catholic institutions of theological

115

and ministerial education in the United States can
thrive in a culturally diverse context, affirming and
sustaining such diversity, it is important to dismantle
the myth of cultural or racial neutrality. U.S. Catholicism is a culturally, racially, and ethnically diverse
experience. This is who we are, and our institutions,
especially those dedicated to ministerial formation,
should not pretend to ignore, bypass, or hide this cultural diversity. The antidote to invisibility is visibility. From a curricular perspective, every program of
Catholic ministerial formation in the United States at
this historical moment should have a cultural diversity
requirement. When one visits or enrolls in an institution committed to cultural diversity, or when one
explores its presence online, one must get the sense
that such commitment is sincere and explicit. Such
visibility is aided by signs that evoke diversity: the use
of multiple languages; creative forms of prayer and
worship that incorporate respectfully different cultural traditions; administrative personnel from various
cultural groups in decision-making positions; student
groups that bring cultural diversity to life; library
collections and exhibits that honor and celebrate cultural diversity; curricula that incorporate culturally
diverse voices as integral to intellectual inquiry as well
as to the everyday life of the school; and so on.

e. *Cultural diversity demonstratively permeates core aspects
of human, spiritual, intellectual, and pastoral formation
espoused by the institution.* A commitment to cultural
diversity should not be an addendum or an ancil-
lary concern in the life of Catholic institutions of
theological and ministerial formation in the United
States. Although we may speak of individual efforts
to develop intercultural competencies among students, faculty, and administrators, such efforts must
be integrated, almost seamlessly, into all aspects of
formation. In doing so, institutions of ministerial
formation model pedagogies and styles of leadership
that will help pastoral leaders to build communion

amid diversity in the contexts where they will serve upon completing their programs.[41]

There is no doubt that this is an exciting time in the history of Catholic theological and ministerial education in the United States. It is, without a doubt, a time of transitions stimulated by the challenges and possibilities of cultural diversity. Whether we look at cultural diversity as a new phenomenon or as déjà vu in the history of U.S. Catholicism, we must respond. Catholic institutions cannot remain passive before such challenges and opportunities. This is a time for creativity and pioneering efforts, a time to adjust what is not working, a time to take risks. Guided by a commitment to an intercultural view and inspired by a spirit of missionary discipleship, Catholic institutions of Catholic theological and ministerial formation are uniquely positioned to develop educational models, pedagogies, programs, and support networks that can inspire other faith-based institutions and communities dedicated to advancing similar goals. After all, we are training the scholars and leaders who will be at the forefront of those institutions and communities. *Carpe diem*!

NOTES

1. Being nonreligiously affiliated (aka, "none") does not necessarily mean that one does not believe in God or some form of divine power. The most comprehensive study of these trends is the multiyear project of the Pew Research Center. See "Religious Landscape Study" at https://www.pewforum.org/religious-landscape-study/.

2. See Hosffman Ospino, *Hispanic Ministry in Catholic Parishes* (Huntington, IN: Our Sunday Visitor, 2015), 8.

3. Francis X. Femminella, "The Impact of Italian Migration and American Catholicism," *The American Catholic Sociological Review* 22, no. 3 (1961): 237.

4. Rev. Alberto Carrillo, "Toward a National Hispano Church," a paper presented at the October 1971 PADRES Congress, cited in Antonio M. Stevens Arroyo, *Prophets Denied Honor: An Anthology on the Hispanic Church in the United States* (Maryknoll, NY: Orbis, 1980), 156.

5. USCCB, *Open Wide Our Hearts: The Enduring Call to Love; A Pastoral Letter against Racism* (Washington, DC: USCCB, 2018), 22.

6. See Charles E. Zech, Mary L. Gautier, Mark M. Gray, Jonathon L. Wiggins, and Thomas P. Gaunt, *Catholic Parishes of the 21st Century* (New York: Oxford University Press, 2017); Timothy Matovina, *Latino Catholicism: Transformation in America's Largest Church* (Princeton, NJ: Princeton University Press, 2011); Peter C. Phan, Diana L. Hayes, and Kevin F. Burke, eds., *Many Faces, One Church: Cultural Diversity and the American Catholic Experience* (Lanham, MD: Rowman & Littlefield, 2005).

7. See Hosffman Ospino, "Rethinking the Urban Parish in Light of the New Catholicity," *New Theology Review* 21, no. 1 (February 2008): 65–67.

8. See Matovina, *Latino Catholicism*, 1–41.

9. "Racism is a sin: a sin that divides the human family, blots out the image of God among specific members of that family, and violates the fundamental human dignity of those called to be children of the same Father. Racism is the sin that says some human beings are inherently superior and others essentially inferior because of races. It is the sin that makes racial characteristics the determining factor for the exercise of human rights" U.S. Catholic Bishops, *Brothers and Sisters to Us: Pastoral Letter on Racism* (Washington, DC: USCC, 1979). "Racist acts are sinful because they violate justice," USCCB, *Open Wide Our Hearts.* See also Bryan N. Massingale, *Racial Justice and the Catholic Church* (Maryknoll, NY: Orbis, 2010), xiv.

10. See Ibram X. Kendi, *Stamped from the Beginning: The Definitive History of Racist Ideas in America* (New York: Nation Books, 2016).

11. See, for instance, Joel Spring, *Deculturalization and the Struggle for Equality: A Brief History of the Education of Dominated Cultures in the United States* (New York: McGraw-Hill, 1997); James D. Anderson, *The Education of Blacks in the South, 1860–1935* (Chapel Hill: University of North Carolina Press, 1988); Rodolfo F. Acuña, *Occupied America: The Chicano's Struggle toward Liberation* (New York: Pearson Longman, 2007); Frances M. Campbell, "Missiology in New Mexico, 1850–1900: The Success and Failure of Catholic Education," in *Religion and Society in the American West:*

Historical Essays, ed. Carl Guarneri and David Alvarez (Lanham, MD: University Press of America, 1987), 59–78.

12. See, for instance, the following influential works: Jamie T. Phelps, ed., *Black and Catholic: The Challenge and Gift of Black Folk; Contributions of African American Experience and Thought to Catholic Theology* (Milwaukee: Marquette University Press, 1997); Orlando Espín and Miguel H. Díaz, eds., *From The Heart of Our People: Latino Explorations in Systematic Theology* (Maryknoll, NY: Orbis Books, 1999); Peter C. Phan, *Christianity with an Asian Face: Asian American Theology in the Making* (Maryknoll, NY: Orbis Books, 2003); Robert J. Schreiter, *Constructing Local Theologies* (Maryknoll, NY: Orbis Books, 2015); Stephen B. Bevans, *Models of Contextual Theology*, rev. ed. (Maryknoll, NY: Orbis Books, 2002).

13. From a theological perspective, see Gerald A. Arbuckle, *Culture, Inculturation, and Theologians: A Postmodern Critique* (Collegeville, MN: Liturgical Press, 2010); Michael Paul Gallagher, *Clashing Symbols: An Introduction to Faith and Culture*, rev. ed. (New York: Paulist Press, 2003); Kathryn Tanner, *Theories of Culture: A New Agenda for Theology* (Minneapolis: Fortress Press, 1997). From the perspective of cultural studies, see the classic works of Homi K. Bhabha, *The Location of Culture* (New York: Routledge, 1994) and Thomas S. Kuhn, *The Structure of Scientific Revolutions* (Chicago: University of Chicago Press, 1962).

14. GS 1.

15. GS 4.

16. GS 53.

17. See Tanner, *Theories of Culture*, 3–16.

18. See Hosffman Ospino, "Foundations for an Intercultural Philosophy of Christian Education," *Religious Education* 104, no. 4 (May–June 2009).

19. Hosffman Ospino, *Interculturalism and Catechesis: A Catechist's Guide to Responding to Cultural Diversity* (New London, CT: Twenty-Third Publications, 2017), 49.

20. Ospino, *Interculturalism and Catechesis*, 24–30.

21. See Mariasusai Dhavamony, "The Christian Theology of Inculturation," *Studia Missionalia* 44 (1995): 1–43.

22. See the classic work by H. Richard Niebuhr, *Christ and Culture* (San Francisco: Harper Collins, 1951). Here I use the category "the gospel" in an analogous way to Niebuhr's use of "Christ."

23. See Orlando Espín, "Intercultural Thought," in *An Introductory Dictionary of Theology and Religious Studies*, ed. Orlando O. Espín and James B. Nickoloff (Collegeville, MN: Liturgical Press, 2007).

24. For more about interculturality from a philosophical perspective, see Raúl Fornet-Betancourt, *Hacia una Filosofía Intercultural Latinoamericana* (San José, Costa Rica: Departamento Ecuménico de Investigaciones, 1994), 21–26; *Interculturalidad y Filosofía en América Latina*, Wissenschaftsverlag (Aachen: Internationale Zeitschrift für Philosophie, 2003), 9–23.

25. Marti R. Jewell, "Practical Theology: Preparing Ministers for Today's Church," *Theological Education* 51, no. 2 (2018): 21.

26. See Philip Gleason, *Contending with Modernity: Catholic Higher Education in the Twentieth Century* (New York: Oxford University Press, 1995); George M. Marsden, *The Soul of the American University: From Protestant Establishment to Established Nonbelief* (New York: Oxford University Press, 1994).

27. Daniel Aleshire, "The Emerging Model of Formational Theological Education," *Theological Education* 51, no. 2 (2018): 35.

28. Aleshire, "Emerging Model," 35.

29. The current edition (fifth) of the *Program of Priestly Formation* serves as a good starting point addressing the need to form priests in the United States to be adequately prepared to serve in culturally diverse contexts. The document, however, maintains a lukewarm approach by making its recommendations about intercultural competence mostly optional. See USCCB, *Program of Priestly Formation* (Washington, DC: USCCB, 2005).

30. Association of Theological Schools, *Standards of Accreditation*, General Standard 2.5. Available online at https://www.ats.edu/uploads/accrediting/documents/standards-of-accreditation-161130.pdf#pagemode=bookmarks.

31. ATS, *Standards of Accreditation*, General Standard 6.2.4.

32. ATS, *Standards of Accreditation*, General Standard 5.1.3.

33. ATS, *Standards of Accreditation*, General Standard 3.3.1.3.

34. ATS, *Standards of Accreditation*, General Standard 4.5.2.

35. See William John Cahoy, ed., *In the Name of the Church: Vocation and Authorization of Lay Ecclesial Ministry* (Collegeville, MN: Liturgical Press, 2012).

36. See *Co-Workers*, 33–50; USCCB, *Program of Priestly Formation*, 70–289.

37. The initiative is called Building Intercultural Competencies for Ministers (BICM), available online at https://www.usccb.org/committees/cultural-diversity-church/intercultural-competencies.

38. BICM.

39. See Schreiter, *Constructing Local Theologies*, 117–21.

40. Much has been written about educational commitments that "raise awareness" and "respond to" culture in culturally diverse contexts. These approaches often fall short of the kind of transformative engagements that create new environments where diversity thrives. There is a growing body of reflections calling for pedagogies and educational commitments that "sustain culture," which demand intentional embrace and cultivation of diverse cultures leading to their flourishing. See Django Paris and H. Samy Alim, eds., *Culturally Sustaining Pedagogies: Teaching and Learning for Justice in a Changing World* (New York: Teachers College Press, 2017).

41. On the idea of building "Communion in Diversity," see Hosffman Ospino, "Building Communion in Culturally Diverse Parishes," *Catholic Update*, Liguori Publications (July 2018).

Chapter Six

CATECHISTS AS STORYTELLERS

African American Tradition of Storytelling as a Catechetical Method

timone davis

Each and every day, we tell stories. It is the way people share ideas, situations, and circumstances. A storyteller weaves a tale, while listeners take it all in and situate themselves around the story being told. Our stories connect our lives. They shape the landscape of understanding. Stories are used in families to recount the past or to explain the current state of affairs. They play a role in business settings as office managers, team builders, leadership trainers, and supervisors use stories to better articulate the points they are trying to make. Storytelling is so much a part of our lives that we often don't recognize it. Richard Bauman writes,

> Like all human activity, [storytelling] is situated, its form, meaning, and functions rooted in culturally defined scenes or events—bounded segments of the flow of behavior and experience that constitute meaningful contexts for action, interpretation, and evaluation.[1]

Catechists as Storytellers

The ancient phenomenon of telling a story is one of the most important ways faith is shared. Throughout the Gospels, we find Jesus teaching and preaching through stories, transforming the lives of people, meeting them where they are, and allowing them to tell their own stories before teaching them with his. On the road to Emmaus, the risen Christ listens to the two disciples first, hearing their story, before reminding them of "all that the prophets have declared" (Luke 24:25). Storytelling offers the Catholic Church a time-honored way to reach those in need of the good news, including those young adults struggling to connect with the Church. The beauty of storytelling as a method of catechesis—particularly when rooted in African oral tradition—is its potential to anchor young adults in the Christian story, while at the same time allowing them to tell their own story.

I first learned about faith through the stories told by my mother. When I was a child, she talked about how God helped her family through hard times when all else was lost. She also talked about "making it through" when the end wasn't in sight. It seemed to me that no matter the problem, my mother's solution was to lean on the Lord. When I was old enough to understand the words of the preacher at church, I found that he, like my mother, relied on stories from the past for solutions in the present. This way of sharing God opened me more fully to other teachings that I might have otherwise disregarded. By recounting her experiences, my mother became a storyteller. When the preacher used examples in his sermons, he too became a storyteller. Each of us, when we recount an experience, becomes a storyteller.

In our Church today, young adults are searching for their place among us. What if the powerful African American tradition of storytelling was used to address the particular needs of young adults? What if storytelling were to help them better understand themselves in relation to God and others? To tell the Christian story, I suggest a process that I call "My Story—Your Story," to show how catechesis resounds not only events from Scripture and the faith tradition, but also events from our own lives. This way of doing catechesis brings to life the Christian story through our shared experiences. To understand better storytelling as a catechetical resource, I first discuss African oral traditions as the context out of which emerged a distinctive

African American culture of storytelling. I then turn to explain My Story—Your Story as a method that opens young adults to receiving and sharing faith. Finally, I discuss some of the implications of using African American storytelling as a method of catechesis for young adults.

AFRICAN ORAL TRADITION

Prior to this research, when I thought of African storytelling, Alex Haley and his book *Roots* usually came to mind. As I began exploring the origin of African American storytelling, I was convinced that it would have "roots" in slave narratives—stories I associated with Africans who fought to keep alive the memory of their native land. I was looking for a direct link between the African oral tradition and the development of slave narratives among African Americans, assured that this link was the foundation of African American storytelling. What I discovered is the fact that the African oral tradition lived on in the African Diaspora more in the form of folktales than in slave narratives.[2] I also discovered that the African American folktale, though the terminology was new, was actually quite familiar to me. Whenever we gathered together, aunts, uncles, grandparents, and friends told tales of yesterday. They didn't call them "folktales"; they just told their stories. What I thought were just favorite stories, told over and over again, I can now see as narratives passing on a history. As Harold Scheub argues, "Story is a means whereby people come to terms with their lives, their past; it is a way of understanding their relationship within the context of their traditions. It is a means of accessing and valuing history: in the end, story is history."[3]

It is important that these stories were *told*. Roger Abrahams observes, "In their African settings (and in oral cultures in general), the spoken word carries great power manifested in several ways. Besides directly addressing deep matters of life, the spoken word can actually create bonds and bring about personal or social transformations."[4] Why is spoken word so important, so powerful? Molefi Kete Asante explains:

There is something musical about the way the story-teller weaves the ups and downs of experience into the fabric of life....Spoken power has a tradition going back to the ancient Africans of the Nile Valley who saw *Mdu Neter*, the language of the ancient Egyptians, as sacred words....Transforming words were placed in the mouths of folk poets from the earliest times in America. Africans in the Americas remembered the storytellers, the griots, who stood in the midst of the children and adults at night and told them rhythmic stories that possessed the special quality of moral and verbal resolution. These memories were to be the memories that would guide the rhymes, rhythms, and raps of the African American. The words were to provide transformations, social and oral, to the hearers.[5]

African storytelling is an oral tradition, Abrahams writes, involving "the sharing of an expressive body of knowledge and values."[6] Through the work of "the elders and the griot (pronounced GREE-oh)," writes Nathan Jones, "the custodians of the collective story, the history, the customs, and the values of [the] people,"[7] African storytelling guided the life of the community, Abrahams writes, by "keeping order, and maintain[ing] its promise of inspiration and illumination."[8]

The African oral tradition continued to play this guiding role even as Africans found themselves ensnared by chattel slavery. Abrahams comments,

The taletelling tradition of blacks in the New World came, directly or indirectly, from the places where the slaves' ancestors lived in the sub-Saharan area of the Old World. The major evidence for this is the relative consistency of the repertoire wherever Africans found themselves transported in the New World.[9]

Story encouraged enslaved Africans to maintain aspects of the past for use in the present. John F. Callahan notes, "Ironically, the dehumanizing conditions of slavery, its prohibitions against literacy, against African language and ritual, reinforced the communal values of the oral tradition."[10]

In order to reinforce values, story has to invite dialogue that results in action. That was the role of the African folktales. According to Abrahams, "In their African setting these tales are called upon not just to deliver a specific message but to initiate talk about that message."[11] The nature of storytelling then is to provide the listener with information that calls forth action. Callahan observes,

> Those listening are responsible to the community for carrying on the work of interpretation begun by storytellers as they tell their tales. A catalytic process, African oral storytelling expresses the flux of social and natural reality through its open form.[12]

AFRICAN AMERICAN STORYTELLING

African slaves were able to keep their culture alive in a strange land while enduring the oppressive conditions of slavery by telling the stories of their homeland. As the griot told the folktales in the new context of slavery, they were transformed. What emerged was a new culture guided by these transformed narratives. Henry Louis Gates Jr. writes,

> Despite the severe restrictions against the preservation of indigenous African cultural forms, and the concomitant legal prohibitions against literacy mastery, black people merged what they could retain from their African heritage with forms that they could appropriate from the various New World cultures into which they had been flung. The blends that they forged... [were] a new culture....In the instance of the African in America, a truly African-American expressive culture emerged from deep inside the bowels of enslavement. This African-American culture was a veritable "underground" culture, shared...by word of mouth.[13]

Oral tradition was a particularly important strategy for slaves who needed to convey information undetected. Again, Gates comments,

> African-Americans nurtured a private but collective oral culture, one they could not "write down," but one they created, crafted, shared with each other and preserved for subsequent generations out loud, but outside of the hearing of the white people who enslaved them, and, later, discriminated against them.[14]

The legacy of this underground culture was expressed in my own life in the stories my mother told me as a child, meant to remind me there are certain "ways of being" in the United States for an African American female. The oral nature of slave culture continued to be important even after emancipation so that Blacks could protect themselves through the time of slavery's heir, segregation. Tempii B. Champion writes,

> The cultural and social practices of West Africa traveled with Africans as they crossed the waters to the United States. Despite the horrors of slavery, Africans [now in Diaspora] still told stories to comfort, teach, and record history in their new home....These storytelling traditions continued from slavery through Jim Crowism, to the Civil Rights movement, and on to present day America.[15]

The centrality of story to the entire history of the African American experience is brought home by Gates in a passage worth quoting at length:

> Telling ourselves our own stories—interpreting the nature of our world to ourselves, asking and answering epistemological and ontological questions in our own voices and on our own terms—has as much as any single factor been responsible for the survival of African-Americans and their culture. The stories that we tell ourselves and our children function to order our world,

serving to create both a foundation upon which each of us constructs our sense of reality and a filter through which we process each event that confronts us every day. The values that we cherish and wish to preserve, the behavior that we wish to censure, the fear and dread that we can barely confess in ordinary language, the aspirations and goals that we most dearly prize—all of these things are encoded in the stories that each culture invents and preserves for the next generation, stories that, in effect, we live by and through. And the stories that survive, the stories that manage to resurface under different guises and with marvelous variations, these are a culture's canonical tales, the tales that contain the cultural codes that are assumed or internalized by members of that culture. For the African American, deprived by law of the tools of literacy, the narration of these stories in black vernacular forms served to bring together the several colorful fragments of lost African cultures in a spectacularly blended weave that we call African American culture.[16]

Rising up out of slavery, African American storytelling differs from other forms of storytelling in that it filters present experience through the lens of oppression, illuminating both sorrows and joys. African American storytelling calls the hearer to freedom precisely because, writes Lee H. Butler,

African American culture, first and foremost, is a resistance culture dynamically constructed around the thematic ideas of freedom and justice....The African American community has always understood that those whom the Spirit makes free are free indeed.[17]

This movement, present to past to present, cannot be done without listeners, who are encouraged to participate in the story. African American storytelling then is not just about sharing yesterday's information. It is also about the assessment of one's present circumstance and its impact on the future. A tradition that arose out of oppressed conditions, African American storytelling invites listeners to hope.

Nowhere is this invitation to hope more creatively expressed than in the way in which African Americans embraced Christianity. Albert J. Raboteau notes,

> In the New World slave control was based on the eradication of all forms of African culture because of their power to unify the slaves and thus enable them to resist or rebel. Nevertheless, African beliefs and customs persisted and were transmitted by the slaves to their descendants.... African styles of worship, forms of ritual, systems of belief, and fundamental perspectives have remained vital on this side of the Atlantic, not because they were preserved in a "pure" orthodoxy but because they were transformed.[18]

By listening to the liberating stories of the Bible, Raboteau adds, the African slaves and their descendants discovered the God who rescues—who "makes a way out of no way."

The story of God at work, in the lives of the people God loves, is told again and again in order to gain new truths. As enslaved African Americans listened to the oft-repeated stories of the Bible, Raboteau comments, "One story in particular caught their attention and fascinated them with its implications and potential applications to their own situation. That story was the story of Exodus."[19] For the enslaved, Jones writes, "[Telling the Exodus story allowed] an ancient, historic event [to] remain an ever-present reality to a faithful people. The telling and retelling of the Story [was] not merely a recollection of the past, but a drawing of the past events into the present."[20] That is the most basic pattern of African American storytelling. Raboteau writes, "By appropriating the story of Exodus as their own story, black Christians articulated their own sense of peoplehood....Exodus became dramatically real, especially in the song and prayer meetings of the slaves who reenacted the story as they shuffled in the ring dance they called the 'Shout.'"[21] This integration of the biblical story into their daily living is precisely the gift of African American storytelling.

MY STORY—YOUR STORY AND *THE* STORY

As young adults continue to search for understanding, African American storytelling has the power to help them form community and gain hope in growing in faith. The narrative nature of the Bible unfolds the Story of God for us and helps us see the importance of that Story in the shaping of our lives.[22] Jones notes, "Each one of us has a story to tell. God is continually unfolding his revelation in our personal and collective lives. This process of reflection/action/reflection is aimed at identifying our story in God's Story and God's Story in ours."[23]

The process that I call My Story—Your Story speaks of our connections—to God, to the tradition, to one another—through story. When I tell my story, you find a point in which to intersect, connecting your story to mine. Our linkage invites us to see one another and ourselves differently. When we hear God's story told in such a way that we are able to find a point of intersection with our own, then we are better able to see our union in God. According to Jones, "Stories invite [us] into a realm of possibility in which [we] may learn new ways of being faithful people in the world."[24] Jones adds, "My story is wrapped up in your story, and it is God's Story."[25] As faithful people, John Westerhoff contends, we realize,

> At the heart of our Christian faith is a story. And at the heart of [catechesis] must be this same story. When we evaluate our corporate lives as a community of faith, this story must judge us. Our ritual life, the experiences we have in community, and the acts we perform in the world, must be informed by this story. Unless the story is known, understood, owned, and lived, [young adults] will not have [Catholic] faith.[26]

Through the process of My Story—Your Story we see more clearly how, write Meghan McKenna and Tony Cowan, "all stories serve that one story, and all tellers serve the universal word that invites us and demands that we become truly human and divine."[27] This one Story has been passed down from generation to generation, first orally, then in written format, and now it speaks to storytelling's ancient use as a catechetical tool. Kenneth Hill observes,

> The Bible is at the center of Christian education. This centrality arises from the Christian Church's basis in the story. The story of God's love is made known in creation, in redemption through the people of Israel, and through the life, death, and resurrection of Jesus Christ. As Christians, everyone participates in this story.[28]

African American storytelling offers an example for catechists to help young adults understand this truth and see themselves in it. Thus, our participation in the Christian Story becomes what Kathleen Hughes calls "a movement from that which is seen and heard and felt to the God who, through them, opens us more to divine encounter, using the whole of our experience to draw us closer if we are open, hospitable, receptive."[29] This encounter calls for participation in and through our words and deeds, our fears, hopes, and dreams.

The My Story—Your Story method shares important resonances with Thomas Groome's shared Christian praxis approach, which he describes as "*a group of Christians sharing in dialogue their critical reflection on present action in light of the Christian Story and its Vision toward the end of lived Christian faith.*"[30] The five movements of his approach (present action; critical reflection on that action; encounter with the Christian Story; dialectical engagement between this Story and one's own story; and determining a response in faith) arcs broadly from *experience* (my story; movements 1 and 2) to the *tradition* (the Story; movements 3 and 4) to *action* with and for others (the continuation of my story within the Story; movement 5).[31]

STARTING WITH MY STORY

Groome's first and second movements invite Christians to think about their own lives and experiences. Inspired by the tradition of African American storytelling, this reflection on experience involves the sharing of stories. My Story—Your Story comes to life by allowing the teller and the listener to find connectedness in their stories, leading to a deeper personal engagement that helps young adults enter the doorway for conversion. Because My Story—Your Story is dialogical, the process facilitates theological reflection in a way that is not judgmental or condemning. It allows a framework, Groome notes, to access and assess daily interactions "physically, emotionally, intellectually, and spiritually."[32]

In accessing the lived experience of young adults today, a My Story—Your Story approach invites catechesis to draw inspiration from a surprising source: hip-hop music. Emerging out of the experiences of Black (and Latinx) youth, hip-hop has come to provide some of the most powerful narratives of contemporary youth culture. And the rapper (or emcee) has become one of the most important storytellers. Although hip-hop came into existence, Efrem Smith and Phil Jackson write, "as a subculture of urban culture, its influence has spread beyond the confines of the city. It has risen from its inner-city roots to influence youth from the American suburbs to Tokyo."[33] The rapper or emcee is the voice of the hip-hop culture, thus offering a contemporary example of African American storytelling, bringing the present into conversation: my story. The rapper or emcee—addressing such topics as relationships and sex, money and poverty, drugs, politics, and identity—is able to express the fears, joys, and sorrows of young adults in a gritty way, reflecting the realism of their actual experiences. This ability to make experiences come to life cuts across cultural borders and offers a lesson to the religious educator.

The rapper or emcee is so influential because of the power of words to transform. As Smith and Jackson note, "The emcee can choose to use their gifts and knowledge in a way that educates and uplifts the listener or degrades and downgrades the listener."[34] Young adults influenced by the emcee are drawn into the rapper's ability to tell a story about their experiences. Through the lyrics, the rapper speaks about situations and circumstances to which many young adults are able to connect. "Hip-hop," Smith and Jackson argue, "has used rap to tell stories of urban youth, poverty, oppression, inner-city life, anger and African American history."[35] With storytelling being used so extensively among young adults, the use of it in catechesis is a natural progression. The notion of catechist as emcee requires an imaginative leap worth taking when you consider the rapper's storytelling abilities. For an emcee-catechist, the lyrics are no longer just about hip-hop culture, but about the broader joys, sorrows, and fears of young adults today.

ENGAGING THE CHRISTIAN STORY

Groome's third and fourth movements turn the catechist's attention to the Christian Story and the transformation that occurs when we bring this Story into dialogue with our own stories. When the risen Christ encounters the two disciples on the road to Emmaus, he first listens to what they have experienced, and then recounts to them "all that the prophets have declared" (Luke 24:25). Today Jesus continues to meet us where we are, listen to our story, and remind us of the larger Story, before helping us find our place in it. Both the listening and the reframing are critical movements. The retelling of the Story is important in that it brings us to an understanding of Christian faith beyond the personal relationship with Jesus.[36] As Nathan Jones explains,

> This living Story is not something you organize and plan to tell and retell, but it is something you feel, something which gives life, which motivates and urges you onward. Furthermore, the Story gives you just what you need in order to deal with life's struggles, hardships, and questions. This Story is *your* Story. It is not just a story that has been passed on by tradition, parents, a priest or a sister. It is a Story you have gratefully claimed as your own. It is an old Story interpreted for a new day.[37]

The new interpretation of the Story helps move young adults beyond their personal relationship with Jesus into the community, which strengthens not only the person but also the community in a way that transforms it into God's kingdom. Central to this movement is Scripture. Hill writes, "The Bible, as a teaching source, illuminates the mind, moves heart, and stirs the soul."[38] It tells the story of God acting in people's lives and people's responses to that action. He adds, "The story in Scripture, told in and through the Church, shapes our understanding of reality. The scriptures provide a grid or set of images by which we may come to believe and interpret our own life experiences."[39]

Here we can again draw on the African American experience to recognize the storytelling power of the preacher. At the beginning of this chapter, I mentioned how my childhood preacher drew upon experiences of the past in order to tell stories for use in the present. Very often, the stories he told allowed me to see a Scripture passage in a new way, in a way that made sense for my life. Jones writes, "The biblical story itself enables the preacher to interpret God's saving Word in light of the lived experiences, struggles, and strides of the people."[40] The preacher's use of story during the sermon "provide[s] connections between the present and the past, to study and explain the past within the context of the present, and vice versa."[41] The preacher then, D'Jimo Kouyate contends, is expected to use the pulpit as "an educational place where its members not only [learn] spiritual truths but also how to apply them to everyday life."[42] Preaching, like story, uses the imagination. The preacher must create images for the ear. In order to become doers of the Word, we must first become hearers.

Looking at preaching through a catechetical lens, it is imperative that Roman Catholic preaching—taking a cue from African American worship—seek to become relevant in the lives of young adults. Dale Andrews comments, "Black preaching and black worship have established traditions centered in nurturing black wholeness and empowerment for living under oppressive conditions. The preaching task has focused on interpreting biblical Christianity in the interests of black humanity and faith development in black life."[43] This way of addressing the needs of African Americans is necessary also for the Catholic Church with regard to young adults; African American storytelling aids the preacher here in crafting sermons that not only contain content important to young adults, but also engaging delivery. Call-and-response, one of the preaching styles employed in many African American churches, helps individuals place their own story within the Story, thereby achieving wholeness and empowerment. It is important to note that wholeness is not just for the individual. Wholeness, Andrews argues, "includes healing amid sustaining and guiding, and the reconciliation of humanity to God, to self and to each other."[44]

In many African American churches, there exists a focus on "nurturing"[45] the Black person, "teaching coping skills and self-worth, and empower[ing] one to seek fullness of life. It [also] addresses the search for meaning and value of life in relation to God and neighbor."[46] Young people need the stories of others in addition to the Story in order to grow and find meaning that opens them more fully to God and others. Storytelling places them in community, so critical to the African American tradition. Scripture tells the Story in which we discover our Christian identity. For, Andrews believes, "Christianity is seen most effectively through the interpretations of meaning and identity derived from Scripture. Therefore, in the formation and agency of black churches, preaching thrives at the center of worship and the communal experience of pastoral care."[47]

The nurturing that takes place in many African American worship services is the same nurturing that needs to take place for young adults to continue growing in faith. Anne Streaty Wimberly writes that African American "worship makes possible discernment through life's opportunities and its darkness."[48] This nurturing is a dialogue that asks young adults not just to be passive, but to be active in the process. It must take the pattern of call-response. And because it is about growth, there will be "growing pains" that call for adjustment.

Wimberly writes,

[Young adults are looking] for a deepening faith and an alive hope that is more than an individualistic orientation to faith and hope. There is a search for a communally shared or "village" faith and hope that evokes in persons a zeal to make faith and hope concretely felt in and beyond the congregation through actions intended to make a better world.[49]

The African American experience of church thereby calls for an integration of the congregation's story with the Story, not just for the individual, but also for the entire community. Storytelling within this context helps shape the future by allowing hope to be heard when it cannot always be seen.

LIVING MY STORY WITHIN THE STORY

Groome's fifth and final movement calls for a response—what C. Vanessa White calls a "transformed" response.[50] Here Groome situates the whole catechetical process within the context of its goal: the kingdom of God, "God's Vision of Creation," and creation's relationship and response.[51] The whole point of bringing our stories into dialogue with the Story is not to discover facts, but to encounter the incarnate God. Megan McKenna and Tony Cowan elaborate:

> The Christian tradition proclaims that The Word became Flesh and dwells among us. In response we, with our words of belief, of assent, of shared hope, must become flesh for others' food. Our flesh must bear witness to the presence of words instilled and cherished, believed and borne witness to in commitment, example and service, and sometimes in the giving of life itself as the final word. It is still the best story, the only story worth telling.[52]

African American storytelling harnesses this concept for young adults. It brings to life the faith of peoples who struggled to grow in faith and love of God and others. Wimberly adds, "Telling and retelling stories from the Bible, from our faith communities, and from our everyday lives as people of faith evokes concrete images and memories that propel us into imaginatively recreating our village connections."[53] Once these connections are reimaged, we move into action; we respond. Stories shared and reflected upon together help people see the future action they should take. One author notes, "We live our lives immersed in stories. While some stories entertain, inform, or teach us, others move us deeply. They change us and bring us closer together. These are sacred stories. Sacred stories...tell us 'who we are and how we relate to the world and our gods.'"[54] The liberating effect of storytelling begins at a deeply personal level. African American storytelling offers a method that gives voice to the young adult spiritual self. Hill comments, "The spiritual journey requires that we attend to our voices and to the possibilities they contain. We cannot walk on the journey of faith if we do not notice our voices and what they reveal to us about ourselves."[55] Since stories provide self-revelation in addition to creating a foundation, it is important that young adults see story as freeing. As we share our stories, we liberate ourselves. When we cannot first find our own voice, we use the voices of our ancestors and past experiences to capture what we are trying to say. African American storytelling has the ability to open young adults more fully to who they themselves are and who the "other" is. In doing so, their voices are freed in a way that both liberates them and challenges them to press forward in faith in God. Catechesis that uses African American storytelling affords young adults the ability to learn and name their faith, offering possibilities for conversion and transformation. This ability sets the person free in faith.

Storytelling invites transformation that ushers in action—calling people to grow in faith through a personal relationship with Jesus lived out in and through relationships with others. When used as a method of catechesis it allows young adults to integrate Scripture and Catholic traditions into their lives in ways that are transforming. It fosters a mode of theological reflection that Anne Streaty Wimberly notes "help[s] us grapple with the realities of our everyday lives and envision how we as Christians can go forward in liberating and hopeful ways."[56] This is a thoroughly communal process. Thus the My Story—Your Story approach helps us see the importance of the ecclesial aspect of religion through which we are called to speak aloud our faith stories. It is through story that one is better able to understand God at work in the world. Kouyate comments, "Stories taught African Americans how to respond to their abilities (that is, responsibilities), even if this was no more than utilizing their gift for memory and an innate understanding of the situations that confronted them."[57] My Story—Your Story is the discovery of God's saving mercy at work in and through us that will teach young adults how to respond to their own abilities and responsibilities.

IMPLICATIONS FOR THE CATECHIST AS STORYTELLER

African American storytelling is an indispensable catechetical method for young adults because it moves beyond memorization into the world of the person. In the dynamic of My Story—Your Story, people enter more fully into the understanding that all persons are not only important, but also connected. McKenna and Cowan observe,

> In general, the oral tradition is stronger and truer, deeper and more meaningful than any written tradition because of its origins in the community. The written traditions, such as scriptures…are inspired. The depth of meanings veiled and hidden in the text and its spaces demands that the reader, the hearer, and then eventually the teller dig down deep to discover and reveal the heart of the message and serve it religiously and devotedly.[58]

The catechist assists young adults in this endeavor. Catechists are religious educators, persons who assist the Church with ongoing faith formation. In this role, catechists are not only storytellers; they are also facilitators of story. This dual role affords the catechist some flexibility in sharing the Story. The catechist becomes more like the African griot, one study argues, who "supplies memory and cultural direction to all people involved in ritual performance."[59] As a storyteller, the catechist provides the hearer with the memories of our Catholic faith, reminding young people how they are to live, thereby calling all to Christian living, a return to the present. Like Jesus in the Emmaus story, the catechist recounts the biblical story. Though we don't like to think of catechesis as performance, we must broaden our thinking to include African American storytelling and how its performative use educates. For, as Ella Mitchell notes, "the oral process…is a legitimate system of teaching and learning."[60]

Edward Wimberly argues, "[Storytelling] enabled African Americans to survive in a culture that denied us the right to define our own value and worth as human beings. Thus…African American storytelling is an artistic and imaginative practice of meaning-making that, although derived from necessity,

focused on God's presence."[61] Since young adults are often marginalized within the Church, African American storytelling will
allow young adults to better learn the Catholic faith. Wimberly
goes on to say,

> A [catechist] who understands the working of God
> through drama can link people with the unfolding of
> God's story. Such a [person] seeks to help parishioners
> develop story language and story discernment in order
> to visualize how God's drama is unfolding in their lives.
> This means that telling and listening to stories become
> central to the caring process. It also means that people
> learn to follow the plots of stories, to visualize how God
> is seeking to engage them in the drama as it affects their
> lives.[62]

Storytelling based on the relationship between storyteller
and listener, moves away from the individualism often called for
in society toward community that is church. According to Jones,

> Like the Afrikan griot, catechists are ministers of the
> community's story....The catechist, like Jesus, invites
> his/her people to see their dying and rising in relation-
> ship to the dying and rising of Jesus. Therefore, the cat-
> echist...must speak to the hearts of the people like a
> poet, an elder, someone who loves them dearly.[63]

By using African American storytelling to catechize young adults,
catechists become narrators opening young adults to the words,
ideas, and practices of the Catholic faith. As two recent scholars
note, "In the process of storytelling, the narrator makes use of
words that are from the womb of tradition, thereby educating the
children in the language of their people."[64] When the narrator
uses images and situations familiar to young adults, it becomes
easier for them to grasp what is being taught.

In reaching deeper into stories, both oral and written, past
and present, McKenna and Cowan write, young adults discover
that "stories are crucial to [their] sense of well-being, to identity,
to memory, and to [their] future."[65] Story, then, teaches us how to

be in relationship with one another. Through story, we recapture our connection to others, better understanding our role in community.[66] Thus, the telling and listening aspect of African American storytelling affords catechists the tools necessary to assist young adults in learning the faith better. As Nathan Jones affirms,

> Story—storytelling and listening—is a central methodology of catechetical ministry. Story is not simply a passing, present-day interest of the religious community, but rather an attempt to recover a lost emphasis. Christian faith did not originally come to us as theology. The Good News came to us as story: "In the beginning was the Word." As the ages have unfolded, this Story has become a cherished tradition handed on down the generations with care.[67]

As ministry educators, we must be the storytellers we wish our students to be. It is important for us to offer ways for ministry students to delve into the richness of their own story in order to be better prepared for the work they do for others. African American storytelling as a method of catechesis does just that. It cultivates a storytelling environment in which students learn their own story and how it can be used in the formation of others, especially diverse contexts. As the first Africans in this country found strength, community, and hope anchored in the stories of their ancestral country and in ancient Scriptures, our young adults can move from the margins, into that place where their lives, the community, and God's story become one.

NOTES

1. Richard Bauman, *Story, Performance and Event* (New York: Cambridge University Press, 1986), 3.

2. A folktale is a "tale or legend originating and traditional among a people forming part of the oral tradition of the common people." *Webster's Unabridged Dictionary of the English Language* (New York: Random House, 2001), s.v. "folktale." Slave narratives are first-person accounts of life as a slave in the United States.

3. Harold Scheub, *Story* (Madison: The University of Wisconsin Press, 1998), 21.

4. Roger D. Abrahams, *African Folktales: Traditional Stories of the Black World* (New York: Pantheon Books, 1983), 1–2.

5. Molefi Kete Asante, *American Storytelling*, ed. Linda Goss and Marian E. Barnes (New York: Simon and Schuster, 1989), 491–92.

6. Abrahams, *African Folktales*, 20.

7. Nathan Jones, *Sharing the Old, Old Story: Educational Ministry in the Black Community* (Winona, MN: St. Mary's Press, 1982), 72. Bucknell University expounds on the meaning of griot at https://www.bucknell.edu/academics/beyond-classroom/academic-centers-institutes/griot-institute-study-black-lives-cultures (accessed October 21, 2018).

8. Abrahams, *African Folktales*, 21.

9. Roger D. Abrahams, *African American Folktales: Stories from Black Traditions in the New World* (New York: Pantheon Books, 1985), xix–xx.

10. John F. Callahan, *In the African-American Grain: Call and Response in Twentieth-Century Black Fiction* (Urbana: University of Illinois Press, 2001), 26.

11. Abrahams, *African Folktales*, 9.

12. Callahan, *In the African-American Grain*, 15.

13. Henry Louis Gates Jr., "Introduction: Narration and Cultural Memory in the African-American Tradition," in *Talk That Talk: An Anthology of African-American Storytelling*, ed. Linda Goss and Marian E. Barnes (New York: Simon and Schuster, 1989), 16–17.

14. Gates, "Introduction," 17.

15. Tempii B. Champion, *Understanding Storytelling among African American Children: A Journey from Africa to America* (Mahwah, NJ: Lawrence Erlbaum Associates, 2003), 3.

16. Gates, "Introduction," 17–18.

17. Lee H. Butler, *Liberating Our Dignity, Saving Our Souls* (St. Louis: Chalice Press, 2006), 8–9.

18. Albert J. Raboteau, *Slave Religion: The "Invisible Institution" in the Antebellum South*, 2nd ed. (New York: Oxford University Press, 2004), 4.

19. Albert J. Raboteau, *A Fire in the Bones: Reflections on African-American Religious History* (Boston: Beacon Press, 1995), 18.

20. Jones, *Sharing the Old, Old Story*, 8.

21. Raboteau, *A Fire in the Bones*, 33.

22. Anne Streaty Wimberly, *Nurturing Faith and Hope: Black Worship as a Model for Christian Education* (Cleveland: The Pilgrim Press, 2004), 4. The capitalization of story is to denote the Jewish-Christian Story from salvation history through the crucifixion of Jesus.

23. Jones, *Sharing the Old, Old Story*, 83.

24. Susan M. Shaw, *Storytelling in Religious Education* (Birmingham, AL: Religious Education Press, 1999), xi.

25. Jones, *Sharing the Old, Old Story*, 8.

26. John H. Westerhoff III, *Will Our Children Have Faith?* (New York: The Seabury Press, 1976), 34.

27. Megan McKenna and Tony Cowan, *Keepers of the Story* (Maryknoll, NY: Orbis Press, 1997), 177.

28. Kenneth H. Hill, *Religious Education in the African American Tradition: A Comprehensive Introduction* (St. Louis: Chalice Press, 2007), 39.

29. Kathleen Hughes, *Saying Amen: A Mystagogy of Sacrament* (Chicago: Liturgy Training Publications, 1999), 27.

30. Thomas H. Groome, *Christian Religious Education: Sharing Our Story and Vision* (San Francisco: Harper and Row, 1981. Repr., San Francisco: Jossey-Bass, 1999), 184.

31. Groome, *Christian Religious Education*, 207–8.

32. Groome, *Christian Religious Education*, 184.

33. Efrem Smith and Phil Jackson, *The Hip-Hop Church* (Downers Grove, IL: InterVarsity Press, 2005), 105.

34. Smith and Jackson, *The Hip-Hop Church*, 155.

35. Smith and Jackson, *The Hip-Hop Church*, 112.

36. Congregation for the Clergy, *General Directory for Catechesis* (Washington, DC: United States Catholic Conference, 1997), no. 144.

37. Jones, *Sharing the Old, Old Story*, 74.

38. Hill, *Religious Education in the African American Tradition*, 28.

39. Hill, *Religious Education in the African American Tradition*, 40.

40. Jones, *Sharing the Old, Old Story*, 65.

41. Scheub, *Story*, 13.

42. D'Jimo Kouyate, "The Role of the Griot," in *Talk That Talk: An Anthology of African-American Storytelling*, ed. Linda Goss and Marian E. Barnes (New York: Simon and Schuster, 1989), 215.

43. Dale P. Andrews, *Practical Theology for Black Churches: Bridging Black Theology and African American Folk Religion* (Louisville, KY: Westminster John Knox Press, 2002), 23.

44. Andrews, *Practical Theology for Black Churches*, 29.

45. My use of "nurture" is based on Wimberly, *Nurturing Faith and Hope*, xiii–xv, where she states that nurture is akin to cultivating, whereas plant life would not grow if it is not nourished or cultivated.

46. Andrews, *Practical Theology for Black Churches*, 40.

47. Andrews, *Practical Theology for Black Churches*, 40.

48. Wimberly, *Nurturing Faith and Hope*, xiii.

49. Wimberly, *Nurturing Faith and Hope*, xvii–xviii.

50. C. Vanessa White, assistant professor of spirituality and ministry at Catholic Theological Union, interview July 7, 2017. While she acknowledges that all theological reflection methods look at culture, experience, and tradition, her distinction is in how she defines those terms and how she engages them within the context of a storytelling methodology.

51. Groome, *Christian Religious Education*, 193.

52. McKenna and Cowan, *Keepers of the Story*, 203.

53. Edward P. Wimberly, *African American Pastoral Care*, rev. ed. (Nashville: Abingdon Press, 2008), x.

54. Charles Simpkinson and Anne Simpkinson, eds., *Sacred Stories: A Celebration of the Power of Story to Transform and Heal* (San Francisco: HarperSanFrancisco, 1993), 1.

55. Hill, *Religious Education in the African American Tradition*, 55.

56. Anne E. Streaty Wimberley, *Soul Stories: African American Christian Education* (Nashville: Abingdon Press, 2005), 1.

57. Kouyate, "The Role of the Griot," 215–16.

58. McKenna and Cowan, *Keepers of the Story*, 176.

59. Bayo Ogunjimi and Abdul-Rasheed Na'Allah, *Introduction to African Oral Literature and Performance* (Trenton, NJ: Africa World Press, 2005), xiii.

60. Ella Mitchell, "Black Nurture," in *Black Church Lifestyles: Rediscovering the Black Christian Experience*, ed. Emmanuel L. McCall (Nashville: Broadman Press, 1986), 50.

61. E. Wimberly, *African American Pastoral Care*, xi–xii.
62. E. Wimberly, *African American Pastoral Care*, 6.
63. Jones, *Sharing the Old, Old Story*, 79.
64. Ogunjimi and Na'Allah, *Introduction*, 22.
65. McKenna and Cowan, *Keepers of the Story*, 196.
66. Westerhoff, *Will Our Children Have Faith?*, 19.
67. Jones, *Sharing the Old, Old Story*, 7.

Chapter Seven

LISTENING TO YOUTH AND YOUNG ADULTS

Insights from Developmental Psychology and Cultural Studies

Tracey Lamont

When I was a youth and young adult minister several years ago, almost every ministerial colleague of mine had on their office shelf a copy of Christian Smith and Patricia Snell's *Soul Searching: The Religious and Spiritual Lives of American Teenagers*. One of my closest colleagues in the field raved about how reading this book gave him new ways to understand the dynamics of the millennial generation. It inspired him with fresh ideas for addressing the challenges of moral formation among youth and young adults beholden to what Smith and Snell call "moralistic therapeutic deism."[1] Once he understood the pitfalls of secular culture, he believed he could develop a thriving countercultural youth ministry program in his parish.

Today, many of my graduate students, most of whom are religious educators, have similar concerns that the secularism, moral relativism, and individualism of contemporary culture are leading people further away from the Church. My students invoke these labels to explain why young people are becoming less affiliated with religious institutions as they enter young adulthood. Such reflections echo Smith and his colleagues, who believe "emerging adults today express many of the difficulties that beset modern and postmodern moral philosophy—skepticism, relativism, [and] subjectivism."[2]

For Smith and his collaborators, the relationship between philosophical currents and everyday beliefs is not merely coincidental; it is causal. They seem to assume that postmodern philosophical theories cause changes in patterns of human behavior—a problematic assumption that often enters conversations such as these. For example, the claim of James K. A. Smith that "cultural phenomena tend to be a product of philosophical movements"[3] is not far from the claim of Christian Smith and his colleagues, who argue, "Few emerging adults have actually read Jacques Derrida or Stanley Fish, but their effects seem to have trickled down in this way into popular pre-reflective consciousness among this population nonetheless."[4] Such a method of interpretation provides a theory-to-practice approach to interpretation, as theoretical or philosophical arguments provide explanations for what emerges in society.

In his analysis of postmodernity, Paul Lakeland warns against attributing too much to the influence of philosophical thought:

> Philosophy does not dictate or direct culture; it mirrors it. Thus, philosophical shifts can be useful indicators in getting a grip on what is happening in the world, but they do not cause to happen whatever it is that we decide is happening. Culture is not best explained philosophically; but philosophy can explain what is happening in culture.[5]

As cultural changes emerge, philosophy can help describe new patterns of human behavior; but that does not mean philosophy causes or creates those patterns. Lakeland's approach is one that resonates with practical theologians. Opting for a practice-to-theory-to-practice method, practical theologians begin by observing and describing peoples' lives, their everyday lived experiences, and then asking what is going on, in what contexts these observations emerge, and why this might be happening.

The many publications coming out of Christian Smith's National Study of Youth and Religion (NSYR)—including *Soul Searching*, and subsequent volumes, *Souls in Transition*, *Lost in Transition*, and *Young Catholic America*—presume a theory-to-practice approach in their interpretation of the data. Particularly in *Lost in Transition*, this approach leads to a normative framework that attempts to explain how young adults *should* and *should not* articulate their moral and religious attitudes. This essay seeks to uncover how young adults *do* and *do not* articulate their moral sensibilities by using the methods of practical theology. Providing "thick description" of young adults' moral and religious sensibilities can enable researchers and educational ministers to understand better the sociocultural influences on contemporary young adults.[6] Such a practice-to-theory-to-practice method involves exploring multiple disciplines, beyond the field of sociology, to interpret the moral reasoning, practices, and deep culture of contemporary young adults.

The NSYR has produced some of the highest quality sociological data on the religious and moral lives of youth and young adults. Thus, despite several other reliable sociological studies, it is the work of Christian Smith and his colleagues that has had the greatest influence on pastoral and academic religious institutions.[7] For this reason, it is important for researchers and practitioners to reflect critically on the NSYR conclusions more fully.

This essay begins by providing an overview of how Smith and his colleagues interpret the NSYR data using a theory-to-practice approach. The first section focuses specifically on their analysis of the moral lives of young adults found in *Lost in Transition*. Two major theoretical assumptions emerge in this work. First, the authors assume that postmodern philosophy offers the best framework for explaining the data they observe. Second, they assume that universal moral truths exist and ought to support normative moral reasoning. These assumptions guide their assessment of young people today.

Rather than presuppose a prior philosophical framework, a practical theological methodology begins with the lived experience of young adults as it surfaces in the qualitative responses collected by the NSYR interviewers. How do young adults articulate their sense of morality? Why do they describe it this way? And what might this reveal? Other disciplinary lenses help to illuminate the way in which young people talk about their process of moral reasoning. Kathleen Cahalan writes, "Practical theology turns to multiple sources to critique practice, holding it up to critical scrutiny by a wide range of sources in philosophy and cultural studies."[8] The following section opens the data up to a critical conversation with various disciplines, including psychology (through the work of Robert Kegan), theology of culture (Richard Cote), and the sociological theory of Robert Wuthnow. These disciplines provide tools to explore what new horizons of meaning emerge when we interpret the lived experiences of contemporary young adults.

This essay concludes by asking how this new horizon of meaning calls us to act. How are researchers, educational ministers, and church leaders called to address these new insights into the religious and moral lives of young adults? Rather than generalize findings on young adults, practical theology uncovers new ways to understand how young adults develop a moral identity in postmodern culture. In conclusion this chapter asks, What should we do and how should we act? What are the implications of this study for the fields of religious education, ministerial formation, and further research projects?

FROM THEORY TO PRACTICE: CONTEMPORARY SOCIOLOGICAL RESEARCH AND INTERPRETATIONS

Christian Smith and his collaborators designed the National Study of Youth and Religion in order to gain insights into the religious and moral lives of contemporary youth and young adults.[9] Their third book, *Lost in Transition: The Dark Side of Emerging Adulthood*, takes a closer look at important data the authors refrained from commenting on in *Souls in Transition*. Their opening chapter, titled "Morality Adrift," points toward their conclusion "that moral individualism is widespread among emerging adults and that a sizable minority profess to believe in moral relativism."[10]

In the course of their argument, Smith et al. report that the majority of contemporary young adults have an "anemic view" of what morality is, as most do not base morality on any universally accepted standards of right and wrong.[11] Contemporary young adults are less concerned with the implications of their moral behavior within the larger world, and they have become less interested in personally contributing to the common good of society. Some cannot even identify what constitutes a moral situation, or mistake mundane issues, like moving out of their apartment, for moral dilemmas. According to the authors of *Lost in Transition*, "these cases make it clear that many emerging adults do not have a good handle on what makes something a *moral* issue or what the specifically *moral* dimensions of situations are."[12]

Smith and his colleagues describe the moral character of contemporary young adults as "a problem," based on an "anemic view" of morality, something "not acceptable," revealing "an overall impoverishment," the "degeneracy" of "a people deprived." The authors believe that moral relativism and individualism are "morally wrong" and "not reasonably defensible."[13] Moreover, they observe that our "American culture and society," including our educational systems and our parenting practices, have failed our young people, leaving them "morally adrift." Many young adults, for example, articulate their moral beliefs relativistically, using expressions like, "I feel that...I believe that...I think that...." These are "unconscious habits of speech reflecting larger cultural norms" that Smith and his colleagues believe express "an essentially subjectivistic and 'emotivistic' approach to moral reasoning."[14] For these young adults, "morality is purely a social construction," and those who struggle to avoid the position of relativism seem to lack the skills to do so.[15] The book concludes that culture and society, by failing to give young adults proper moral education, have let young people down.[16]

THEORETICAL ASSUMPTION 1:
POSTMODERN PHILOSOPHY

Smith et al. describe some of the social and cultural changes affecting the subjects of their study, including the dramatic growth of higher education, delayed marriage, emerging adulthood as a new life phase, longer financial support from parents, the availability of contraception, and the influence of postmodern theory.[17] In describing this last factor, the authors note how the last quarter of the twentieth century "saw the widespread diffusion and powerful influence of the theories of poststructuralism and postmodernism in U.S. culture."[18] Somehow "all of this high theory thus became democratized and vulgarized in U.S. culture. Simplified versions of Nietzsche, Foucault, and Derrida were now a driving influence evident on MTV and in high school 'world cultures' classes."[19] Overall, Smith and his colleagues are concerned that postmodern philosophy has had a negative influence on the moral sensibilities of young adults and the larger culture.

THEORETICAL ASSUMPTION 2: MORAL TRUTH

The authors are up front about their more subjective approach to sociological research. They follow Emile Durkheim's sociological perspective by offering a normative reading of the data, rather than the descriptive approach common to the Weberian perspective.[20] The authors, in following Durkheim, believe sociologists can and should make claims about what young adults *ought* to believe and how they *should* behave, arguing that "sociology need not always be value free."[21] In fact, they believe empirical sociology should be steadfast in upholding what is good or right, while making every effort to avoid bias. The authors believe unequivocally that it is *good* for people living in a diverse society to know how to articulate what is morally right and morally wrong. They state,

> So, not only do we in this book not try to hide our ideas about what is good, we unapologetically state them in black and white for all to inspect. We think it can only help social science and American society more broadly to be more straightforward about its beliefs about the good in human life....We think it is good for people to be able to think coherently about moral beliefs and problems, and to explain why they believe whatever they do believe...for people to be able to understand different moral positions, to consider how different assumptions

shape moral beliefs....And almost no emerging adult today is able to do much of that, as we show below. We think that is a problem.[22]

In a section titled "Morality Adrift," within a chapter by the same name, each paragraph begins with the authors' beliefs on certain core values, then outlines how young adults struggle to meet these values, and ends with an evaluative remark similar to, "And that, we think, is a problem."

Thus philosophical and moral assumptions provide the framework through which the authors interpret the moral sensibilities of contemporary young adults. They believe postmodern philosophy has negatively influenced contemporary young adults' ability to reason morally and that "moral relativism and individualism are simply intellectually impossible and socially unsustainable positions," arguing that "moral realism is the only position that makes sense."[23] Smith et al. favor a more modern, or antipostmodern, worldview of morality that believes in the universality of moral truths. The authors conclude that the solution to this individualism and relativism is more parental support and moral education.

FROM PRACTICE TO THEORY: APPROACHING THE DATA THROUGH PRACTICAL THEOLOGY

Practical theology and qualitative research, according to Josh Swinton and Harriet Mowat, are like a detective story, involving the same "painstaking and complex process of unpacking the detail of who did what, when, and why, within a particular situation and formulating this into evidence that will enable a fair judgement to be made."[24] However, Swinton and Mowat continue, "unlike a detective, the qualitative researcher does not seek to *solve* the problem or 'crack the case.'...The evidence can tell many stories and all of them may contain truth."[25] Smith and his colleagues reduce several possible stories to one story, prejudging the case by fitting the clues into a predetermined explanation. This section tells another story, a more complex story of how and why young adults articulate their moral sensibilities the way they do. By drawing on insights from psychology and alternative socio-logical studies, it fleshes out the narrative in revealing ways.

To begin this retelling, or thick description, take the three features Smith et al. identify as pertinent to contemporary moral development: moral individualism, moral relativism, and sources of moral authority.

Of the 230 young adults interviewed, 60 percent were reported to have a "highly individualistic approach to morality. Many said morality is a personal choice, entirely a matter of indi-vidual decision."[26] In their responses, young adults use phrases like "for me," "that would be wrong," or "personally" I would not do that.[27] These young adults also discuss how they refrain from judging the right or wrongness of another person's moral deci-sions, based on the belief that morality is personal, so "who am I to judge?"[28]

Approximately 47 percent of young adults surveyed agreed with the statement that "morals are relative, there are not defi-nite rights and wrongs for everybody."[29] One respondent stated, "I don't know if there really is a good and bad. I mean, yeah, there is. Certain things are bad, I mean inhumane, some things. But other than that, basically the world is built on corruption so bad, really it's a fine line."[30] Many young adults said they could not gauge the moral validity of a specific scenario because it just "depends on the situation."[31]

Furthermore, the majority of young adults interviewed stated that they "do not or would not refer to moral traditions or authori-ties or religious or philosophical ethics to make difficult moral decisions, but rather would decide by what would personally make them happy or would help them to get ahead in life."[32] Thirty-four percent of all young adults could articulate no moral referent or standard to judge what is right or wrong. Forty percent base their moral judgments on how others might perceive them, and sixty percent feel the basis of morality could be determined by "whether or not anything *functionally improved people's situations*."[33] When asked to explain why some people have different "personal moral codes," most suggested it was because of "the influence of par-ents...friends...religion or the media."[34] Moreover, many young adults struggled to identify the sources for their moral beliefs, if they had any at all.

Lost in Transition concludes that the majority of young adults struggled to articulate what a moral dilemma entailed, whether they had ever faced one, or what would constitute a moral conviction. Of the one-third who could describe a moral issue, they usually referenced scenarios involving relationships, substance abuse, their future, or an issue involving a job or career.[35]

INSIGHT FROM CONSTRUCTIVE-DEVELOPMENTAL PSYCHOLOGY

In taking a closer look at what these responses reveal about the moral development of young adults, this section asks, What can we learn about how young adults make moral decisions in contemporary society, and why do the majority of young adults respond to moral scenarios with what sounds like indifference, confusion, or ambiguity? What do their sources of moral authority tell us about their self-understanding? If their moral outlook is not simply moral relativism or individualism, then how might we describe the moral fabric of their lives?

Robert Kegan's theory of human personhood provides rich insights into the developmental characteristics and transitions emerging in the young adult years. According to Kegan, a person's moral perspective is embedded in his or her perceptions of self and world; therefore, a person's sense of morality will be directly related to the ways in which a person finds meaning in the world.[36] As individuals grow, their ways of knowing become more complex and their moral perceptions and ability to recognize moral truth evolve as well.

Kegan's theory of human personhood describes five constructive-developmental stages of knowing. In *stage one* (from infancy through approximately age seven), children have momentary fleeting attachments followed by more impulsive feelings and illogical thoughts.[37] It is in *stage two*, adolescence, that the individual starts to organize knowing around her or his own needs and self-interest. Often, other people become objects of the adolescent's own interests, existing only to fulfill the adolescent's needs. Beginning in the teenage years, adolescents start to evolve toward *stage three*, what Kegan calls the traditional or socialized level of knowing. At this point, the young person begins to share in the needs of others by developing interpersonal relationships. Teenagers adopt the values and beliefs of parents, coaches, mentors, and others, thus becoming socialized into a way of living. When one transitions out of stage three and moves toward *stage four*—the modern or self-authoring way of knowing—the young adult slowly begins to develop a new sense of identity. One's own internal voice and experiences become the authority by which decisions are made.

The movement from self-authorship to *stage five*, the postmodern or self-transformative mind, emerges only when a person develops the ability to see the interrelatedness of self-systems.[38] Stated differently, when individuals at stage five encounter divergent views or conflict, they "focus on ways to let the conflictual relationship transform the parties rather than the parties resolving conflict."[39] Where the fourth level of knowing is content with "letting bygones be bygones," the fifth level of knowing "uses the conflict to transform one's identification with one's own 'side.'"[40] Those arriving at stage five have a new ability to carry multiple perspectives as they distance themselves from their own internal voice of authority.

The early young adult years (beginning around age eighteen) often mark the beginning of a slow transition from adolescent ways of knowing toward the socialized way of knowing (stage three).[41] This transition comes with an ability to live up to the expectations of those who are closest to the individual, and, in turn, the external expectations of others become integrated into one's moral identity.[42] In the third level of knowing, one cannot internally critique or evaluate how or why they believe what they do. They are socialized in relationship to external authority figures, like parents, teachers, and coaches, and begin to share in their beliefs and values. People at this level follow the rules of their communities—home, school, and society—because they are socialized into doing so and they do not want to let parents, teachers, coaches, or others down. If moral authority is external to the individual, then it would be quite natural that 40 percent of young adults "referred to how other people would think of them (at least partly) in defining what for them would be morally right and wrong."[43]

In the socialized way of knowing, young adults focus their moral reasoning around living up to the expectations of society or other authority figures. Many young adults at this stage of development cannot internally assess how or why they believe what they do. In desiring to live up to the expectations of those around them, young adults may "relativize or subordinate their own immediate interests on behalf of the interests of a social relationship."[44] Smith and his colleagues' observation that many young adults "turn out to be highly oriented to the interests, needs, or desires of social relations" reflects this characteristic of young adult development.[45] Many of these young adults also explained that they refrain from judging other people's moral decisions or behaviors *precisely because* they see that other people have different parents, friends, or religious communities that provide them with other morals or ways of living different than their own. This dynamic explains why young adults struggle to evaluate their sources of moral authority when their moral conclusions differ from others.

In the young adult years, people begin to develop their own internal sense of authority. This is the transition Kegan describes from the socialized way of knowing to the self-authoring way of knowing (fourth level). As young adults develop a new sense of identity, their voice and history of experiences become the authority that guides decision-making. At this stage of life, they become aware of their responsibility to themselves, rather than feeling responsible to the opinions and needs of others. Only at this stage can young adults begin to reflect critically on why they hold the values and beliefs they do.[46]

Young adults may refrain from making judgments when they are transitioning from one way of knowing toward another, more complex, way of knowing because they are still in the process of developing their own moral identity. Young adults who responded to survey questions by stating that morality is an individual choice reflect a sense of transitional development. As this transition progresses, young adults may no longer hold the same moral stance they held as a teenager, but they have not fully developed a new way of understanding morality and of making moral judgments. These responses reflect a *transitional* moral relativism, which is a natural part of human development. Expecting young adults to have a fully developed internal sense of moral authority places modern (fourth level) expectations on young adults who may still be operating at the traditional (third) level, or are perhaps transitioning from one level to the next. These societal expectations run the risk of overwhelming young adults or making them feel "in over their heads."[47]

Developmentally, many young adults are struggling to carve out a new way of making sense of the world as they transition toward adulthood. Kegan notes that the family unit surrounds children and adolescents with a set of values, rules, and beliefs that guide them in day-to-day activities, and in the way they perceive themselves and the world.[48] Moving beyond the social surrounds of childhood and adolescence provides new opportunities for young adults to adhere, question, reshape, relativize, or even reject the values, rules, and beliefs of their family of origin. What is more, studies show that few young adults will evolve past the third level of knowing before leaving college.[49] In fact, according to Kegan's research, approximately two-thirds of adults between the late twenties and mid-forties have not transitioned to the fourth level of knowing.[50]

EXPLORING DEEP CULTURE

The fact that many young adults are in a state of developmental transition does not mean that their evolving worldviews are superficial. Practical theology pays attention to the deep sociocultural realities embedded in peoples' experiences by contextualizing the stories that give rise to their self-understanding. Taking a closer look at contemporary postmodern culture reveals a sharp distinction between the surface culture and deep culture of young adults. Smith and his collaborators acknowledge that postmodernity has changed the landscape of contemporary young adulthood in dramatic ways; yet their analysis moves away from the context of young adult lives, instead interpreting their stories through abstract philosophical theories. This approach only scratches the surface. An alternative can be found in Robert Wuthnow, who argues that sociologists should work to uncover the deep cultural symbols in society. According to Wuthnow,

> Culture as *deep meaning*...is concerned with the tacit knowledge that guides human behavior without our needing to think very much about it. It is composed less of beliefs and values and more of orientations and understandings....[It] lies beneath the surface of what is actually said or written.[51]

Richard Cote also explores the importance of understanding deep culture as it relates to the mission of the Catholic Church. He states, "One of the most disquieting aspects of the Church's dealing with culture in the past...is its tendency to appraise a culture or its parts largely (sometimes exclusively) on the basis of what 'meets the eye,' that is, on the outer epidermal surface of a culture. It has not always paid sufficient heed to the deeper 'invisible' strata of culture, the dynamic myths and mobilizing symbols that burn like a fiery furnace within."[52] What meets the eye—often the "isms" of contemporary culture (e.g., relativism, individualism)—does not reveal deep culture. There is an "unfortunate tendency," Cote writes, "to equate ideologies with fundamental cultural values." He continues, "Although ideologies can and do enter cultural structures, they are not *constitutive* of culture as fundamental values are; they are more like viral infections that weaken or distort a culture, but which do not belong to its essential nature."[53]

To suggest that moral relativism and individualism are synonymous with deep culture in the United States overlooks important cultural cues and symbols of meaning essential to understanding how young adults view themselves and their role in society. When we associate deep culture with the "isms" of contemporary society, not only do we misperceive the deep meaning of important values and beliefs, but also, Cote argues, "culture itself is made the scapegoat for every conceivable ill that is visited upon humanity. It then becomes virtually impossible to perceive culture...as being redeemable (let alone evangelized); it also explains why culture is often regarded as a most unlikely marriage partner for faith."[54]

The way to interpret these deeper layers of cultural meaning is, according to Wuthnow, by "pay[ing] closer attention to personal narratives and their role in framing cultural assumptions about the individual."[55] Cote and Wuthnow help us explore the deep cultural meanings revealed through the stories young adults tell of their lives. Their narratives provide a powerful way to explore their self-understanding. When someone begins telling their story, Wuthnow notes, "one remembers the lessons and, in a small way, relives the process of learning it."[56] He states, "Personal narratives are often told to illustrate a specific transition or insight, such as a lesson that was learned or a moral that was driven home by the context in which it occurred."[57] Sociological studies that offer a thick description of life stories can thus help educational ministers discover how young adults find meaning in contemporary society.[58] Religious educators and ministers can develop mentoring relationships with young adults that encourage young adults to retell portions of their life story, to tell their personal narrative and then reflect on the meaning of that story in their lives. When we listen to people's life stories, we start to see the links between a person's self-understanding and how our culture conceives of individuals in society.

Cultures are composed of complex, multilayered, interconnected webs of socialization, interaction, and meaning. On the surface, we hear young adults struggle to make sense of their moral convictions, articulate moral beliefs, or identify where they turn for guidance on moral dilemmas. Below the surface, we hear young adults starting to develop their independence and autonomy. Their moral reasoning was once based on their relationships to those closest to them, and now they are searching for their own inner moral authority. Many young adults experience deep changes in their self-understanding when they move away from the social surrounds of adolescence, causing them to rethink their experiences in light of what they once believed. This process of developing one's own inner voice from which to reflect and make decisions takes time, but supportive mentoring environments can nurture this transition. It is in listening to the personal narratives of young adults that we can begin to understand how they make meaning, what experiences brought them to believe what they believe, and how we might support and accompany them in their ongoing growth.

CONCLUSION

Why do so many ministers, educators, and church leaders believe that the "isms" of contemporary culture are responsible for leading young adults away from the Church and leaving them morally adrift? One answer is that such an explanation is easy. It is easier to offer solutions that come with clear directives and well-marked road maps. Young people, the thinking goes, just do not know what is morally right and morally wrong. The "problem" is moral relativism, and the solution is more moral instruction. When we package our efforts at evangelization this way, it sounds less daunting to practitioners. Such an approach provides one way to address the challenges faced by young adults. However, simply blaming the "isms" of contemporary culture cuts short any attempt by religious educators to explore the lived experiences and life stories of young people. A different approach would be to help young adults think about their moral positions by listening to their life stories, so that theologians, ministers, and pastoral leaders might more fully understand why they believe what they do. Religious educators and other ministers can create networks of mentors, or partners in ministry, within the faith community, by collaborating with campus ministers, college professors or counselors, other lay ecclesial ministers in the surrounding dioceses, lay apostolate movements, religious communities, and even leaders from other faith traditions. Mentors can help young adults grow beyond a transitional moral relativism and encourage them to take into consideration the authority of the Catholic faith tradition and other wise practitioners as they develop their own inner moral voice.

Christian Smith and his colleagues rely heavily on the theoretical in their interpretations of the practical. The result is a portrait of contemporary young adults driven by the expectations of a modern moral vision that presupposes all moral truths are self-evident. Without the benefit that comes from dialogue with developmental psychology, they place unrealistic expectations on young people who are in the process of transitioning into more adult ways of knowing, thus failing to notice the deep cultural meaning revealed in the questions young adults ask and the stories they tell. Such causal explanations attribute too much to philosophical theories. "Our contemporary world," Paul Lakeland reminds us, "is not the way it is because of the work of Derrida and Foucault and Rorty, any more than the medieval world was the product of Aquinas or Ockham."[59] Insofar as postmodern theory enters in to the analysis of Catholic practical theologians, it enters not as the impetus for cultural changes, but rather, to offer "systematic explorations of cultural practices and insights that arise within postmodernity."[60] Starting not with ideas about young adults, but with the young adults themselves, practical theology invites educational ministers and church leaders to listen to the life stories of young adults as a way of becoming more attuned to the deep patterns of meaning and to recognize the developmental aspects of transitional moral relativism common to young adulthood.

NOTES

1. For this particular description, see chapter 4 in Christian Smith and Patricia Snell, *Souls in Transition: The Religious Lives of Emerging Adults in America* (New York: Oxford University Press, 2009), for an analysis of the survey data from this cohort at the ages of eighteen to twenty-three.

2. Smith et al., *Lost in Transition: The Dark Side of Emerging Adulthood* (New York: Oxford University Press, 2011), 55.

3. James Smith, *Who's Afraid of Postmodernism? Taking Derrida, Lyotard, and Foucault to Church* (Grand Rapids: Baker Academic, 2006), 21.

4. Smith and Snell, *Souls in Transition*, 48–49.

5. Paul Lakeland, *Postmodernity: Christian Identity in a Fragmented Age* (Minneapolis: Fortress, 1997), 36.

6. Clifford Geertz argues that to understand the meaning and significance of cultural patterns, we need to move past "thin descriptions," or our own observations and assumptions, to

explore "thick descriptions," or the layers of meaning and complexity behind what is happening. See Clifford Geertz, *The Interpretation of Culture* (New York: Basic Books, 1973), 312–14.

7. See, e.g., Mary E. Bendyna and Paul M. Perl, *Young, Adult Catholics in the Context of Other Catholic Generations: Living with Diversity, Seeking Service, Waiting to Be Welcomed* (Center for Applied Research in the Apostolate at Georgetown University, 2000); and William V. D'Antonio et al., *American Catholics Today: New Realities of their Faith and Their Church* (Lanham, MD: Rowman and Littlefield Publishers, 2007). For a list of ministry and professional presentations and resources referencing the NSYR data, see Tom Beaudoin, *Witness to Dispossession: The Vocation of a Post-modern Theologian* (Maryknoll, NY: Orbis, 2008), 174n7.

8. Kathleen Cahalan, "Locating Practical Theology in Catholic Theological Discourse and Practice," *International Journal of Practical Theology* 15, no. 1 (2011): 15.

9. Smith and Denton analyzed the first sampling of this generation as teenagers between the ages of thirteen and seventeen in the first book in this series, *Soul Searching: The Religious and Spiritual Lives of American Teenagers* (New York: Oxford University Press, 2005). The second and third wave of data explored this cohort between the ages of sixteen and twenty-one, and then again at ages eighteen to twenty-three; see Smith and Snell, *Souls in Transition*. Christian Smith et al. later published *Lost in Transition*. The final book explores what the data says specifically about Catholic young adults from the same sample (ages 18–23). See Christian Smith, Kyle Longest, Jonathan Hill, and Kari Christoffersen, *Young Catholic America: Emerging Adults In, Out Of, and Gone from the Church* (New York: Oxford University Press, 2014).

10. Smith et al., *Lost in Transition*, 60.

11. Smith et al., *Lost in Transition*, 65.

12. Smith et al., *Lost in Transition*, 59, italics in original.

13. Smith et al., *Lost in Transition*, 44, 65, 60, 31, 68, 69, and 31–69, respectively.

14. Smith et al., *Lost in Transition*, 251n5, citing Alasdair MacIntyre.

15. Smith et al., *Lost in Transition*, 33.

16. Smith et al., *Lost in Transition*, 61.

17. Smith et al., *Lost in Transition*, 13–15.

18. Smith et al., *Lost in Transition*, 15.

19. Smith et al., *Lost in Transition*, 15.

20. In contrast, Gabriel Abend argues sociologists should follow Weberian sociological framework, arguing sociologists are not and should not be moral philosophers. They should remain neutral as much as possible and offer no value judgements on empirical research as they are not "moral philosophers in disguise." For more on this distinction, see Gabriel Abend, "Two Main Problems in the Sociology of Morality," *Theory & Society* 37, no. 2 (April 2008): 90.

21. Smith et al., *Lost in Transition*, 6.

22. Smith et al., *Lost in Transition*, 6–7.

23. Smith et al., *Lost in Transition*, 60–61.

24. John Swinton and Harriet Mowat, *Practical Theology and Qualitative Research* (London: SCM, 2006), 29.

25. Swinton and Mowat, *Pracical Theology*, 29.

26. Smith et al., *Lost in Transition*, 21.

27. Smith et al., *Lost in Transition*, 22, emphasis added.

28. Smith et al., *Lost in Transition*, 27.

29. Smith et al., *Lost in Transition*, 27. For the list of interview questions, see 249n1. Note: several of these questions are rather leading questions.

30. Smith et al., *Lost in Transition*, 38. The authors labeled this response as a "consequentialist view of morality."

31. Smith et al., *Lost in Transition*, 42, 49.

32. Smith et al., *Lost in Transition*, 60.

33. Smith et al., *Lost in Transition*, 36–38.

34. Smith et al., *Lost in Transition*, 21.

35. Smith et al., *Lost in Transition*, 59.

36. Robert Kegan, *The Evolving Self* (Cambridge, MA: Harvard University Press, 1982).

37. Robert Kegan, *In Over Our Heads: The Mental Demands of Modern Life* (Cambridge, MA: Harvard University Press, 1994), 29.

38. As noted below, this transition occurs for very few adults (between the ages of twenty-five and fifty-five) and will generally not begin until at least middle age (beyond the age of about fifty). See Kegan, *In Over Our Heads*, 191–96. While many will not reach this level in young adulthood, it is important to be familiar with

later stages so that we can support the cognitive growth of young adults toward maturity.

39. Kegan, *In Over Our Heads*, 320.

40. Kegan, *In Over Our Heads*, 318.

41. Kegan, *In Over Our Heads*, 37.

42. Kegan, *In Over Our Heads*, 47.

43. Smith et al., *Lost in Transition*, 38.

44. Robert Kegan, "What 'Form' Transforms? A Constructive-Developmental Approach to Transformative Learning," in *Learning as Transformation: Critical Perspectives on a Theory in Progress*, ed. Jack Mezirow and associates (San Francisco: Jossey-Bass, 2000), 64.

45. Smith et al., *Lost in Transition*, 35.

46. Kegan, *In Over Our Heads*, 132.

47. Kegan, *In Over Our Heads*, 132.

48. Kegan, *In Over Our Heads*, 267.

49. Philip Lewis et al., "Identity Development during the College Years: Findings from the West Point Longitudinal Study," *Journal of College Student Development* 46, no. 4 (2005): 357–73; and Kegan, *In Over Our Heads*, 267.

50. Emily Souvaine Lahey et al., *A Guide to the Subject-Object Interview: Its Administration and Interpretation* (Cambridge, MA: Harvard University School of Education, Subject-Object Research Group, 1988).

51. Robert Wuthnow, *American Mythos: Why Our Best Efforts to Be a Better Nation Fall Short* (Princeton, NJ: Princeton University Press, 2006), 25.

52. Richard G. Cote, *Re-visioning Mission: The Catholic Church and Culture in Postmodern America* (New York: Paulist Press, 1996), 92.

53. Cote, *Re-visioning Mission*, 97–98.

54. Cote, *Re-visioning Mission*, 98.

55. Wuthnow, *American Mythos*, 41.

56. Wuthnow, *American Mythos*, 65.

57. Wuthnow, *American Mythos*, 65.

58. For a survey of Catholic young adult life stories, see John Fulton, "Young Adults, Contemporary Society and Catholicism," in *Young Catholics at the New Millennium: The Religion and Morality of Young Adults in Western Countries*, ed. John Fulton et al. (Dublin: University College Dublin Press, 2000), 1–26.

59. Lakeland, *Postmodernity*, 36.

60. Harold D. Horell, "Cultural Postmodernity and Christian Faith Formation," in *Horizons and Hopes: The Future of Religious Education*, ed. Thomas H. Groome and Harold Daly Horell (Mahwah, NJ: Paulist Press, 2003), 82.

Chapter Eight

FORMATION FOR MISSION INTEGRATION

Forming Lay Leaders of Catholic Institutions

Celeste Mueller

BACKGROUND

In the 1985 article "Can Church Education be Theological Education?" Edward Farley inquired,

> How is it that the Christian faith, committed as it is to relate faith to reality, world, knowledge, and learning, continues to restrict this relating to its ordained leadership and to withhold it from the laity?...Why is it that *theological* education, ongoing studies in disciplines and skills necessary for the understanding and interpretation of Scripture, doctrines, moral principles, and policies, and areas of praxis, defines something needed by Christian clergy but never by Christian laity?[1]

It has been over three decades since Farley challenged theologians, seminaries, and schools of ministry to recognize the need for "ordered learning" for the laity; that is, substantive theological education including "disciplined efforts to equip the believer to interpret reality."[2] We can safely admit that in that time neither parish leaders nor those who prepare Christian ministers and educators have responded with a comprehensive approach to equipping the faithful with a "cumulative, rigorous educational process and post-Enlightenment tools of analysis and interpretation (historical, literary, social, psychological, philosophical)" through which they can meaningfully appropriate the wealth of the Christian tradition for personal formation and social transformation.[3]

Catholic parishes in these years, in fact, have steadily relied more heavily on a formative approach that emphasizes piety and devotion. Pastors have required less, not more, theological expertise in hiring directors of religious education and pastoral ministers, despite the number of excellent graduate programs in ministry and the guidelines for preparation of lay ministers outlined in *Co-Workers*. The impact of this hiring trend has reverberated in schools of theology and ministry. In 2013, the Auburn Center report of enrollment in degree programs in ministry described major losses in master of divinity degree programs and even greater losses in nonministerial master's degrees in theological studies.[4] The programs that provide rigorous and comprehensive theological study, and have the greatest potential to enable parish ministers and educators to facilitate a genuine theological formation in parishes, have been steadily declining in enrollment.

During the same period, which parallels the emergence of lay ecclesial ministry and the years of the development of *Co-Workers* until today, Catholic health care organizations have experienced a very different trend as they have given steadily increasing attention and resources to the work of formation. From an early wariness of the word *formation* and suspicion of what it might entail, leaders of Catholic health care organizations have moved to a clear expectation that formation is essential to sustaining Catholic identity and advancing the mission. Catholic health care in the United States and beyond, with the many diverse challenges it faces, has been functioning as a laboratory for approaches in formation. Our efforts in designing, developing, and facilitating formation over the last fourteen years at Ascension—a large Catholic health system in the United States—have produced and affirmed an approach that explicitly engages theology, spirituality, and ethics, that incorporates the four elements of formation identified in *Co-Workers*, and that corresponds to Farley's description of "ordered" learning.

Participants experience formation as an opportunity for reflection on identity in community, specifically, reflection on personal identity, professional identity, and organizational identity in dialogue with the riches of the Catholic tradition, which has shaped and continues to sustain Catholic health care. The outcomes we observe, through a 360 degree assessment process, in our formation participants include greater professional and organizational fidelity to the identity and mission of Catholic health care as a ministry of the Church, and personal growth that integrates mind, body, and spirit. Ascension's experience of what we name *ministry formation* demonstrates a resounding "Yes!" to Farley's question, and realizes hopes for the personal and organizational integration of theology, spirituality, and ethics that surpass, perhaps, Farley's own imagination. The evolving work of ministry formation in Catholic health care offers rich examples and resources to assist dioceses and other Catholic organizations in their efforts to provide personal formation and to sustain Catholic identity. The fact that ministry formation is being led and facilitated in Catholic health care primarily by theologically educated laywomen and -men suggests emerging opportunities for practical theologians and for schools of theology and ministry.

FORMATION IN CATHOLIC HEALTH CARE: FOUNDATIONAL FRAMEWORKS

The ecclesial foundation for formation of leaders[5] in Catholic health care is the same as the primary root identified in *Co-Workers*, answering the universal call to holiness through the transformation of the secular realm:

> [The] laity, by their very vocation, seek the kingdom
> of God by engaging in temporal affairs and by order-
> ing them according to the plan of God. They live in
> the world, that is, in each and in all of the secular pro-
> fessions and occupations...called there by God that by
> exercising their proper function and led by the spirit of
> the Gospel they may work for the sanctification of the
> world from within as a leaven.[6]

From that common root, however, a distinctive branch has
emerged through the gradual recognition of Catholic health
care as a ministry of the Church. Leaders in Catholic health care
have an opportunity through their professional responsibilities to
transform the world according to the gospel *both* as individuals
called to personal holiness *and* as leaders of a corporate ministry
of the Church, that is, as *ministry* leaders.

What is needed by health care leaders so that they can fulfill
this dual role? The desired outcomes of formation are twofold:
personal flourishing in community—holiness and wholeness—and
the *organization's integrity as a ministry of the Church.* These dual
aims hold together the *individual* experiences of the leaders and
the *collective* experience of the health care organization as a community; they implicate the *interior* life of the *individual* (values, dispositions, motives) and the *interior* life of the *community* (culture,
shared values, morale), as well as the more visible *exterior* life of
individuals and the community seen in decisions, actions, policies, processes, and organizational structures. To reach the aims
of formation in an integrated way, each of these four dimensions
of human experience needs to be addressed, and a graphic rep-
resentation, based on the integral theory of Ken Wilber, provides
an "integration map" for our work in formation.[7] (See figure 1.)

The process of developing greater awareness of each of
these dimensions of leaders' individual and communal experience and intentionally pursuing greater alignment and integrity
between the dimensions is a continuous exercise of practical wisdom that is the core mechanism of formation. Thus, in its sim-
plest articulation, we define *formation* as "reflection on practice
in community," which involves a disciplined cycle of seeing, judging, and acting.

Our Formational Map for Integrity and Alignment

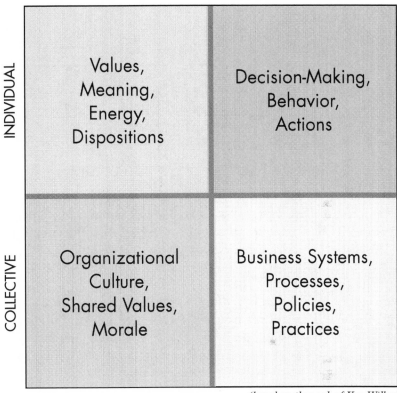

INTERIOR   EXTERIOR

INDIVIDUAL

Values,
Meaning,
Energy,
Dispositions

Decision-Making,
Behavior,
Actions

COLLECTIVE

Organizational
Culture,
Shared Values,
Morale

Business Systems,
Processes,
Policies,
Practices

(based on the work of Ken Wilber)

Fig. 1: Four Dimensions of Human Experience

The corporate context of health care means that what is called "formation" is introduced into a culture that highly prizes the process of continuous learning and leadership development common to most of the business world. While in some ways the career advancing goals of what is usually understood as "development" can seem to be at odds with the formation goals of holiness and ministerial integrity, in fact expanding the scope of "leadership development" in collaboration with those responsible for Organizational Development and Learning can unite formation and learning into a single framework of integral human

169

Fig. 2: Spiritually Centered Leadership Development

development. (See figure 2.) As Pope Francis has said, quoting St. Paul VI, the foundation stone of integral human development is "development of each person and the whole person."[8]

Health care organizations routinely offer learning and development programs that equip individuals with the professional and organizational skills needed for the work they are doing. *Professional* formation addresses what workers do in their individual roles, where individual performance is governed primarily by standards of behavior, professional standards of excellence, and expectations of quality and reliability. *Organizational* formation addresses skills needed for working in complex organizations: communication, strategy, managing the performance of workers, maintaining accountability, navigating organizational politics, developing teams, and "building talent." Most often, leadership development programs are oriented toward personal career success and the corporate good of the organization. Both professional and organizational formation programs are necessary, but alone, they are insufficient to constitute integral human development that promotes personal flourishing and an organization's integrity as a Catholic ministry. Integrating spiritual and theological formation into this broader picture of development introduces theological reflection, which Richard Gula identifies as a "*distinguishing* characteristic of ministry leaders,"[9] as a leadership competency. The critical bridge highlighted here is that an integrated framework for development of the whole person makes it more possible to invite leaders to theological reflection on the specific contexts of their leadership in ways that include both the descriptive and strategic tasks of practical theology.[10] Leaders can build skills to recognize and analyze theological claims embedded in their day-to-day decisions and organizational policies, and from that analysis to interpret and lead organizational processes—strategic, operational, financial, and clinical—according to Catholic health care's identity as a ministry of the Church.

Pope Francis notes that integral human development must always be a matter of integrating body and soul, because "no work of development can truly reach its goal if it does not respect that place in which God is present with us and speaks to our heart."[11] When the practice of theological reflection is consistently accompanied by opportunities for spiritual reflection, leaders discover within the contexts of their work deeper awareness and deeper connections to their true selves, to others, to the wider community, and to God. Paying attention to their inner life, leaders can recognize themselves as unique and precious beings created in love and called to personal flourishing as whole persons; they can learn to listen more attentively to the God whose "voice echoes in [their depths] summoning [them] to love the good," and can cultivate the virtues necessary to lead in ways that promote greater organizational integrity.[12]

THEOLOGICAL FORMATION FOR EXECUTIVES

The foundational elements described above constitute frameworks that make it possible to pursue "ordered learning" in the health care context in the sense described by Farley. However, which theological content and learning methods ought to be used with health care leaders is not self-evident. A debate about the degree to which leaders should be invited to rigorous theological study is taking place among Catholic health care systems in the United States, even though it is rarely in the form of an explicit dialogue. Rather, the debate is evident through the diversity of approaches used in formation programs in different health care systems. What is at issue is the question of what is necessary to sustain the identity of Catholic health care as a ministry of the Church. What is at stake is the Catholic identity of health care institutions, and the transformative good that they can do as Catholic ministries in society. In a recent essay, Charles Bouchard asserts,

> Whatever shape…formation takes, it is clear that there can be no meaningful appropriation of the term "ministry" to describe Catholic health care unless it is nourished with serious theology and spirituality at a number of levels. Senior leaders, board members and sponsors will have to have fluency in theological questions that impact health care just as they have fluency in organizational development, finance, and strategic planning.[13]

The groups of leaders that Father Bouchard identifies, executives among them, have the highest degree of accountability for protecting, sustaining, and advancing the identity of Catholic health care as a ministry of the Church. This accountability for ministry identity is carried out by leaders who daily articulate a vision for their organizations, set strategy, establish structures, policies, and practices, and make decisions that shape the culture, expectations, work life, and experience for thousands of associates, and for the hundreds of communities and millions of patients served.

The challenges in offering substantive theological study in a formation program are real. Executives have widely divergent understandings of what "formation" might mean and can be suspicious of a subtle form of proselytizing. Often those joining Catholic health care from secular and for-profit corporations are simply perplexed by the invitation to formation. Audiences for formation have broadly diverse occupations, perspectives, religious practices, faith commitments, levels of education, and degrees of religious literacy, and the pace of work and volume of responsibilities for executives would seem to preclude theological study. Implicit in the debate, beyond the obvious challenges, I fear, is the very same axiom that Farley invites us to challenge. Despite the scope and significance of the responsibilities of health care executives, even many among the vowed religious whose communities founded Catholic health care organizations in the United States and beyond, do not seem to be able to imagine that ordered learning in theology is necessary, possible, and achievable within an executive formation program. The details of our Executive Ministry Leadership Formation program illuminate a pathway for how theological learning can be ordered within the parameters of a corporate setting, for a diversity of learners who have little or no previous theological or even religious formation, for the sake of their personal flourishing and capability to lead the organization as a ministry of the Church, which we hope can stimulate a wider imagination of possibilities.

CONTENT AND APPROACH

We begin with a set of expectations that presuppose leaders' willingness to support and advance the mission of the organization.[14] All executives at Ascension are expected to

- Be personally committed to practices and habits of spiritual reflection that foster deeper relationship with self, God, others, community, and the world as part of their ongoing formation journey.
- Be professionally committed to the healing ministry and mission of Jesus with special attention to those who are poor and vulnerable.
- Consistently integrate and practice virtuous servant leadership while being and building community.
- Articulate foundational concepts from the Catholic theological, moral, and spiritual tradition in order to communicate our ministry identity and mission.
- Interpret and lead integrated strategic, operational, financial, clinical, and organizational processes through the lens of Ascension's identity as a ministry of the Church.

Three elements of the Catholic theological tradition are so closely tied to these expectations and so vitally important for executives to articulate and use in their leadership of organizational

173

processes that they form an essential core for each of our formation programs. First, the nature of the human person made in the image of God—intrinsically relational, possessing inherent and inviolable human dignity, and destined for union with God. The understanding of the human vocation, emerging from the reality of being created in love, for community, and gifted to serve the common good, is the foundation for personal and social ethics and every principle of Catholic identity for which health care leaders are accountable: justice, solidarity, subsidiarity, participation, stewardship, and respect for human life. Significantly, the implications of the nature of the human person apply equally to nonclinical subsidiaries or partnerships involved in health care today as they do in direct care and clinical settings.

The second theological notion essential to our conceptual framework for formation is the nature of Catholic ministry. Our health care system is a business that is a Catholic ministry; that is to say, it is a community called and animated by the Holy Spirit to serve the good of all persons on behalf of the Catholic Church, through witness to the gospel. Discussions of ministry, especially lay ministry, in Catholic circles are often "bedeviled by confusion," invoking widely variable pastoral practices and questions of authorization and limits of individual ministry.[15] At Ascension, we have opted, therefore, to focus on what have been described as the *functions* of ministry. All authentic ministry, including the corporate ministries of healing, education, and social service, accomplishes the following functions: *sustaining, guiding, reconciling, nurturing, empowering, liberating.*[16] Executives easily understand how the practice of medicine can accomplish these functions through the healing arts, and profound conversations are stimulated by analogous questions: How is it that the whole organization offers guidance, nurturing, reconciliation, and sustenance? Do executives function as agents of empowerment and liberation through the work of management and leadership?

The third core concept is Jesus's proclamation of the reign of God, which identifies the widest horizon of the mission of Catholic health care. Like Jesus's own ministry of healing, Catholic health care is called to be a witness to the good news of God's reign of justice, peace, and mercy. In this truth, executives find hope. They are able to see that their vocation is oriented beyond their immediate concerns and our present moment and at the same time to see that God's gifts of justice, peace, and mercy have been given and are available to them in this moment. They can see their work and the work of the organization in light of the bigger picture of God's designs and the work God is doing on earth.

Each of the three elements of our theological core also guides the Formation Department's approach. We provide formation both to sustain organizational identity as a ministry and because our Christian anthropology compels us to provide a workplace in which persons can thrive in community. We endeavor to provide formation that is person centered and holistic, and we attend to each of the functions of ministry in the work of formation. We do all of this with our eyes on the horizon of God's reign, trusting that we are cooperating in the work God is doing, and with hope that our organization can be an ever more faithful sign of God's reign.

Building on this essential three-dimensional core, we extend theological study in our executive formation program through five eight-week courses.[17] These courses are built around a specific set of eight theological claims or affirmations, which were selected because we have experienced the direct connection of each to the discernment and decisions health care leaders are making every day. Together these affirmations create a theological spine for the entire program that is reinforcing but not redundant, focused but not reductive, and that maximizes the impact of learning within the parameters of our context. From the perspective of faculty in the program, the affirmations limit the scope of topics, but do not constrain creativity of approach and engagement. From the perspective of the participants, the affirmations are bite-sized portions that become entrees into the profound theology being introduced as well as anchors for their learning. Reciting the entire list aloud when the group gathers in retreat provides the ritual reinforcement of a litany.

COURSE 1. THE MYSTERY OF GOD WHO CALLS

- God is known and knowable: revealed through experience.

- God is mystery: transcendent and immanent.
- God is a community of persons.
- God is good; God is love.
- God is Creator who invites cocreation; we are made in the image of God.
- God is just and merciful.
- God acts on behalf of the poor and vulnerable.
- God wills the wholeness of all creation.

COURSE 2. JESUS: MISSION AND MINISTRY

- The mission of Jesus is to proclaim and embody the reign of God.
- Jesus acts as Servant in boundary-breaking solidarity with those on the margin.
- Jesus heals, restoring the wholeness of persons and communities.
- Jesus gathers the disciples and sends them on mission.
- Jesus suffers with and for us.
- Jesus destroys the power of death.
- Jesus frees us.
- Jesus reveals the fullness of humanity; Jesus reveals the fullness of divinity.

COURSE 3. CHURCH: MISSION AND MINISTRY

- The Church is the community of the faithful.
- The Church is the Body of Christ in the world: one, holy, catholic, apostolic.
- The Church is both human and divine.
- The Church is a "field hospital."
- The Church worships, preaches, teaches, heals, and cares for the poor.
- The Church is sacrament.
- The Church is a communion of communions: an "ordered" communion.

- The Holy Spirit fills the Church with gifts for the work of mission.

COURSE 4. CATHOLIC MORAL VISION: PERSONAL AND SOCIAL

- The human person is made in the image of God: holy, social, self-giving.
- The human person is both limited and created for transcendence: destined for intimate union with God.
- The human person possesses inalienable dignity.
- The human person is called to serve the common good.
- The human person has rights and responsibilities.
- The human person is both spiritual and embodied.
- All are called to serve the poor and vulnerable.
- All are called to care for all of creation.

COURSE 5. ETHICS: CLINICAL AND ORGANIZATIONAL

- Moral reasoning seeks full human flourishing.
- Catholic ministries seek human dignity and the common good in all things.
- One may not do evil to achieve good.
- Catholic health care is animated by the gospel of Jesus and guided by the moral tradition of the Church.
- The gift of life calls Catholic health care to protect human dignity at the beginning and end of life, and all points in between.
- Catholic health care limits participation in immoral activities, according to the principles of formal and material cooperation.
- Discernment is decision-making that reaches into the heart of our beliefs about God, creation, others, and oneself.
- An ethical organization is sustained by virtue.

METHOD

Each online course is set between face-to-face retreats. In both the retreats and the online format, we utilize five teaching and learning practices in order to engage substantively the identified theological content for professional appropriation and to support personal flourishing. The five teaching and learning practices that we employ reflect Alasdair McIntyre's understanding of practices as coherent and complex socially established activities "through which the goods internal to that form of activity are realized."[18] Practices are broader and more open-ended than what may be more commonly understood as teaching techniques or classroom strategies. These practices, which echo our understanding of the nature of the human person, are akin to an art form that may come to life through a variety of particular strategies or techniques:

1. Create a welcoming, safe environment conducive to internal reflection.
2. Invite awareness and consideration of personal and communal experience.
3. Promote inquiry and learning in community.
4. Engage the dynamic of action and reflection.
5. Integrate prayer and ritual.

Hospitality, acceptance, and assurance of confidentiality are critical to inviting leaders to internal reflection. For many of our leaders, the inner life is a foreign territory, and in the words of Parker Palmer, "The soul is like a wild animal—tough, resilient, savvy, self-sufficient, and yet exceedingly shy."[19] Establishing a habit among the leaders of accessing and sharing their experience provides a pathway to the inner life, builds trust that creates safety, and increases their willingness and ability to be vulnerable with one another. This, in turn, creates greater openness to inquiry-driven learning.

The importance of building a learning community among the leaders and faculty cannot be overstated. Learning as a community reflects the communal nature of persons in the image of God, enables a clearer and more experiential recognition of the communion we share as humans and with God, equips leaders for the increasingly collaborative leadership that health care demands, and fosters personal growth. Joretta Marshall writes,

> Communities are places where we are held and nurtured...places where we discover a sense of contradiction and where we find ourselves struggling to discern how to move into something new, risking the loss of some aspects of our old selves in order to participate in a newness that we do not yet know or understand.... [They provide] a space for persons as they change and grow and a place to which they may return anew.[20]

Further, learning in community, which affirms the active role of each in the learning process, is a critical reinforcement of the authority with which the leaders are expected to incorporate their learning in the organization. Parker Palmer proposes a model of a community of truth: colearners gathered around a topic of inquiry in which each individual is actively engaging each other, and all together are actively attending to the subject being studied.[21] The model graphically highlights the subjectivity and, therefore, the agency of each participant in the conversation, as well as the significance of each member's contributions to uncovering deeper truth of the subject around which they are gathered. Faculty members meet face-to-face with the participants twice, at the retreat that precedes the course and at the one that follows the course. Faculty precede their course with an introduction that uncovers the participants' experiences and current knowledge of the topic, and follow the course with an activity that encourages the participants to demonstrate and apply what they have learned to their specific leadership context. Members of the Ascension Formation Department, who also hold terminal degrees in theology or spirituality, serve as master facilitators for the retreats, and guide participants in their use of the "See-Judge-Act" model to engage the dynamic of action and reflection at retreats and within their online course discussions. (See figure 3.)

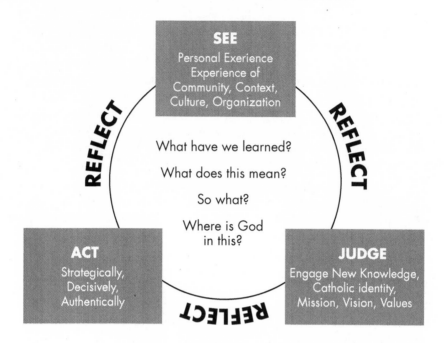

Fig. 3: See-Judge-Act Model

Over the span of the eight retreats, the participants develop skills in contextual analysis—"seeing" and developing a "thick description" of the complexity of their personal, professional, and communal experience, and practice assessing it in light of their theological learning. In between retreats, during the online portions of the courses, participants are also invited to engage their learning through a specific practice at work, which promotes both personal and professional reflection on action. For example, during the course "Jesus: Mission and Ministry," participants are asked to solicit direct feedback frequently from peers, direct reports, supervisors, and others on the quality of their presence and interactions as leaders. Reflection questions help connect their experience to Jesus's question, "Who do people say that I am?" and lead to deeper awareness of their own sense of vocation as a leader. The entire program concludes with an integrative capstone project in which participants engage what they have learned, and who they have become in the process, to address collaboratively a specific challenge in their area of responsibility and to plan for their own ongoing formation.

During the program, leaders move through a familiar hermeneutical pattern: (1) engaging experience that reveals presuppositions or "first naïveté," (2) critical inquiry, in which leaders often have an experience of distanciation, and (3) transformational appropriation or "second naïveté"[22] that promotes transformed action. This pattern corresponds to what research in neuroscience has identified as the pattern of learning in the brain, and it offers leaders a way to reflect on the experience they are having in the learning process. Both of these insights guide formation facilitators and reflect elements that help to maximize the impact of learning within time constraints faced by our leaders.[23]

Introducing prayer and ritual to a religiously diverse group is a delicate endeavor because ritual is such a powerful experience, and precisely because of its power, ritual is essential in the learning process. "Ritual practices, times, and spaces bracket our experiences so that they achieve a heightened potency, both to sustain and transform us."[24] The dynamic of ritual is the dynamic of "living as if." Participants are absorbed into the liminal space and time that ritual creates, and multiple parts of their brains are engaged by the array of meanings that rituals symbolically present. Ordinary time and space are suspended, and participants can embody the possible worlds projected. Many rituals are incorporated in the learning process, including simple practices of awareness involving the senses, breathing, movement, and body posture. The most enthusiastically received ritual prayer is communal *lectio divina*. Participants are invited to discover and nurture their own unique human spirit and, if they are persons of faith, to listen for God's voice and action in their experience. Each person is free to bring to the practice their own system of beliefs, and individuals are always welcome to opt out, but in our experience that is a very rare occurrence.

Leaders in our organization are expected to lead prayerful reflection at the beginning of every meeting, and leading *lectio divina* gives leaders an opportunity to practice and model leadership that is hospitable, inclusive, safe, humble, and courageous. Careful attention to the power of ritual also provides an opportunity to invite participants into a greater consciousness of the ritual power of their other actions at work. Whether or not leaders hold an explicit faith, they are invited to consider that prayer is a stance of humility and courage, daring to invite the Holy to do what we are unable to accomplish on our own. Prayerful reflection, or simple reverence, orients us to a vision wider than we might imagine possible—an essential stance for servant leadership.

This pattern of practices, which appear in our formation experiences like a fractal in nature, serve to unite and integrate the theological and spiritual, the individual and communal, the personal and professional, and shape a process of ordered learning that is holistic and fully human. Gradually, through the five courses and eight retreats, leaders grow in each of the areas defined by the formation outcomes and expectations, and particularly develop the skills to interpret and lead the integrated strategic, operational, financial, clinical, and organizational processes of the organization as a ministry of the Church.

The following comments from the participants' reflections on their formation journey are indicative of the outcomes we have witnessed:[25]

> During this time of formation, I have discovered some different ways of thinking about God, the Church, and ministry. I believe the shift in my perspective, though subtle, will have profound effects on my leadership. It already has....Very specifically, the ethics exercises challenged my thinking and were emotionally challenging. Having spent a professional lifetime practicing Obstetrics and Gynecology, I find that objectivity still eludes me when it comes to reproductive issues. The mechanisms of discernment and the language of different forms of dialogue and discernment remain frustrating and opaque. That being said, this experience has given me an opportunity to learn to listen and engage in healthy dialogue about issues that have been closed books to me for many years. The practices required for ethical discernment have further shown me how difficult true listening, dialogue, forgiveness, and acceptance are. I understand that formation is a lifelong pursuit. This formation time provides me a

community through which to pursue it. (A chief medical officer)

Not having had much exposure to Catholic teachings during my lifetime I have always had a very rigid view of the belief system—primarily because of sensationalism in the media. So while there are still elements with which I might personally hold different perspectives, this experience has given me a new awareness of the inclusiveness of Catholic teachings and the rich world view. Our studies on the Church were also very helpful to me personally, because they gave me perspective on how the role of the Church has evolved over the centuries, as well as the concept of a "communion of communions," and the multiple relationships and stakeholders that must be honored and fostered. This concept was so helpful to me when thinking about how our own hospital ministries function with our communities.

Perhaps the most powerful component of formation for me was on suffering because I have always struggled mightily with it; I still do, but our studies greatly enhanced my understanding of the different views on suffering, which helped me (even if ever-so-slightly) to find a bit more peace with the subject. Overall, I was surprised at how well all these teachings integrated with and even enhanced my own spiritual development, despite not being Catholic. The program has helped me to see that spirituality is a lifelong journey that is shaped by the Divine Mystery and not limited by one particular doctrine or set of beliefs. (An executive in quality, risk, and safety)

[I have come to] recognize that God formed me specially and uniquely in his image for his purpose and called me to service as a ministry leader even with my unique gift in technology. One part of that calling is to be a leader in a faith-based, Catholic organization where I consciously and unconsciously use all of who I am, and what I come with, to make decisions on behalf

183

of the organization, and to behave and act in a manner consistent with the reign of God as demonstrated through Christ. I can therefore serve the people I work with, and for, in ultimately providing health-care services to all, especially those who are struggling and are most vulnerable. (An executive in Ascension Information Services)

CONCLUSIONS

Our formation programs have cultivated a community of leaders who are more theologically articulate and spiritually mature, and who are deeply committed:

> Serving all persons with special attention to those who are poor and vulnerable...dedicated to spiritually-centered, holistic care, which sustains and improves the health of individuals and communities, [and] advocates for a compassionate and just society through [their] actions and [their] words.[26]

The fruits of our labor suggest significant implications for the Church and for ministry formation. The integrated model of spiritual, theological, and ethical formation described here can be fruitfully applied in the formation of disciples working in a variety of fields, of lay leaders in Catholic education, social services, and other ministries in the Church, and can be adapted with integrity to serve other Christian communities and faith-based, mission-driven organizations. If, through their magisterial leadership, Catholic bishops become even more vocal advocates and champions of an integrated and substantive theological, spiritual, and ethical formation for all members of the Church, they may realize in fresh ways the vision of active and mature discipleship articulated in *Gaudium et Spes, Apostolicam Actuositatem,* and so many of Pope Francis's writings and speeches.

Farley concludes the article quoted at the start of this essay with this observation:

If the Church ever does repudiate and move beyond its inherited axiom that church education cannot be theological education, comprehensive reconstruction will be involved....A new population of a very different kind of church teacher will be called for. The educator on the church staff will have to be a theologian-teacher.[27]

In order to extend and expand opportunities for the integrated formation described here, we need to develop not only "theologian-teachers" for parishes and organizations; rather, we also need formation leaders who have a unique constellation of knowledge, skills, and internal dispositions. Formation leaders need to have facility in theology, spirituality, ethics, and psychology, and in the contributions of neuroscience to adult learning strategies and methods. They need to be adept in practices of self-awareness, spiritual and theological reflection, and group dynamics and collaboration, and they need to be skilled in contextual analysis, as well as have skills for leadership that include emotional intelligence, communications, influence, and accountability. Further, they need to exhibit their own commitment to ongoing personal formation, spiritual maturing, integrity, and leadership. There is not currently a single graduate program in which this set of knowledge, skills, and dispositions converge to advance the emerging discipline of formation leadership for Catholic or other faith-based organizations and ministries, and this is a great challenge and an opportunity for schools of theology and ministry.

The vowed religious women and men who are currently members of the congregations and communities that founded Catholic health care do not see the work of formation within Catholic organizations as a remedy for their declining numbers, nor exclusively as a perpetuation of their congregational charisms, but as a wholly new work of the Holy Spirit. "I am about to do a new thing; now it springs forth, do you not perceive it? I will make a way in the wilderness and rivers in the desert" (Isa 43:19). The variety of streams and rivers springing forth to refresh the Church and the world are a testament to the faith, hope, and courage that empowered these same religious women and men to entrust the ministry of Catholic health care to the sponsorship and leadership of the laity. In this loving and prophetic act, they mirror the powerful image and legacy of the women and men who endured hardship and danger with an indomitable spirit to bring Catholic health care to birth in the United States. We honor their spirit and extend that same spirit as we equip the lay faithful to fully engage and integrate the Catholic theological, spiritual, and ethical tradition into their work and leadership.

NOTES

1. Edward Farley, "Can Church Education Be Theological Education?" *Theology Today* 42, no. 2 (1985): 158.

2. Farley, "Church Education," 163.

3. Farley, "Church Education," 171.

4. Barbara G. Wheeler and Anthony T. Ruger, "Sobering Figures Point to Overall Enrollment Decline," *In Trust* (Spring 2013): 6–7.

5. Building on the common foundation described here, Ascension offers formation opportunities to all associates, including staff, care providers, nurses, physicians, managers, and board members. This essay focuses on our programs for executive leaders. See also *Co-Workers in the Vineyard of the Lord: A Resource for Guiding the Development of Lay Ecclesial Ministry* (Washington, DC: The United States Conference of Catholic Bishops, 2005), 7–10.

6. LG 31.

7. Ken Wilber, *A Theory of Everything* (Boston: Shambhala, 2001), 43. This is just one of the many works in which Wilber explores his integral vision.

8. Pope Francis, "Address of His Holiness Pope Francis to the Participants in the Conference Organized by the Dicastery for Promoting Integral Human Development, Marking the 50th Anniversary of the Encyclical '*Populorum Progressio*,'" April 4, 2017, http://www.vatican.va/content/francesco/en/speeches/2017/april/documents/papa-francesco_20170404_convegno-populorum-progressio.html.

9. Richard Gula, *Ethics in Pastoral Ministry* (New York: Paulist Press, 1996), 54.

10. Don Browning, *Fundamental Practical Theology* (Minneapolis: Augsburg Fortress Press, 1991).

11. Francis, "Address," 4.

12. GS 16.

13. Charles Bouchard, "The Meaning of Ministry in Health Care," in *Incarnate Grace: Perspective on the Ministry of Catholic Health Care*, ed. Charles Bouchard (St. Louis: The Catholic Health Association, 2017), 205.

14. The Mission of Ascension reads, "Rooted in the loving ministry of Jesus as healer, we commit ourselves to serving all persons with special attention to those who are poor and vulnerable. Our Catholic health ministry is dedicated to spiritually-centered, holistic care which sustains and improves the health of individuals and communities. We are advocates for a compassionate and just society through our actions and our words." Ascension, "Mission, Vision, and Values," accessed July 19, 2019, https://ascension.org/our-mission/mission-vision-values. Willingness to support this mission is an aspect of the selection process for leaders.

15. Bouchard, "Ministry in Healthcare," 202.

16. Carroll Watkins Ali, "A Womanist Search for Sources," in *Feminist and Womanist Pastoral Theology*, ed. Bonnie J. Miller-McLemore and Brita L. Gill-Austern (Nashville: Abingdon Press, 1999), 51–64. Ali recalls the evolution of understanding of the functions of ministry through the works of Seward Hiltner, preface to *Pastoral Theology: The Ministry and Theory of Shepherding* (Nashville: Abingdon Press, 1980); W. A. Clebsch and C. R. Jaekle, *Pastoral Care in Historical Perspective* (London: Harper Torchbooks, 1967); and Edward P. Wimberly, *Pastoral Care in the Black Church* (Nashville: Abingdon Press, 1983).

17. See Celeste DeSchryver Mueller, "Connect the Practical to the Theological," *Health Progress* (March–April 2011): 52–55, for the logic of the course sequence.

18. Alasdair McIntyre, *After Virtue: A Study Theory* (Notre Dame, IN: Notre Dame Press, 1981), 175.

19. Parker Palmer, *Let Your Life Speak* (San Francisco: Jossey-Bass, 2000), 9.

20. Joretta Marshall, "Learning and Teaching in Community: Lessons for Faculty Development," *Teaching Theology and Religion* 8, no. 1 (2005): 31.

21. Parker Palmer, *The Courage to Teach: Exploring the Landscapes of a Teacher's Life* (San Francisco: Jossey-Bass, 1998), 101.

22. Paul Ricoeur, *Interpretation Theory: Discourse and the Surplus of Meaning* (Fort Worth: Texas Christian University Press, 1976), 92–94. Sandra Schneiders, *The Revelatory Text: Interpreting the New Testament as Sacred Scripture*, 2nd ed. (Collegeville, MN: The Liturgical Press, 1999), 158, 172. Schneiders's term *aesthetic surrender* describes the transformative engagement of the whole self in interpretation.

23. James E. Zull, *The Art of Changing the Brain* (Sterling, VA: Stylus Publishing, 2002).

24. David A Hogue, *Remembering the Future, Imagining the Past: Story Ritual and the Human Brain* (Cleveland: The Pilgrim Press, 2003), 160.

25. Each participant granted permission to publish comments; names are withheld for privacy.

26. Ascension, "Mission, Vision, and Values."

27. Farley, "Church Education," 171.

Chapter Nine

LEARNING LITURGICALLY

The RCIA as Paradigm for Ministry Education

Diana Dudoit Raiche

This chapter aims to invite and inform a fruitful discussion concerning theory and praxis as they relate to the formation of those entering the Catholic Church. According to Matthew Lamb, the relationship between theory and praxis goes right to the core of the entire theological enterprise; and the catechumenal ministry is a particularly important locus of debate over this relationship.[1] How does knowing relate to doing and how does doing relate to knowing? Is the relationship between knowing and doing a real one—discernible in a concrete historical situation—or is it a relationship that is merely posited theoretically? The very way in which such questions are posed betrays a polarized understanding of theory and praxis. For example, one approach simply reduces theory to the abstract life of the mind and collapses praxis to lived experience without any connection to underlying principles, structures, and recurring patterns. Another perspective argues that all theory is rooted in praxis and is therefore subject to change as cultural currents shift. This chapter argues that such polarization is an unfortunate historical remnant that obfuscates understanding theory and praxis in relation to the Rite of Christian Initiation of Adults (RCIA).[2] In fact, the catechumenal process put forth by the Rite implies a dialectical, mutually beneficial relationship between theory and praxis. Recognizing this dialectical relationship not only aids practical theologians who train catechetical and catechumenal ministers, but benefits everyone involved in this ministry.

The argument proceeds in four parts:

> **Part one** surveys some key voices of the past (from Plato to Habermas) that have engaged in the ongoing conversation about theory and praxis.
>
> **Part two** addresses the dialectical processes developed in the praxis-oriented approaches of Latin American liberation theologians, particularly Clodovis Boff.[3]
>
> **Part three** draws on the dialectical approach of Boff to understand the praxis of education and initiation found in the RCIA, spread over four periods and three steps.[4]
>
> **Part four** recognizes that the dialectical relationship of theory-praxis advanced through liberation theology, and the guidelines and principles of the RCIA resolve perceived polarizations in the content-method debate.

Inherent in the RCIA are both content (Scripture and doctrine) and a methodological praxis (reflection on liturgical rites) that deliver an educational-formational process for initiatory and ongoing catechesis.

PART ONE

THEORY-PRAXIS IN HISTORY
From Distinctions to Dichotomies

Ever since Plato (ca. 427–347 BCE), theory and praxis have been defined as opposing poles: idea and reality; concept and object; thought and action. It is no wonder, then, that contemporary pastoral ministers have inherited and unconsciously adopted the language of polarization with regard to the relationship between theory and praxis. Aristotle attempted to gain greater clarification by introducing further distinctions: *theoria* connoted theoretical or contemplative thought for its own sake; *praxis* communicated that knowledge for the purpose of ethical action in the practical realm; and *poiesis* meant technical ability in human work and productive ways of living.[5] Aristotle was probably the first to use *praxis* as a technical term.[6] However, when Aristotle translated Plato's complex, but less differentiated, scheme into the threefold pattern of *theoria, praxis,* and *poiesis,* he also reduced it to an opposition between the "theoretical" and the "practical" life.[7] These earliest accounts of handling the theory-praxis polarization confirm the significance of the problem and its culturally and philosophically conditioned perspectives echoing through history.

A Christian treatment of theory-praxis furthered the dichotomy between theory and praxis and took over a thousand years to arrive at dialectical notions, that is, a method of reasoned discourse that aims to resolve competing points of view by seeking to understand the other's point of view. Early Christian society, increasingly defined by secular and sacred duality, at first appropriated a slightly Christianized version of the Neoplatonic ideas of "theory" and "practice." However, Christian thinkers in the third and fourth centuries gradually began to discover two ambiguities in the notion of practice, which were passed on through St. Augustine (354–430): (1) the life of faith is appropriate to every walk of life, and (2) the demands of charity and concern for one's neighbor militate against a leisurely lifestyle.[8] The "practical life" was a life concerned with the works of justice and welfare of others. Discussions about active and contemplative life became the prerogative of specialists in ascetic and mystical theology.[9]

St. Thomas Aquinas (1225–74) would cling to the notion of two distinct walks of life (active and contemplative)—with the active life centered on activities in accordance with right (virtuous) reason.[10] Even though Aquinas had learned from Aristotle that nothing is ever in the intellect that is not first in the senses, he espoused a pedagogy that moved from a way of knowing based on theory to a way of knowing based on practice, overlooking biblical language in favor of Greek philosophical categories.[11]

Blessed John Duns Scotus (ca. 1266–1308), the first Latin scholar to use the word *praxis*, was also the first medieval thinker to ask explicitly, What exactly is practice? His definition also shows his prejudice for the primacy of theory: "*Praxis*, to which practical cognition extends, is the act of a faculty other than the intellect which, by its very nature, succeeds intellection and may be elicited in accordance with right intellection so as to become right."[12] For a number of reasons pertaining to developments in the natural and mechanical world, as well as the historical context of the time, philosophers from the thirteenth through the sixteenth centuries began to question many of the theories concerning the natural world.[13]

Francis Bacon (1561–1626) signaled one of the major shifts in a theory-praxis relationship when he argued that experimentation and induction (from experience to fundamental principles) creates the path to knowledge. Bacon introduced a new concept of pragmatism: scientific knowledge should be of some practical usefulness.[14] Unlike Aristotle and Aquinas, Immanuel Kant (1724–1804) focused on the subject to make his distinction between theory and practice, acknowledging that philosophy should maintain theoretical and practical divisions. Instead of allowing practice to remain a mere application of theoretical propositions to actions and objects, Kant subordinated practice to practical reason.[15]

From Dichotomy to Dialectics

According to Richard Bernstein (1932–), a theory-practice dichotomy fundamental to modern philosophy tends to cloud our understanding of G. W. F. Hegel (1770–1831). Hegel's whole philosophy turns on the problem of theory-practice, which he presents under the heading of the opposition between what ought to be and what is.[16] Hegel conceived of philosophy as the "highest form of *theoria*, which has the *telos* of understanding and comprehending reality."[17] While Hegel's treatment of theory-practice is anything but traditional, he reduces practice to theory by treating the distinction between the two in psychological terms (that is, from will to thought).[18] Hegel's philosophy had signaled a turning point; for him practice is simple being, a material that consciousness explains and transfigures.[19]

The early nineteenth century produced Polish Count August von Cieszkowski (1814–94), less well-known but critically important. According to N. Lobkowicz (1931–), Cieszkowski wanted to overcome Hegel's theoretical philosophy by developing a justification of the alleged superiority of "post-theoretical practice" over theory.[20] Cieszkowski also advanced a philosophy of action that serves as a link to Karl Marx (1818–83), who was intent on changing the world. For Marx, history had to be linked with praxis, but praxis with a shift in meaning.[21] If Marx turned Hegel upside down, it was to "place the world on its feet, rather than on its head where Hegel had left it."[22] Marx saw Hegel as the "last philosopher" and determined that after philosophy reached a definite degree of universality, it ceased to be contemplative and became active: the spectator had to become the actor.[23]

CRITICAL THEORY

Jürgen Habermas (1929–), the acknowledged leading contemporary representative of the school of critical theory at the Frankfurt Institute, claims that since knowledge is the product of society, it can never be entirely free of distortions and, in fact, can participate in the perpetuation of those distortions. Evaluating Marxism based on epistemology,[24] Habermas notes that Marxism still leaves theory and praxis with two poles: scientific Marxism and critical Marxism.[25] He, too, attempts to resolve the problem of polarization by exploring the role of critical reflection to address the deficiency in Marxist thought.[26] For him, praxis involves critical reflection, which is the basis for emancipation from oppressive social structures and traditions. This becomes important for liberation theologians. Language, too, plays a central role in the work of critical reflection, since language originates from social labor and institutional structures, serving to legitimize relations of organized force.[27] Habermas's work moved from an attempt at unity to a "dialectical expansion of communicative rationality beyond the narrow purview of ideal, argumentative speech" and signals a real paradigm shift, what David Ingram calls "a profound change in the critical agenda."[28]

These multiple proposals to explain the relationship between theory and praxis indicate that while the problem of polarization has been a thread woven throughout history, over time, a more fruitful understanding of praxis emerged in the theory-praxis conversation. This development is especially evident in the praxis-action orientation of liberation theology, which has relevance for the formation process in the catechumenate, and to which we now turn.

PART TWO

LIBERATION THEOLOGY

In the last half of the twentieth century, liberation theology drew attention to social sin and the sinful structures kept in place by oppressive political and economic systems. Critical reflection on the situation of the poor in Latin America by its best-known champions, Gustavo Gutiérrez, Jon Sobrino, and Pablo Richard, first gave birth to an articulation of a theology of liberation.[29] Theology as critical reflection on historical praxis becomes a liberating theology capable of transforming not only the history of humankind but also that portion of the human family, gathered into *ecclesia*, that confesses Jesus as the Christ.[30] Liberation theology emerged contemporaneously with the RCIA, and catechumenate ministers recognized its emphasis on historical praxis as relevant to the catechumenal process. Its praxis-action and dialectical orientation pointed to the value of and need for the kind of reflection recognizable in liturgical and mystagogical catechesis.

Gustavo Gutiérrez (1928–)

As one of the first major voices to articulate the concerns of a theology of liberation, Gutiérrez situates the general landscape. First, Gutiérrez understands theology to be a secondary discourse on faith: an engagement in reflection. It possesses a critical attitude, and is a second, not a first, step. Theology is what follows the life of faith. To use Hegel's words about philosophy, "It rises only at sundown."[31] Gutiérrez's program for reflection engages

194

in a dialogue with Marxism. First, he proposes theological reflection with the poor, oppressed, marginalized, and disenfranchised. Second, Gutiérrez articulates a process for doing theology that acknowledges the life of faith as both the point of departure and the terminus for theological reflection.[32] Christ is the one in whom faith-filled Christians believe. Therefore, liberation theology has a soteriological and an eschatological dimension. According to Gutiérrez, the relationship of faith to historical reality is the basic constitutive element of liberation theology.[33] The faith of the theologian and the faith of the oppressed play a critical role in liberation theology. Third, persons of faith yield to the gospel values in Scripture. The Bible aids in interpreting concrete historical reality and so plays a prominent role in the life of faith-filled Christians who engage in a theology of liberation.

Fourth, the community engages in theological reflection on its own behalf. Thus, the real-life experience of poor, oppressed people of faith is not just the object of critical reflection. Subjects themselves who are oppressed engage in theological reflection by bringing the exigencies of faith as hermeneutically mediated in the biblical tradition to bear on their specific and oftentimes politically oppressive situation. It is not just some historical situation that cries out for critical reflection; it is a particular personal history-in-the-making situation that becomes the object of theological reflection. Fifth, liberation theology communicates a particular ecclesiology that "uncenters" the Church through gatherings of believers that happen in small base communities. Sixth, Gutiérrez also understands the unique relationship of theory and praxis within liberation theology. He acknowledges the dependence of theory on some, but not all, dimensions of praxis, and recognizes a problematic gap between theory-praxis in his own work.[34]

As one of the first to call attention to the role of the community in the theological process,[35] Gutiérrez expands an understanding of theological reflection and liberates theology from the confines of academic and ecclesiastical settings.[36] His practical theology identifies society with the Church as the people of God, the *ecclesia*, the ones who live *koinonia*, making theological reflection on real-life situations accessible to believers.

Clodovis Boff (1944–)

Clodovis Boff takes up the concern of theory and praxis in a reworking of his doctoral dissertation, *Theology and Praxis: Epistemological Foundations*. His proposal for a theology of the political—or liberation theology—helps to clarify the problematic identified in the theory-praxis relationship:

> The theology of the political is constructed on the basis of two fundamental theoretical mediations: socioanalytic and hermeneutic. The former furnishes the material object of this theology, the latter its specific means of production. Further, the (theological) theory that functions here is continuously determined by the dialectical relationship it maintains with praxis (the praxis of faith), and at the same time brings to bear its own determination of this praxis, in its proper manner—that is, theoretically. Finally, although both mediations are to be understood as falling in the category of the *medium quo* of this theology, praxis is related to it as its *medium in quo*.[37]

Boff acknowledges that any relationship between theology and the social sciences is determined by the "existence and demands of Christian praxis."[38] For him, praxis has a political connotation, for the only way to exert influence on social structures is through a political intermediary.[39] He clearly means, however, to articulate a proposal that maintains both the autonomous and dependent nature of theology with respect to praxis.[40] His is not merely a pragmatic proposal. He does not mean to make theology or theory the voice of praxis any more than he means to place them over praxis.

Boff unpacks his thesis in terms of three mediations for a theology of liberation: socioanalytic, hermeneutic, and practical. First, a socioanalytical mediation is "required by theology principally in virtue of its point of departure, in function of praxis, and in a particular manner."[41] He posits that the political (as material object) has a place in the theological enterprise on ethical grounds, and that the social-scientific mediation ought to be

Marxist. Second, a hermeneutical mediation requires that a theologian of faith reflect on theological pertinency by asking how a particular discourse relates to the word of revelation. Finally, the practical mediation takes praxis as its object for consideration. Boff proposes that praxis influences theory insofar as theory takes up the real problems of praxis under the form of (theoretical) questions. For Boff, "theory has its origin in praxis," and "is always marked by praxis, even when it effectuates a 'rupture' in its regard."[42] Likewise, political praxis exerts influence insofar as theory is involved in the interplay between social interests and political strategies.[43] He determines the role of theory on the social level by the extent to which the dialectical relationship between theory and praxis is operative between socioanalytic mediation and hermeneutic mediation.[44] He also asserts that theory and practice are not situated on a continuum; a radical discontinuity exists between them that can be bridged only in a leap of creative freedom. It is in this sense, he contends, that praxis transcends theory.[45]

To demonstrate the dialectical relationship between theory and praxis, Boff draws some distinctions regarding criteria and theory-praxis. If praxis were to be valued as the *sole* criterion of truth, as such a valuation, it would imply empiricism, and lead to pragmatism. Rather, he advances a dialectic of theory and praxis whereby praxis becomes *a* criterion of truth. The dialectic of theory and praxis functions, not according to a formal manner, but according to an axiom: "praxis exerts pressure on theory (thesis); theory, reacting, modifies praxis (antithesis); theory and praxis are transcended, and sublimated in a synthesis; and so on in that order."[46] He distinguishes theological criteriology, which is of a theoretical order (orthodoxy), from the criteriology of faith, which is of a practical order (orthopraxy). The practice of faith and the practice of theology are distinct, but not really separated.[47]

Boff likens the dialectical nature of theory and praxis to minor and major keys. My position is that the dialectic "plays" in two distinct and coordinated registers or "keys." The first is a minor key, the second a major key. The minor key is that of the restricted field within which the process of cognition occurs: the sphere of theory or theoretical practice. The "major key" is that of the broader terrain in which historical movement unfolds: the world of praxis, in its capacity as producer of social reality and by this very fact the abode of theory.[48]

Theology and Praxis makes a significant contribution to a fuller understanding of the relationship of theory and praxis as a dialectical, mutually self-correcting process.[49] When Boff asserts that "every theologian must adopt a liberation theology," he speaks of a theology that is not merely historical, but one that is also personal and eschatological. He means a theology that is necessary for the Church and connects the great truths of faith to a development of their social and political context.[50]

Boff's call for such a theology resonates with anyone familiar with the Christian initiation process in the RCIA. The dialectical relationship between theory and praxis that Boff details, together with the characteristics of liberation theology (Scripture, ecclesial community, eucharistic liturgy, small intentional communities, apostolic action informed by the mission of the Church to build the kingdom of God in a concrete historical reality), correlate to the praxis-action orientation and theological pertinency inherent in the Christian initiation process.

PART THREE: RITE OF CHRISTIAN INITIATION OF ADULTS

A NEW WINESKIN FOR NEW WINE

The *Rite of Christian Initiation of Adults* is more than a liturgical document that retrieves the so-called golden age of the catechumenate (the third through fifth centuries). The RCIA fits within the theory-praxis conversation because it signals such a significant paradigm change with regard to our understanding of conversion and the symbiotic relationship between catechesis and liturgy, and thus, between theory and praxis. Because this symbiosis is an educational process linked to a family of liturgical rites, it defines a new methodology. The particular pastoral agenda of the RCIA, conversion to Christ and incorporation into his body the Church, is brought about through a cohesive, structured formation process that represents a paradigm shift in catechesis—one that is doctrinally sound, grounded in both the lectionary and the liturgy, and occurs in the midst of a faith-filled community that lives the gospel message.

The paradigm shift in the RCIA also reflects a dialectical approach to formation in faith that mirrors a more contemporary dialectical relationship between theory and praxis that is the topic of this chapter. Integrating human experience, Scripture, liturgy, community, and mission in an educational-formation process, ordered toward conversion, describes what the *General Directory for Catechesis* calls a "catechumenal style" of catechesis.[51] The paradigm shift it signifies is not just for initiatory catechesis, but for ongoing catechesis, the process of educating in faith after initiation.[52]

The paradigm shift evident in the RCIA retrieves the foundational catechetical and liturgical practices for Christian initiation from the ancient catechumenate and melds it to a dialectical understanding of theory and praxis that attends to the human person. While Augustine's *De Catechetical Rudibus*, a fourth-century example of catechesis for catechumens, may conform to a more didactic presentation style of content consistent with the rhetoric of its time, it also pays attention to the make-up of the audience, taking care to adapt to the needs of those receiving the teaching.[53] The mystagogical homilies of the early Church demonstrate that extended doctrinal catechesis followed the celebration of baptism, in order to effect a more robust reflection on the mysteries of faith experienced through the rituals and ritual symbols of initiation.

CONSTITUTIVE ELEMENTS OF THE RCIA

The *Rite of Christian Initiation of Adults* (January 6, 1972) transformed a pre–Vatican II approach to bringing adults into the Church and tied renewal in the Church after the Council to liturgical reform. The degree introducing the revised rite states,

> The Second Vatican Council prescribed the revision of the rite of baptism of adults and decreed that the catechumenate for adults, divided into several steps,

should be restored. By this means the time of the catechumenate, which is intended as a period of well-suited
instruction, would be sanctified by liturgical rites to be
celebrated at successive intervals of time. The Council
likewise decreed that both the solemn and simple rites
of adult baptism should be revised, with proper attention to the restored catechumenate.[54]

The RCIA unfolds its faith formation process over a period of several years, as needed, in three distinct steps: the Rite of Acceptance into the Order of Catechumens, the Rite of Election, and
the Rites of Initiation (baptism, confirmation, and Eucharist).
Taken together, "these steps lead to periods of inquiry and growth;
alternatively, the periods may also be seen as preparing for the
ensuing step."[55] First, the period of evangelization and precatechumenate prepares for the Rite of Acceptance; second, the period
of the catechumenate prepares for the Rite of Election; third, the
period of purification and enlightenment follows election and
coincides with the season of Lent in preparation for the initiatory
sacraments at the Easter Vigil; and fourth, the period of mystagogy
follows full initiation into the Church as an intentional period of
apprenticeship that should become a way a life.

Woven from these periods and steps, the RCIA proposes four
dialectically and integrally related elements that guide the initiation process: word, liturgy, community, and mission.[56] Scripture
figures prominently in both the period of evangelization and the
period of the catechumenate, although it does so in different
ways.[57] In the precatechumenate, the life of an individual leads
one to explore the word of God; in the period of the catechumenate, the Sunday readings from the lectionary guide the process
of reflecting on one's life, the Church, and the world. Throughout the process, the RCIA raises to new prominence the role of
the community, particularly for sponsors and witnesses. Their
presence and participation in the rites, along with catechumens
and candidates, are clearly prescribed:

The initiation of catechumens is a gradual process that
takes place within the community of the faithful. By
joining the catechumens in reflecting on the value of

the paschal mystery and by renewing their own conversion, the faithful provide an example that will help the catechumens to obey the Holy Spirit more generously.[58]

Preparation for and celebration of the accompanying rites gives the entire process its focus and propels the newly initiated into the world to transform it according to gospel values.

The Rite of Christian Initiation of Adults signals a paradigm shift in the relationship between knowledge and action in the process of catechesis on three levels. First, the vision of initiation in the rites attends to the foundational human dimension of conversion as an ordered process.[59] Second, the liturgical rites and Scripture that undergird them exert a formative and hermeneutical pertinency that attends to doctrine, yet challenges a doctrine-only approach to initiation formation. Finally, the emergence of an initiatory method that joins knowledge and action constitutes a suitable catechesis that attends to the exigencies of liturgy (praxis), mission (praxis), and theology or doctrine (theory). The implications of this shift, from a theory-only-based approach to one that incorporates elements of both theory and praxis, are yet to be fully realized, but the shift itself clearly signals that a new horizon for formation in faith and catechesis beckons.

PART FOUR: EDUCATIONAL-FORMATIONAL PROCESS OF THE RCIA

Drawing on the implications of a contemporary understanding of praxis found in liberation theology, part four addresses the methodology inherent to the RCIA. Such a proposal engages in a discussion of educational process, not from a position of mere educational methodology, but from a dialectical praxis-theory-praxis perspective that supports conversion and formation in faith.

THE RCIA: AN EDUCATIONAL PROCESS

It is important to recall that the catechumenate is a model for all catechesis.[60] Understanding that model helps to put the mistaken perception that the catechumenal process lacks content into perspective. Mary Boys (1947–) sees the RCIA affirming the place of an affective knowledge that effects a change of heart, not merely a change of opinion. Some proponents of the rite have emphasized the experiential quality of the teaching and shun the language of instruction and curriculum as "inappropriately didactic, a judgment resulting from a tendency to understand education reductionistically, as well as an indication of the dichotomy and polarization that has developed between the specializations of liturgy and religious education."[61] Traditionalist and conservative religious educators who accuse the RCIA of being "content deficient" reveal an attitude, whether conscious or unconscious, that values theory over praxis—missing the praxis-theory-praxis dialectic at work. They fail to appreciate that the RCIA is an educational-formational process and not just an educational program.

Boys affirms what seasoned practitioners already know about the RCIA: it is a formation process that leads people toward conversion of life; although the RCIA is a *liturgical* rite, it ought to be considered an expression of Catholic educational philosophy; it witnesses to the inextricable link between liturgy and education.[62] Making explicit the link between liturgy and liberation, she goes on to say,

> [A] communal context for reflection is oriented toward a reordering of society: the base communities offer a way for those whose voice is seldom heard to join in solidarity so as to cry out against injustice. The knowledge these communities seek is one that gives rise to action. Hence their focus is on praxis, that is, on the dialectical movement of action and reflection.[63]

The *General Directory for Catechesis* corroborates her judgment and offers some relevant insights that have implications for a praxis-theory-praxis discussion relevant to the RCIA. The *Directory* names two categories of catechesis: initiatory and ongoing.[64] Acknowledging that content and method are interdependent in the RCIA, the *Directory* insists, "Catechesis must have a catechumenal style, as of integral formation rather than mere information"; and "catechesis must act in reality as a means of arousing true conversion."[65] It asserts that a catechetical process based on the RCIA's catechumenal style helps people (1) to experience radical transformation in conversion to Christ; (2) to begin to interpret the signs of the times using Scripture and liturgy as criteria of truth; and (3) to become moved to remedy unjust political situations of oppression and bondage. The *Directory* affirms that "catechesis is an essentially ecclesial act";[66] "catechesis is nothing other than the process of transmitting the Gospel, as the Christian community has received it, understands it, celebrates it, lives it, and communicates it in many ways."[67] Finally, recognizing the soundness of the RCIA as a model for all catechesis, the *Directory* says that "post-baptismal catechesis, without slavishly imitating the structure of the baptismal catechumenate and recognizing in those to be catechized the reality of their baptism, does well to draw inspiration from 'this preparatory school of Christian life' and allow itself to be enriched by those principle elements which characterize the catechumenate."[68] Clearly, the Church intends the educational process inherent in the RCIA to influence all catechesis.

CONVERSION: STARTING POINT FOR CATECHESIS

Bernard Lonergan notes, "Conversion is basic to Christian living, so an objectification of conversion provides theology with its foundations."[69] By foundations, Lonergan does not mean the doctrines of fundamental theology, but rather the "horizon within which the meaning of doctrines can be apprehended."[70] Such a horizon is the life world of a human being in a concrete historical reality. It is within this horizon that conversion is understood as a transformation of both the subject and the world of the subject.

The RCIA begins with evangelization for conversion to Jesus Christ. The precatechumenate period is marked by welcome, meeting others in the community, evangelization, and a suitable explanation of the gospel.[71] It unfolds as a gradual process of formation involving not just the intellect (what one knows), but the entire being as an acting subject in a concrete historical reality. Employing Boff's analysis of the three mediations of liberation theology (socioanalytic, hermeneutic, and practical) are helpful in analyzing select aspects in the praxis-oriented, educational process inherent in the RCIA.

SOCIOANALYTIC MEDIATION: ACCOMPANYING CONVERSION

The period of evangelization is ordered to conversion to Jesus Christ. Socioanalytic mediation of liberation theology exposes particular instances of human bondage and oppression that cry out for liberation. Practical theologians reflecting on initiation would be well served in adapting an intentional socioanalytic mediation in relation to the spiritual journey of those who are inquiring—a mediation rooted in life experience and examined in relation to Scripture. The period of evangelization introduces inquirers to Jesus and his followers. By God's grace, conversion to Jesus Christ happens; by creating appropriate conditions (welcome, listening, sharing Scripture, and prayer), catechumenal ministers create the conditions for a person to cooperate with God's grace. The RCIA as a "school of faith" begins in the praxis of life, helping people recognize and name particular needs, wishes, desires, and actions that hold them in bondage.[72] This is more than personal compunction for past sins; it is an opening of the spirit through the practice of prayerful reflection. Recognizing the spiritual challenges in a journey to conversion, the rite advocates for and insists upon companions: sponsors, priests, catechists, and the entire faith community.[73] Admittedly, it may be easier to "teach" timeless truths by which one can live one's life than to act as a companion to a person who embarks on this spiritual journey; however, those who guide the Christian initiation process have learned that helping people reflect on their *human* experience in light of Scripture is a more reliable method for companioning a person toward radical reorientation to Jesus Christ.

HERMENEUTIC MEDIATION: SCRIPTURE AND LITURGY

According to St. Jerome, ignorance of Scripture is ignorance of Christ. In the process of evangelization, a person begins to experience the depths of spiritual poverty in a life devoid of Christ. According to the ritual text, the signs of initial conversion are evidence of first faith, the first stirrings of repentance, calling upon God in prayer, a sense of the Church, and contact with members of the community of faith.[74] How are these manifestations called forth? Those who are responsible for companioning the inquirers are listeners, holding the life story of the person seeking initiation, and guiding a conversational process for connecting their personal story to the story and vision of Scripture. Such a connection cannot be assumed, but requires knowledge of Scripture on the part of the companion and catechist and an indeterminate amount of time. This is the first instance in which Scripture plays an interpretive mediating role between human existence and human existence oriented to Christ through God's word.

The period of the catechumenate offers another opportunity in which Scripture mediates between human experience and human experience touched by a desire for deeper conversion to Christ in faith. This occurs when the Sunday Scripture readings from the lectionary drive the catechetical agenda for initiation catechesis.[75] The period of the catechumenate "should extend for at least one year of formation, instruction, and probation" from at least the Easter season of one year until the next, preferably beginning before Lent of one year and extending until after Easter of the next year.[76] As the liturgical year unfolds Sunday after Sunday, catechumens can test personal transformation against the demands of the gospel. This gospel is manifest in liturgical celebrations and in the life of the community, which catechumens engage explicitly through reflecting on the homily, lectionary-based catechesis centered on the readings or prayers from the Roman Missal, and extended doctrinal catechesis based on the Sunday readings.

A third instance of hermeneutic mediation occurs through undergoing any of the ritual celebrations that accompany a deepening sense of conversion. Each particular liturgical rite celebrates what has already occurred on an interior level within a self-transcending subject. The ritual text affirms an ancient teaching of the Church that places liturgy in both a theoretical and praxis position: *lex orandi, lex credendi* (as the Church prays, the Church believes). This ancient maxim sums up the integral relationship between doctrine and liturgy. The rituals themselves have formative power to further conversion according to the grace of God, for before the doctrines of the faith were cast into theological statements, they were prayed in the liturgy of the

Church.[77] With this perspective in mind, liturgy is constitutive of both theory and praxis. The rites belonging to the catechumenate mediate faith and tradition in the actions of the Church at prayer.

PRACTICAL MEDIATION: LITURGY AND MISSION

Liturgy functions as both a hermeneutical and a practical mediation, for celebrating liturgy constitutes a work of the people that is wedded to a theory-praxis-action orientation. In the context of Vatican II, the liturgy "became a privileged place to carry out the struggle for the integration of the Church with the modern world." The Rite of Christian Initiation of Adults is one of those privileged places where the Church engages the modern world at the level of conversion: individual conversion to Jesus Christ that brings liberation to the church and society. Before the paradigm shift effected by the liturgical reform, sacraments were associated with personal sanctification; ecclesiology was reduced to institutionalism; piety, to mere individualism.[78] The revised rites of the catechumenate manifest a significant paradigm shift in approaches to Christology and ecclesiology, as well as sacramental theology and practice. Individuals who undergo the rites know the shift experientially, as well as intellectually. Through a process of critical reflection on the rite as experienced, any lingering interior dissonance is brought to light and to language for an individual. In this integrated experience-reflection interplay, formation and instruction occur in the catechumenal process.

When liturgy is seen as a theological source, the dialectical relationship between doctrine and liturgy (theory and praxis) becomes more apparent. The rites for the catechumenate demand an educational process that connects to and complements the ritual so that what is celebrated is true. Understanding the truly dialectical relationship between doctrine and liturgy (theory and praxis) advances an understanding of what is at stake in the content-method debate that surrounds the practical mediation.

Mission as the fourth element in the catechumenal formation process is comparable to the practical mediation that Boff describes in the dialectical relationship between knowing and doing in a political and liberation theology. Mission is the manifestation of praxis in a pure form. It also makes clear that conversion to Christ is not for mere personal gain, grounding in Scripture is not for mere personal spiritual nourishment, and participation in liturgy is more than for mere obligation or personal satisfaction. Conversion facilitated through Scripture and liturgy leads to apostolic service and points a self-transcending subject toward action that builds the kingdom of God in a particular concrete historical reality. The Two-Thirds World is not the only place for a liberation theology, as Clodovis Boff reminds us. There are lessons to learn from returning to the epistemological foundations of a theory-praxis relationship manifested in a theology of liberation. Those lessons appear to have significant relevance in furthering an understanding of a theory-praxis relationship in liberation theology and its implications for the Rite of Christian Initiation of Adults as an educational process.

CONCLUSION

The fact that the relationship between theory and praxis has been a topic for reflection for philosophers, theologians, and educators from Plato to the present time demonstrates that it is a topic of no small importance. Its treatment in this chapter signals the desire to bring light to a content-method debate that hampers a catechumenal style of education and formation according to the Rite of Christian Initiation of Adults.

When catechists continue to use a standard curriculum-based educational method for the catechumenate, then too little attention is given to (1) the personal situation of an inquirer and the necessity of conversion; (2) a praxis oriented theological reflection on liturgical rites; and (3) an intentional process for practical mediation in the period of the mystagogy. Using socioanalytic, hermeneutic, and practical mediations, seasoned RCIA practitioners are able to avoid a tendency toward polarization inherent in the content-method approach that emanates from religious educational approaches that have not yet begun to model themselves on a catechumenal style of education and formation.

Clodovis Boff demonstrates the importance of a dialectical relationship between theory and praxis through the metaphor of minor and major keys. The image of "figure and ground" may amplify this metaphor to explain the dynamic interaction between theory and praxis. Figure has nothing to differentiate it without ground. Ground, acting as a backdrop that allows a figure to stand out, brings figure into view and focus. Figure is analogous to a theoretical world; ground is analogous to the world of praxis. Without figure, ground ceases to be ground; without ground, figure is lost or undifferentiated. Whether referring to theory and praxis, minor and major keys, or figure and ground, each pair is inherently dynamically and dialectically related. Both elements are necessary, but neither one can be privileged over against the other. Praxis forces theory to be theoretical, but not ideological; praxis is not the mere verification of empirical theory, but when submitted to theological reflection, creates a mutually self-correcting dialectic that leads toward a clearer understanding of the relationship of theory and praxis in the RCIA.

NOTES

1. Matthew L. Lamb, "The Theory-Praxis Relationship in Contemporary Christian Theologies," in *Proceedings of the 31st Annual Convention of the Catholic Theological Society of America*, ed. Luke Salm (Washington, DC: June 9–12, 1976), 178. Field practitioners use the terms *practice* and *praxis* interchangeably; therefore, the terms are used interchangeably here. However, *praxis* is the richer, preferred term, as the body of research literature shows.

2. USCCB, *Rite of Christian Initiation of Adults* (Chicago: Liturgy Training Publications, 1988). The 1988 edition replaces the provisional text issued by the International Commission on English in the Liturgy (ICEL) in 1974 and contains the approved English translation of the 1974 emended second printing. References to this document are to paragraph numbers, not page numbers.

3. See the works of Gustavo Gutiérrez: *A Theology of Liberation*, trans. and ed. Sr. Caridad Inda and John Eagleson (Maryknoll, NY: Orbis Books, 1973), and *The Truth Shall Make You Free*, trans. Matthew J. O'Connell (Maryknoll, NY: Orbis Books, 1990). See also Clodovis Boff, *Theology and Praxis: Epistemological Foundations* (Maryknoll, NY: Orbis Books, 1987).

4. See RCIA, nos. 42, 75, 138–49; and nos. 244–51 of part 1 of the RCIA.

5. See Werner Post, "Theory and Practice," in *Sacramentum Mundi*, vol. 6 (New York: Herder and Herder, 1970), 246, and Matthew Lamb, "Praxis," in *The New Dictionary of Theology*, ed. Joseph A. Komonchak, Mary Collins, and Dermot A. Lane (Wilmington, DE: Michael Glazier, 1990), 786.

6. Lamb, "Praxis," 786.

7. Nicholas Lobkowicz, *Theory and Practice: History of a Concept from Aristotle to Marx* (Notre Dame, IN: University of Notre Dame Press, 1967), 4–5. Thomas Groome adds that as ways of knowing, *poiesis*, *praxis*, and *theoria* differ in their intended outcomes or their telos. Groome also notes that Aristotle's preference for *theoria* reveals his context: he was reacting against Sophists of his day who had reduced knowing to practical or technical efficiency. Aristotle was arguing against reductionism and pragmatism in making his distinctions. See Thomas Groome, *Christian Religious Education: Sharing our Story and Vision* (San Francisco: Harper & Row Publishers, 1980), 152, 156.

8. Lobkowicz, *Theory and Practice*, 59–74.

9. Lobkowicz, *Theory and Practice*, 66–69.

10. Lobkowicz, *Theory and Practice*, 70–71.

11. Groome, *Christian Religious Education*, 160.

12. Lobkowicz, *Theory and Practice*, 71–72, citing *Ordinatio*, prologus, pars V, qu. 2, no. 1, ed. Vaticana (1950 ff.) I, 155ff. Lobkowciz notes that after Scotus, the question *quid sit praxis* became commonplace; it was raised either in connection with the question originally asked by Scotus (Is the nature of theology practical or theoretical?) or in connection with subtleties about *habitus*, e.g., in Suarez, *Disp. Met.*, XLIV, 13, 20ff., ed. Paris (1866) II, 728ff. Some thinkers (even Thomists) argued, however, that intellectual operations are *praxis* as well. See Capreolus (e.g., *Defensiones theologicae*, prologus, q. 2, conclusion 4,) and Ockham (*Ordinatio*, prologus, qu. 4, a. 1).

13. Lobkowicz, *Theory and Practice*, 109–11.

14. Groome, *Christian Religious Education*, 161–62.

15. Post, "Theory and Practice," 247.

16. Lobkowicz, *Theory and Practice*, 143.

17. Richard J. Bernstein, *Praxis and Action* (London: Lowe & Brydone Ltd., 1972), 32.

18. Bernstein, *Praxis and Action*, 151–54.

19. Lobkowicz, *Theory and Practice*, 143.

20. Lobkowicz, *Theory and Practice*, 198–99.

21. Lobkowicz, *Theory and Practice*, 275.

22. Groome, *Christian Religious Education*, 165.

23. Lobkowicz, *Theory and Practice*, 239–41.

24. Groome, *Christian Religious Education*, 169.

25. Lamb, "Praxis and Generalized Empirical Method," 57, quoting A. Gouldner, *The Two Marxisms: Contradictions and Anomalies in the Development of Theory* (New York: The Seabury Press, 1980), 177–98, 8–37; L. Kolakowski, *Main Currents of Marxism*, vol. 1, *The Founders* (Oxford: Clarendon Press, 1978); D. McLellan, *Marx before Marxism* (New York: Harper & Row, 1970).

26. Groome, *Christian Religious Education*, 179; and Terry Hoy, "The Hermeneutics of Hans Gadamer: Towards the Renewal of Aristotelian Praxis," in *Praxis, Truth and Liberation: Essays on Gadamer, Taylor Polanyi, Habermas, Gutierrez and Ricoeur* (Lanham, MD: University Press of America, 1988), 6.

27. Hoy, "Hermeneutics," 6.

28. David Ingram, "The Theory-Practice Problem Revisited," in *Habermas and the Dialectic of Reason* (New Haven, CT: Yale University Press, 1987), 173.

29. Leonardo Boff and Clodovis Boff, *Introducing Liberation Theology*, trans. Paul Burns (Maryknoll, NY: Orbis Books, 1996), 11, 46–49. See also T. Howard Sanks, and Brian H. Smith, "Liberation Ecclesiology: Praxis, Theory, Praxis," *Theological Studies* 38 (1977): 8.

30. Gutiérrez, *Theology of Liberation*, 15.

31. Gutiérrez, *Theology of Liberation*, 11. Also see Boff, *Theology and Praxis*, 70–73.

32. See Gutiérrez's correlation of the community to Eucharist, which "points forward to its complete fulfillment," in *Truth Shall Make You Free*, 17–18.

33. Boff and Boff, *Introducing Liberation Theology*, 11.

34. John J. Markey, "Praxis in Liberation Theology: Some Clarifications," *Missiology: An International Review* 23, no. 2 (April 1995): 184–85.

35. Gutiérrez, *Truth Shall Make You Free*, 6.

36. Gutiérrez's proposal for a theology of liberation that acknowledges the pastoral dimension of theology correlates to the practical theology in Tracy's three publics, who describes three types of theology: the academy for fundamental theology; the Church for systematic theology; and society for practical theology. See D. Tracy, *Analogical Imagination: Christian Theology and the Culture of Pluralism* (New York: Crosssroad, 1991), 3–28.

37. Clodovis Boff, *Theology and Praxis: Epistemological Foundations*, trans. Robert R. Barr (Maryknoll, NY: Orbis, 1987), 221.

38. Boff, *Theology and Praxis*, 4.

39. Boff, *Theology and Praxis*, 6.

40. Boff, *Theology and Praxis*, 15.

41. Boff, *Theology and Praxis*, 4–8, 221.

42. Boff, *Theology and Praxis*, 175–78, 230.

43. Boff, *Theology and Praxis*, 186–89, 230.

44. Boff, *Theology and Praxis*, 194.

45. Boff, *Theology and Praxis*, 231–32.

46. Boff, *Theology and Praxis*, 213–16, 232.

47. Boff, *Theology and Praxis*, 198–205, 231.

48. Boff, *Theology and Praxis*, 207.

49. Notwithstanding the value of Boff's analysis, Markey critiques Boff for (1) defining theory as rational scientific thought process that renders theory too narrow, (2) raising praxis to a quasi-metaphysical category, and (3) identifying theory-praxis dualism without completely bridging the gap between them. See Markey, "Praxis in Liberation Theology," 182–83.

50. Clodovis Boff, "Epistemology and Method of the Theology of Liberation," in *Mysterium Liberationis*, ed. Ignacio Ellacuria, SJ, and Jon Sobrino, SJ (Maryknoll, NY: Orbis Books, 1993), 61.

51. *General Directory for Catechesis* (GDC), 29. This "style of catechesis" is in distinct contrast to the way adults were brought into the Catholic Church prior to Vatican II when conversion was assumed and six weeks of private instruction with a priest was considered adequate "preparation" for entry into the Church. It is also in distinct contrast with the kind of direct instruction that flows only in one direction from a teacher to a student, is bound by a specific timeframe, or is characterized by a topical curriculum that does not relate to the people who are in formation.

52. GDC, 91g.

53. Thomas Groome reminds his readers that Augustine was forward-thinking in his style of catechesis in *Christian Religious Education*, 178n36. Augustine stressed love and trust in the student-teacher relationship. He advised teachers to concentrate on a central unifying theme in their presentations; to explain material without losing focus and wandering; to use a variety of teaching styles so as not to lose the student's interest; to adjust the material to the capacity of the student; to summarize material often; and to give good examples.

54. RCIA, v.

55. RCIA, no. 7.

56. RCIA, no. 75. The periods and steps discussed in this section refer only to the unbaptized who are called catechumens.

57. Each period and step incorporates Scripture; these two periods are highlighted as exemplars.

58. RCIA, no. 4.

59. On intellectual, moral, and religious conversion, see Bernard Lonergan, *Method in Theology* (Toronto: University of Toronto Press, 1990), 237–43. Also see Rosemary Houghton, *The Transformation of Man: A Study of Conversion and Community* (Springfield, IL: Templegate Publishers, 1980).

60. GDC, no. 90.

61. Mary Boys, *Educating in Faith: Maps and Visions* (Kansas City: Sheed and Ward, 1989), 138.

62. Boys, *Educating in Faith*, 138.

63. Boys, *Educating in Faith*, 139.

64. GDC, no. 67; See also U.S. Catholic Conference, *Sharing the Light of Faith: National Catechetical Directory* (1979), no. 32.

65. GDC, no. 29; See also John Paul II, Apostolic Exhortation *Catechesi Tradendae* (October 16, 1979), no. 19b.

66. GDC, no. 78.

67. GDC, no. 105.

68. GDC, no. 91g.

69. Lonergan, *Method in Theology*, 130. Lonergan has a longer treatment on the differentiation of types of conversion as intellectual, moral, and religious conversion.

70. Lonergan, *Method in Theology*, 131.

71. RCIA, no. 36.

72. USCCB, *National Directory for Catechesis* (2005), no. 35D.

73. RCIA, nos. 4, 10, 11.

74. RCIA, no. 42.

75. RCIA, no. 75.

76. RCIA, 75. RCIA National Statutes, no. 6.

77. Alexander Schmemann, "Liturgical Theology: Remarks on Method," in *Liturgy and Tradition: Theological Reflections of Alexander Schmemann*, ed. Thomas Fisch (Crestwood, NY: St. Vladimir's Seminary Press, 1990), 138. Schmemann makes a distinction between "theology of the liturgy," where theology determines a priori what within liturgy constitutes *locus theologicus*, and "liturgical theology," where liturgical theology is based upon the recognition that the liturgy is not just an object of theology but is above all its source. The *lex credendi* finds its principal criterion and standard in the *lex orandi*.

78. Schmemann, "Liturgical Theology," 143.

Chapter Ten

INTERDISCIPLINARY, INTERCULTURAL, AND INTERRELIGIOUS LEARNING

Ministry Education for Postmodern Border Crossing

Maureen R. O'Brien

Sr. Anne Arabome, a Nigerian American theologian committed to the empowerment of girls and women in Africa, informally "adopted" six teenage girls living in the massive Nairobi slum of Kibera. From her location in the United States, she cared for them through frequent phone calls, financial support, and much prayer. She was able to visit only occasionally. Yet she yearned to give them *more*—especially, the sense that *more* was possible for them, that their lives need not be defined by the desperate circumstances in which they lived. So she imagined a new experience for them. While attending a theological conference in Nairobi, Sr. Anne obtained beautiful cloth and helped the girls design festive dresses. She taught them some liturgical dances. Then she brought them to the conference for a day to meet the theologians, participate together in the Eucharist through their dance ministry, and share a meal. As she explained, it was vital not simply to tell, but to *show* them that a different future could unfold for their lives.[1]

Elizabeth, a Euro-American lay ecclesial minister, reflected on her experiences working in her home parish in the northeastern United States:

> I've found that working in one's home parish has its own set of rhetorical questions. How do I address the many different needs that those whom I know so well feel are most important in the parish? How do I separate me from my work? How do I minister justly to those parishioners who, because of recent events, are tearing apart rather than building up the parish by their words and/or actions? How do I find time for my own personal spiritual development? I've found these to be some of the difficulties faced when working in my home parish. Over the past year, they've been complicated by facility closings, clergy transfers, and looming consolidations or mergers. All of these create strain on numerous parish relationships: parish community—diocese, parish community—parish leadership, parish community—other local parishes, and often, parishioner—parishioner. I struggle with the fact that many times my integrity is challenged when I have to set aside my own feelings as a member of the parish in order to deal with these complications as a member of the parish staff. I don't know if the conflict in being both parish staff and parishioner is a common one for LEMs [lay ecclesial ministers] in such positions, if it's heightened because of the recent events in this parish, or if it's my own inability to see ministry as just a job. My "dream job" hasn't yet turned into a nightmare, but it has caused some restless sleep. This is the "betwixt and between" that I find myself surrounded by in my ministry.[2]

In very different contexts, these two accounts speak to the problematic realities and hopeful possibilities of "border crossings" in our lives and ministries. For Sr. Anne and her girls, the intractability of poverty could give way, a little, in the experience of crossing the boundaries of Kibera to go to a new place and don new clothing, in offering a gift of dance ministry to others and having this gratefully received, and in sharing in food and conversation. For Elizabeth, a heartfelt embrace of ministry in her home parish became a simultaneous coexistence in multiple identities, within a shifting environment that kept her continually "betwixt and between," navigating boundaries in her attempt to balance roles and relationships. Sr. Anne, Elizabeth, and many others like them could benefit from opportunities for reflective learning on their experiences in order to aid them in the negotiation of their changing ministerial identities "on the edge."

Ministry educators today live out their own stories, composed of multiple life dimensions and relationships, at the same time they seek to educate others, especially laity, who assume ecclesial roles in the fluid landscapes of contemporary church and society. There is both opportunity and risk in recognizing and navigating the inherent tensions of existing "in-between."[3] It is not unlike the challenge to go continually to the "peripheries" of our world, as Pope Francis continually reminds us, to bring the gospel of joy and love to those in greatest need. In his own example, Pope Francis models the crossing of boundaries—socioeconomic, religious, cultural, and others—for the sake of forging new connections in humble service and mutuality.

In this chapter, I hope to illuminate some of the contemporary challenges in ministry education as shaped by two major convictions: first, the need to face squarely the realities of postmodernity (with a focus on the contemporary United States, but also cognizant of these realities worldwide); and second, the importance of engaging theological and educational sources attentive to these postmodern realities. Accordingly, I begin with a brief overview of important aspects of postmodernity. I then draw on theological sources to highlight two key aspects of the postmodern self—namely, existing as a "many-storied" hybrid and engaged in questing and border crossing. This treatment leads to an examination of religious and theological education approaches that can help ministry educators address postmodern challenges, highlighting three key dimensions of such strategies: the interdisciplinary, intercultural, and interreligious.

At the heart of my argument is the conviction that through the combination of these perspectives, ministry educators can help to form ministers proficient in "border crossing," leading to the creation of new connections and communities.[4] With such sensibilities, ministry educators can orient their students toward effective service amid shifting, liminal positions, in a culture characterized by ambiguity and fluidity. Through these educational efforts, ministers can learn to move through and beyond the givenness of their situations into a more deliberate stance—one that offers a path of greater faithfulness to their baptismal call and pastoral vocation to serve the reign of God. Like Sr. Anne Arabome, they might opt for a painfully challenging connection with "others" such as the Kibera girls, for the sake of their empowerment through supportive relationships and new opportunities. Like Elizabeth, they might become better able to live the everyday, in-between struggle of their complex ministerial relationships with greater self-awareness, grace, creativity, and continued growth, allowing ministers to better support their parishioners in their own struggles.

Before embarking on this effort, two words of explanation are in order regarding terminology. First, when citing authors for the first time, I will generally offer an identity qualifier such as "Euro-American" or "Korean American." As engagement with plural voices in society, Church, and scholarship makes evident, our sociocultural location matters and is important to acknowledge. (Acknowledging my own angle of vision as shaped by my Euro-American context and heritage is also vital in writing this essay.) Second, while working mainly with the metaphors of "border crossing" and "forging connections," I also will include some reference to sources that employ the language of "margins" and "centers." The danger of the latter juxtaposition is that we can assume a single, normative "center"—whether it be a church, our particular group or social location, or some other locus—from which we generously go to the "margins" to "help" the needy others. This, of course, can become patronizing and exploitative. However, some approaches, such as that of Korean American theologian Jung Young Lee, offer an alternative perspective. In Lee's words, "When everyone becomes marginal, there is no centrality that can marginalize anyone. Thus marginality is overcome through marginality."[5]

When marginal people resist oppressive marginality and freely build new, creative "centers," justice, peace, love, and reconciliation can be realized.

THE REALITIES OF POSTMODERNITY FROM A CHRISTIAN PERSPECTIVE

Writing about postmodernity quickly leads into a complicated tangle of theories, assumptions, diagnoses, and prescriptions. For our purposes, I will work from the Christian minister's foundational commitment to service in the name of Jesus Christ. This will allow us to use a specific faith stance to surface several key characteristics of the postmodern condition as well as evocative metaphors and strategies for responding to them.

In all times and places, Christians are called to follow Jesus through their lives of faith and service. Spurred on by Vatican II's emphasis on baptism as constituting a community on mission, the U.S. Bishops' 2005 document *Co-Workers in the Vineyard of the Lord* states,

> Baptism initiates all into the one priesthood of Christ, giving each of the baptized, in different ways, a share in his priestly, prophetic, and kingly work. And so every one of the baptized, confirmed in faith through the gifts of God's Spirit according to his or her calling, is incorporated into the fullness of Christ's mission to celebrate, proclaim, and serve the reign of God.[6]

Such discipleship, if it is to be faithful to Jesus's example, will reach out to people in the concrete circumstances of their lives. Thus disciples today will "celebrate, proclaim, and serve the reign of God" by seeking to heal, reconcile, and work for justice and peace within the realities in which we find ourselves in this present moment. In the mode of *Gaudium et Spes*, they will take responsibility for "reading the signs of the times and of interpreting them in the light of the Gospel."[7]

How can we responsibly read those "signs" so as to describe the contemporary circumstances for our ministry and ministry education, in order to respond to these faithfully and effectively? I believe it is crucial to frame our interpretation with reference to postmodernity. European religious education scholar Friedrich Schweitzer identifies four important aspects of the postmodern condition, especially as these relate to religious identity: *pluralization, individualization, privatization,* and *globalization.* First, many people across the globe, but certainly in Schweitzer's context of the Global North, are conscious that they live amid multiple identities and perspectives, including many types of religious beliefs—or none at all. Second, this nonnegotiable reality of pluralism, along with the endless consumer choices of modern capitalism and the ease of these selections through ever-faster technological means, feeds the individual's capacity and desire for personal choice in all areas of life. Third, such choice, whether religious or otherwise, is understood as one's private affair and viewed separately from larger societal ramifications. Fourth, the driving forces of economic globalization have been accompanied by clashes of cultures and civilizations, and have strengthened the trends of pluralization and individualization, often through the victimization of some cultures and peoples by others.[8]

In their *National Directory for Catechesis,* the U.S. Bishops echo these trends, focusing especially on the American prioritization of "freedom" in religious and economic terms, their pragmatism, their interest in science and technology, the impact of globalization and mobility, and the religious, cultural, and regional diversity found in this country.[9] This analysis is also sharpened by a recent study of young, disaffiliated Catholics, in which the authors note, "There is a persistent and perhaps even growing culture of personal autonomy and 'choice' among young families and children. Parents are more likely than in the past to allow their children to choose their faith."[10]

Within these realities, certain dispositions have emerged as "postmodern." Euro-American religious education scholar Harold Daly Horell presents a concise overview of what he calls "cultural postmodernity" as the context for contemporary North American religious education. He finds within it six major features. First, "a movement away from reliance on meta-narratives" means that postmoderns, in the face of pervasive pluralism, are likely to dismiss any single mode of viewing the world as definitive—including the central narrative of one's own faith tradition. Second, and following from the first, postmoderns accept that knowledge is socially constructed rather than proceeding from a foundational and unquestioned source. This in turn shapes the third feature, a view of oneself and one's social identity as "projects or goals" rather than as preestablished certainties. Fourth, in seeking to know themselves and the world, postmoderns accordingly embrace "specificity, contingency, and limitation in knowing." Fifth, postmoderns recognize the importance of critical reflection on how we are shaped by large institutions, which accompanies the sixth aspect, a greater awareness of how power dynamics shape one's life and view of reality.[11]

Horell names two broad stances within which cultural postmoderns may respond to these dispositions. The first, "trivializing" mode, tends toward nihilism in emphasizing our limited ability to construct meaningful knowledge and negotiate the limitations that social forces place on us. It can take on an ironic and wounded quality.[12] However, the other approach, "questing postmodernity," holds promise for Christians and thus for ministry educators. Horell maintains that people of faith can be encouraged to greater honesty about our limitations and "promote imaginative creativity and the pragmatic construction of new patterns of self-identity and social solidarity," if they are willing to take a reflective, questing attitude.[13]

If I were to "check in" with Sr. Anne and Elizabeth from my introduction, they might find resonance with some of the postmodern categories I have described. Sr. Anne would likely point out how globalization has had a long historical reach in Africa. The massively negative effects of European colonization on the indigenous peoples, including its modern-postmodern industrialization and urbanization, have contributed directly to the current plight of her Kibera girls. She would undoubtedly urge that U.S. ministry educators help their students understand how a "trivializing" stance toward postmodernity can be taken only by people of privilege, and advocate that they learn to reject the ease of endless consumer choices in favor of options for solidarity with the poor and oppressed. Elizabeth might observe how her "betwixt and between" feelings concerning parish relationships illustrate the postmodern complexity of shifting identities and roles, and the challenge the Catholic Church in the United States now faces to support all ministers and members in negotiating the resulting difficulties. She would probably note that in parishes like her own, varied responses to changing conditions coexist and place differing demands on her as a minister.

The stories of these two women, and of many other ministers today, point us toward further theological examination of the varieties of the postmodern self and the need to build connections among the diverse "selves" we encounter in postmodernity. In doing so, I will focus on two themes that I find especially helpful for ministry education in postmodernity: the notion of postmodern persons as having hybrid identities containing many stories, and the imperative toward questing and border crossing.

MANY-STORIED, HYBRID IDENTITIES

Since its beginnings, Christianity has been challenged to come to terms with diversity and to embrace the "other." Jesus sought out the outcasts of society, and even allowed himself to be challenged by outsiders like the Syro-Phoenician woman. The Pentecost event shines in our tradition as catholicity in action, with the Holy Spirit making the good news intelligible to people speaking every language on earth. Jesus's followers struggled to understand how to become a community of Jews and Gentiles, and later generations of Christians found in the Great Commission a mandate for bringing the gospel to every corner of the earth—an enterprise fraught with human failures yet impelled by the model of Christ.

Today, postmodern currents have led people to experience themselves as diverse not only interpersonally, but also *intra*-personally. Elizabeth, in being pulled "betwixt and between," discovers in herself the seemingly competing narratives of parishioner and lay ecclesial minister. Sr. Anne, in nurturing relationships with her Kibera girls, attends not only to the stark disparities of economic, gendered, and cultural differences, but also the ways in which her multiple identities as Christian, vowed religious, American, Nigerian, and now adoptive "mother" shape her spirituality and praxis. In these women and in ourselves, we can identify the need for intentional self-construction as influenced by diverse others, along with negotiating diversity even within the self.

In this vein, Euro-American theologian Michele Saracino offers a rich theological anthropology for Christians committed to identifying and claiming the positive value of "borders" and being "about borders." Key to this analysis is her understanding, drawing on theologies of liberation and intercultural engagement, that each of us is essentially a "hybrid" being throughout our lives, existing at the intersection of many distinct "stories" of gender, race, culture, sexual orientation, and other aspects. As in postmodernity's rejection of a single "master narrative," each of us has no single story. Our hybrid identities will therefore be both porous and shifting as their constitutive stories shift. Because this is often uncomfortable and provokes strong emotional responses, we tend to try to shore up more secure borders for our personal identities—as the discordant tribalism and attempts to build stronger walls (both literal and figurative) in our current U.S. political debates illustrate all too well. Yet the Christian is challenged to resist this temptation. Saracino advocates,

> [This situation] obligates us to surrender the one true story that brings us comfort, to acknowledge that our *many-storied selves* are connected to those of others at borders, and to face the affective floodgate that such a realization unhinges....Through converting to, or what I like to call "incarnating," hybridity, Christians are compelled to grapple with the many stories of themselves and that of another, as well as to the ambiguity of all the spaces in-between.[14]

The acknowledgment of "many-storied selves" leads us, then, to challenge rigid borders within the person, as well as among persons.

QUESTING AND CONNECTING THROUGH BORDER CROSSING

The Christian tradition carries strong references to metaphors of pilgrimage and journey, from Israel's travel to the promised land to the "people of God" and "pilgrim church" ecclesial images evoked by Vatican II.[15] In a postmodern context, the metaphor of "questing" is apt for Christians who seek to be faithful to their calling in Christ while working responsibly within the cultural conditions that shape the journey. Since those conditions include diversity and fluidity, the quest will inevitably involve encounters with difference—again, both among others and within the self.

Acknowledging both hybridity within oneself and multiple stories beyond oneself, then, becomes a calling from God to a journey of crossing borders for open engagement with otherness, rather than making these boundaries rigid or collapsing them. Again, Saracino finds in Jesus the Christian's model. As he said, "The Son of Man has nowhere to lay his head" (Matt 8:20), and so his followers are called to be "homeless" in their refusal to be confined by restrictions—even those that offer the comforts of home. So, for Christians, growth in charity requires awareness of and passing through "the borders of difference, both within and outside ourselves."[16]

Saracino goes on to identify evidence in the foundational teachings of Christianity for God's own activity and presence in salvation history as being "about borders" and as calling God's people to continuous border crossing on the faith journey. God's creation of humans in *God's image and likeness* implies for her a kind of divine-human hybridity. Catholic *sacramental sensibility* makes manifest how God's existence is porously available among the contours of our everyday life. The *incarnation* shows the hybridity of the Jesus of history with the Christ of faith, not as a confusion of human and divine natures but in their close coexistence. "In becoming human, Jesus Christ *relinquishes the primacy of the one story*, kenotically surrendering himself to a hybrid existence that undercuts any absolute identity, creating room for the other."[17]

As our currently polarized society makes all too evident, we are tempted to strengthen our borders and demonize those different from us—to take refuge in "the primacy of the one story." While Saracino admits that cultivating the habit of being "about borders" can be difficult and exhausting, she nevertheless develops several creative examples of it, ranging from parenting to the post-9/11 engagement between Christians with Muslims. Sr. Anne could find in Saracino the basis for a relational vulnerability through which she and others could enact their Christian commitments by "being about" the borders of race, culture, and socioeconomic class in forging connections with the girls of Kibera. Elizabeth could reflect on how the hybridity of each parishioner and staff member in her parish—formed in their particular experiences, generations, ethnicities, family lives, and other spheres—means that each member of the community is, like her, "betwixt and between," as they live into their collective identity and shape their many stories, day by day and year by year. She, like all ministers, must meet people precisely where they are in order to offer them new possibilities for transformation.

Fostering persons and communities that can negotiate the multiple borders becomes ever more imperative as postmodernity continues to spiral into greater pluralization, technological acceleration, globalization, and problematic encounters with others. We as ministry educators face a tall order as we seek to address postmodern realities with our students in ways that will equip these students for effective ministry. I am convinced that ministers who hope to respond meaningfully to these trends will find themselves crossing boundaries among Christians of various degrees of belief and practice, as well as diverse cultural and religious identities—indeed, encountering people with many stories. Ministry educators, then, must attend to not only our students' human, spiritual, theological, and pastoral formation for Catholic Christian identity and ministry, but also help to develop their capacities for negotiating the complexities of self-identity and reflection, in order to foster growth at the borders of these identities. And while we must begin with the particularity of each life narrative, we cannot end there. Well-educated ministers must also be equipped to forge new connections with others, facilitating their transformative capacities in turn and creating new connections for viable postmodern engagement.

To that end, I maintain that the fields of religious and theological education can offer us valuable resources in three interwoven dimensions: interdisciplinary, intercultural, and interreligious. The rest of this chapter will explore key aspects of these dimensions and their implications for ministry education in a postmodern world.

ENGAGING POSTMODERN REALITIES

INTERDISCIPLINARY, INTERCULTURAL, AND INTERRELIGIOUS DIMENSIONS FOR MINISTRY EDUCATION

Interdisciplinary

While the phrase *religious education* is often used synonymously with catechesis, catechetics, faith formation, and Christian education, the scholarship of religious education per se has been explicitly interdisciplinary. Religious education brings together the insights of educational research with that of religion and theology for the sake of teaching religious believers effectively in faith communities, as well as fostering public engagement on religious issues. Further, those who work in religious education scholarship often do so as theological educators in academic institutions, and thus there is frequent overlap in their interests among the spheres of faith community, academy, and larger world.[18] Thus I will use "religious" and "theological" education interchangeably. In this section, I focus on themes and strategies, arising from the work of European and Euro-American scholars in education and religious or theological education, that I find suggestive for helping ministry educators in the United States develop capacities in their students for negotiating cultural and ecclesial border crossing, and forging connections, conscious of the challenges of postmodernity and the many-storied selves of postmodern people.

Education as conversation: Euro-American education scholar Nicholas Burbules has done important research on what he calls the four models of dialogue for use in pedagogical strategies. For religious educators, his model of dialogue as "conversation" has been the most evocative. In this model, Burbules posits conversation as "inclusive-divergent" dialogue, with "inclusive" connoting an epistemological openness and willingness to cooperate, and "divergent" signifying that while understanding is sought, agreement will not necessarily result. Education in this mode requires working toward a shared language across values and cultures, cognizant that both understanding and misunderstanding will occur throughout the process.[19] A number of religious educators have embraced the conversation model for classroom teaching and adult interreligious learning. For example, Euro-American Mary C. Boys details a set of vital "spiritual virtues" for teachers and learners to cultivate for educative conversation. These virtues include humility, faith, self-denial, and the cultivation of attentive listening skills.[20] Euro-American Theresa O'Keefe explicitly adopts the inclusive-divergent strategy in designing an adult education program for dialogue between Christians and Jews.[21] As these authors illustrate, fostering dialogue in deliberate and spiritually open ways shows promise for the postmodern requirements of border crossing among the many identities and stories of participants.

Education practiced in transitional communities and languages: Religious education scholars today, including those working most explicitly in interreligious modes, typically insist on the importance of forming believers in faith communities that help *both* to sustain members amid multiple and shifting roles, *and* to build competency for engaging in informed and open ways with others. We will treat interreligious dimensions more fully below, but for now it is helpful to note that the postmodern condition involves plural selves participating in multiple subcultures. Thus people of faith must be equipped to form and participate in subcultures and languages that foster multicontextual fluency.

Addressing the role of such subcultures is the work of Euro-American education scholar Kenneth Bruffee, who has influenced a number of those involved in theological learning and ministry education. In his struggles as an instructor to help college freshmen from urban and underserved areas gain necessary academic skills, Bruffee found success through creating small "transition groups" for a process he called "collaborative learning." These groups functioned as liminal spaces in which students could translate between their familiar home cultures and new, disorienting expectations for college learning.[22] Commenting on Bruffee's relevance for her own work as a theological educator, Euro-American Judith Berling reminds her colleagues in similar settings that "their authority as teachers lies in their skill at *the boundaries between their disciplines and the many worlds from which their students come*"—language clearly resonant with Saracino.[23] Thus, educators are called to facilitate collaborative, transitional groups in the classroom that assist students in making meaningful connections among these "worlds." Berling, drawing on the work of African American educator bell hooks, asserts that such subcultures are not meant to provide "safety," but rather to foster a shared sense of a learning community committed to the common good.[24]

Those of us in ministry education are likely no strangers to the importance of forming supportive communities, facilitating transformative conversations, and honoring diverse backgrounds among our students. Yet I believe that religious education's interdisciplinary resources offer valuable opportunities to rethink some of our practices. For example, since religious education as an interdisciplinary field takes seriously the complexities of identity development in postmodern, liminal societies, it can help to remind us and our students that there is no one-size-fits-all model for Catholic Christian belief and practice. Ministry students, rather than being frustrated by "questing postmodernists," can learn to meet them on their particular journeys by offering opportunities for lifelong formation, raising key Christian metaphors to sustain the postmodern quest, highlighting spiritual formation through worship and prayer that acknowledges the complexities of liminal identities, providing for good moral formation, and so on.[25]

We as ministry educators can assist students in identifying the crucial "conversational virtues" needed to engage with plural perspectives, emphasizing respect and openness. We can teach them how to discern when pastoral situations require "inclusive-divergent" approaches, and when other dialogical modes involving "critical" or "convergent" approaches are more effective.[26] Finally, ministry education and formation can be practiced in ways that establish "transitional" subcultures with porous borders, teaching multiple fluencies in the "languages" of these subcultures that prepare students, in turn, to build these with the people they serve.

INTERCULTURAL

Attention to multiculturalism has long characterized ministry education for laypeople. *Co-Workers* states,

> Every person preparing for lay ecclesial ministry has already been formed by the cultural context(s) which that person has experienced. Formation programs need to be mindful of the words of Pope John Paul II: that formation should "take the greatest account of local human culture, which contributes to formation itself....Attention should be paid to diverse cultures which can exist in one and the same people or nation at the same time."[27]

Further, across fields of ministry formation and education, we have expanded our notions of multiculturalism beyond ethnic and racial identities to include gender, sexual orientation, class, (dis)ability, and other aspects.

In this section, I introduce Christian religious and theological education perspectives that affirm multicultural realities, yet I also argue for an "intercultural" approach. This move is especially pertinent, I believe, for fostering competencies in negotiating border crossing and forging connections among ministry students, cognizant of their many stories and the stories of those they serve. Scholarly guides in this process, unsurprisingly, are frequently people of nondominant cultural identities. For my discussion I will draw primarily on one Hispanic American (José Irizarry), one Korean American (Boyung Lee), and one Euro-American (Anne Carter Walker).[28] These writers assume the postmodern framework of multiple and shifting identities discussed above, and build upon it to address effective religious education cognizant of borders and intersections, margins and centers, and the power dynamics inherent in these fluid realities. To my knowledge none of these authors is Catholic, and so their work provides

Catholic ministry educators the further benefit of dialogue with ecumenical partners.

José Irizarry claims that while some forms of religious education are properly called "multicultural"—focusing on distinctive aspects and interplay of various ethnic and racial groups—all religious education should be "intercultural." He calls for a less narrow and more comprehensive use of anthropological and ethnosocial tools. This would push educators to avoid easy generalizations, prioritizing instead "the ability to diagnose the different expressions of a cultural composition *before* culture is identified with any particular grouping of people (i.e., racially or ethnically)."[29] Communities are always cultural, holding a shared yet fluid sense of identity; thus, our entry into new communities transforms our cultural "selves."[30] Consequently, religious educators must become skilled cultural actor-reflectors, able to understand themselves as inherently cultural and compare their pedagogical assumptions with those of learners so as to "negotiate cultural differences on educational expectations and be ready to understand and create an atmosphere of respectful tolerance and fair critique."[31]

In Irizarry, we see echoes of Bruffee's "transitional subcultures" and the need to cultivate mediating languages across their borders for effective learning. Similarly, Anne Carter Walker works from her position as a white, and inherently "privileged," religious educator to urge that others like her cultivate a "border-crossing" pedagogy. While white people cannot fully abandon their privileged status, through such pedagogy they can learn to tolerate ambiguity in themselves and in interactions with others, and to decenter self in order to foster identification with multiple groups. "This identity is multi-vocal, drawing upon many systems of meaning, speaking in multiple languages."[32] Walker challenges white teachers and learners to live as both insider and outsider, alert to the patterns of privileged hegemony.

In a related critique, Boyung Lee finds in "multicultural" religious education a tendency to identify a singular, imaginary "center"—white, Western, and male in nature—causing groups identified as "marginal" relative to it to compete among themselves for access to power. For her, doing *intercultural* religious education requires instead a transformed orientation characterized as "liberating interdependence." Rather than seeking to gain influence by cultivating relations with a single cultural power center, marginalized groups would benefit from fostering interdependence with one another, as well as with the plurality of "center" groups. This would help marginalized people to avoid seeking power at the expense of others. Rather than a zero-sum game, intercultural religious education becomes a shared learning experience, which produces more fruit—though not without conflict and tension.[33]

For ministry educators, these analyses strike me as pointing to two key implications. The first is likely already reflected in our ministry education efforts: the need to treat students as cultural selves and to help them do likewise in their own pastoral settings. Here I believe that using religious and theological education sources like those I have discussed can build on good foundations, helping aspiring ministers become more culturally sensitive through the readings, assignments, and learning activities we offer. Especially through integrative forms of contextual education and classroom assessments, students can develop the ability to detect and mitigate cultural biases. We are also likely already to be teaching pastoral skills for building culturally sensitive faith communities, cognizant of the ongoing changes in the ethnic and racial composition of U.S. parishes and dioceses. Proceeding from these strengths, the religious education approaches outlined here could be especially helpful for an analysis and critique of the margin-center dynamics associated with the role of lay ecclesial minister. In their "in-between" status as neither clergy nor undifferentiated layperson, lay ecclesial ministers require border-crossing strategies that keep them personally and spiritually healthy and ministerially engaged. Thus, for example, these approaches could assist in healing adversarial relationships with pastors and parishioners by encouraging creative conversations that bring various parish groups together. Elizabeth would likely recognize the value of this "intercultural" orientation in facing her own parish challenges.

A second implication seems to me more challenging, especially for members of the academy such as those in the Association of Graduate Programs in Ministry. Can ministry educators in graduate-level educational institutions give time and energy to serious questions regarding our social location in these "power centers," especially as relative to ministry formational and educational efforts occurring in nonacademic settings? Can we structure our academic borders to be more open to these "others"? Particularly for lay ministers and aspiring permanent deacons, ministry formation occurs in many contexts outside the institution of higher education, especially for people who are educationally, financially, and culturally marginalized. In the major shifts occurring in U.S. parish life, can academicians learn to be less attached to privileged "centers" and move into collaboration with other formational programs? What might a serious collaborative effort at the national level between graduate education and other ministry formation efforts—especially efforts aimed at marginal groups—look like as a border-crossing pedagogy, where those in academic contexts relinquish privileged status and construct what Walker calls "a third way of identity," "a decentering epistemology"?[34]

INTERRELIGIOUS

This third dimension of my engagement is one for which Catholic ministry educators find ample justification in official teaching, yet it is often the most difficult to address. Vatican II's *Nostra Aetate* and ensuing decades of interreligious dialogue provide strong theological and ecclesial foundations for engagement with non-Christian religions. *Co-Workers* encourages an "ecumenical and interfaith dimension" in intellectual formation.[35] The Alliance for the Certification of Lay Ecclesial Ministers Certification Standard 2.8 (under Spiritual Formation) states that these ministers should "display an openness to ecumenical prayer, work, and practices that promote Christian unity, and acknowledge the gifts afforded the human community from the various world religions."[36] Yet ministry educators in academic, diocesan, and other settings typically provide little attention to this area within their crowded curricula.

Once again, I find in religious and theological education scholarship some valuable perspectives that can encourage our efforts at interreligious or interfaith initiatives for ministry education. The field offers constructive methods for teaching and learning among individuals and faith communities from multiple religious and spiritual traditions. Students in ministry education will benefit from theological-reflection methods that inspire them to learn from such traditions—encouraging their willingness to interact at their own ecclesial borders, open to being transformed by religious "others" and forging new connections with them.

In this section, I will rely on white, Euro-American Christians (Judith Berling, Mary Hess, and Kristin Johnson Largen) and one Japanese American Christian (Sheryl Kujawa-Holbrook) who work in interreligious forms of teaching and learning, principally in Protestant theological schools and congregations. These scholars provide helpful theological-educational foundations and motivations that can help ministry educators grow in this direction.

As Sheryl Kujawa-Holbrook reminds us, Jesus is a model for interreligious openness as a Jew who engaged with religious others and invited them into kingdom relationships—think of the Samaritan woman at the well and the Roman centurion at the cross. Today, our religiously plural world calls us to such efforts as well. For the authors examined here, it is essential to practice religious and theological education in a way that nurtures one's own faith, as well as one's commitment to dialogue with those of different faith traditions.[37]

Calling seminary professors to adopt comparative-theological approaches, Kristin Johnston Largen wryly opines that God will not sulk if Christians pay attention to non-Christians' beliefs, and asserts that "Christian theology as a whole is strengthened and enhanced through the engagement with non-Christian religions."[38] Such engagement is vital to help seminary students and those with whom they minister avoid not only the extremes of relativism and fundamentalism, but also "religious irrelevance."[39] She continues,

> Thus, as a means of going forward in a direction both fruitful and faithful, while navigating a "middle way" between these two obstacles, I want to offer a Christian rationale for appreciative, yet academically rigorous, interreligious engagement that encourages interreligious conversation while at the same time emphasizes

one's rootedness in one's own tradition—and the ultimate value such conversation has for that tradition."[40]

If interreligious learning is practiced effectively, Christians will not only gain appreciation for other traditions—they will also find their own faith deepened. Judith Berling, for example, couples her appreciation of comparative theologians like Paul Knitter with her extensive teaching experience to name two poles for learning another religion: "(1) understanding another religion faithfully and (2) reappropriating Christian tradition in light of new understandings and relationships."[41] In border-crossing conversations with religious "others"—which might be written texts, as well as other persons—Christians are called to articulate key dimensions of their own faith in transformed ways, making new connections both with others and within their own hybrid selves as well, fashioning new religious stories of themselves and others.

Scholar-practitioners of interreligious teaching and learning also warn that entering these conversations, while seeking to promote capacities of openness, respect, compassionate listening, healing, and hospitality, will not be conflict free. Moving between Berling's two poles is likely to spark dissonance within participants as well as periodic misunderstandings among participants, which she believes is essential for meaningful learning. Hess draws on Euro-American educator Robert Kegan's spiral schema of "connection, contradiction, and continuity" to suggest how Christians might be encouraged to risk such learning.[42] Even the most fundamentalist among them, Hess believes, can be reached through empathetic affirmation of the student's convictions as rooted in Christian truths:

> One possibility—and there are many—would be to help that student recognize that their own conviction of God's power contains within it an answer: that it is God's power at work, not human power. Therefore, trusting in God's gift of faith, in God's overwhelming grace, frees one from responsibility for another's journey, while yet inviting one into wonder and joy at sharing faith.[43]

From this point of *connection* in shared wonder and joy, students can be invited to risk the *contradictions* of engaging with religious others, and move toward a reappropriation characterized by *continuity*. "Continuity is the name for that process by which we come to a new understanding which is connected to our previous way of making meaning, but which grows beyond it."[44] Contradictions are not ignored, but through the willingness to entertain what Saracino would call porous boundaries among religions, we might reconstruct the stories of our own religious identities in ways that do not devalue the identities of others, and with the possibility of knowing ourselves more fully through knowing something of the many-layered faith stories of other believers.

I see in the interreligious orientation of religious education a series of implications for ministry educators. First, at the basic curriculum level, it challenges us to consider whether we have a serious commitment to engagement with other religions in our educational and formational efforts. Second, incorporation of interreligious dimensions can provide another testing ground for the educational and formational approaches that already characterize many of our programs' orientations in practical theology and adult learning. We are probably no strangers to the importance of fostering dialogue and pastoral care for diverse populations, as evident in our multicultural priorities and our theological reflection efforts to read the signs of the times and interpret them in light of the gospel. However, our world today also cries out for creative ways to foster respectful conversation among those of diverse religious traditions, rather than uncivil and uninformed (or misinformed) polarization. Interreligious engagement increasingly emerges as an imperative for ministers committed to serving God's reign.

Finally, forming community with those of other faiths provides yet another opportunity for ministers and those who educate them to celebrate and sponsor new life through ecclesial and religious border crossing. If we embrace the Catholic notion of sacramental imagination, we are called to offer possibilities for our students to glimpse God's image in unexpected places and open themselves to transformation through such awareness. Creating new spaces of connection, where those of diverse religions can learn from one another—in family ministry, adult faith formation programs, joint justice and service activities, and other initiatives—can foster authentic border crossing that brings religiously diverse people into new, life-giving configurations and connections, while enriching our own experiences and understandings of our particular traditions.

CONCLUSION

The postmodern condition raises important questions for ministry educators seeking to help students develop the dispositions and skills necessary to negotiate the varied and fluid stories that constitute the world today. We need to cultivate the gift of respectful border crossing—whether within the very selves of ministers like Elizabeth and Sr. Anne, among the people they care for, or between all these people of God and the disorienting, complex societies in which they find themselves. Engagement with the rich resources of religious and theological education, conducted with postmodern awareness and critical appropriation, offers abundant possibilities for ministry educators.

NOTES

1. I am grateful to Sr. Anne Arabome, SSS, for introducing me to her work.

2. Unpublished, online journal entry from a qualitative research study by Maureen R. O'Brien, "Emerging from the Vineyard: A Reflection and Writing Project" (entries made in 2010–12). The participant's name has been changed.

3. See Maureen R. O'Brien and Susan Yanos, eds., *Emerging from the Vineyard: Essays by Lay Ecclesial Ministers* (Barberville, FL: Fortuity, 2014), for essays by lay ecclesial ministers exploring theological and pastoral tensions they experience; and Maureen R. O'Brien, "Relational Theologies of Ministry and Implications for Plural, Missional Identities," in *Mission for Diversity: Exploring Christian Mission in the Contemporary World*, ed. Elochukwu E. Uzukwu, Interreligious Studies 8 (London: LIT Verlag, 2015), 235–42, for an analysis of key findings from the Emerging from

the Vineyard project, with a focus on the marginal status of lay ecclesial ministers and relational theologies of ministry.

4. While the use of metaphors such as "borders" and "border crossing" abound in the literature, see, e.g., the sources by Michele Saracino and Anne Carter Walker that I will use later in the chapter.

5. Jung Young Lee, *Marginality* (Minneapolis: Fortress, 1995), 151. Another treatment of multiple "centers" and the problems that arise when those from multiple "margins" focus on a single, hegemonic power "center" is provided by Korean American religious educator Boyung Lee, discussed below.

6. *Co-Workers in the Vineyard of the Lord: A Resource Guide for Guiding the Development of Lay Ecclesial Ministry* (Washington, DC: United States Conference of Catholic Bishops, 2005), 18.

7. *Gaudium et Spes* 4, at http://www.vatican.va/archive/hist _councils/ii_vatican_council/documents/vat-ii_const_19651207 _gaudium-et-spes_en.html.

8. Friedrich L. Schweitzer, *The Postmodern Life Cycle: Challenges for Church and Theology* (St. Louis: Chalice, 2004), esp. 14–15.

9. USCCB, *National Directory for Catechesis*, 21–40.

10. Saint Mary's Press of Minnesota and Center for the Applied Research in the Apostolate, *Going, Going, Gone: The Dynamics of Disaffiliation in Young Catholics* (Winona, MN: Saint Mary's Press of Minnesota, 2017), 32.

11. Harold Daly Horell, "Cultural Postmodernity and Christian Faith Formation," in *Horizons and Hopes: The Future of Religious Education*, eds. Thomas H. Groome and Harold Daly Horell (Mahwah, NJ: Paulist Press, 2003), 83–89; quoted phrases from 86. As trenchantly noted by North American theologian Paul Lakeland, the stance that Horell calls "trivializing" can lead economically secure postmodern people to an ironic and superficial pursuit of pleasure—"playing our computer games and whiling away the time with the toys that material success brings" (Paul Lakeland, *Postmodernity* [Minneapolis: Fortress, 1997], 9).

12. Horell, "Cultural Postmodernity," 90.

13. Horell, "Cultural Postmodernity," 91. Horell believes that among the questing postmodernists found in North American Catholic congregations today, some are more "reluctant" and others more "wholehearted" in this disposition. He offers a number

of strategies for engaging these postmodernists through religious education, especially in parish settings (91–97). Similarly, Lakeland affirms the potential for postmodern thinkers to prompt realistic ("nonutopian") engagement with the world in local and pragmatic ways (*Postmodernity*, 9). Recent sociological research on young, disaffiliated Catholics has similarly identified some who are open to continued "questing," though this is unlikely to take place within a faith community. See Saint Mary's Press, *Going, Going, Gone*, esp. 29–31.

14. Michele Saracino, *Being about Borders: A Christian Anthropology of Difference* (Collegeville, MN: Michael Glazier/Liturgical, 2011), 17; emphasis added.

15. See *Lumen Gentium*, esp. nos. 2, 7, at http://www.vatican .va/archive/hist_councils/ii_vatican_council/documents/vat-ii _const_19641121_lumen-gentium_en.html.

16. Michele Saracino, "Hybridity and Trespass: With Jesus at the Borders of Identity," *Horizons* 33, no. 2 (2006): 230.

17. Saracino, *Being about Borders*, 42; emphasis added.

18. The Religious Education Association, e.g., explicitly identifies its interests within these three spheres. See Religious Education Association, "The REA Mission," accessed September 12, 2018, https://religiouseducation.net/mission.

19. Nicholas Burbules, *Dialogue in Teaching: Theory and Practice* (New York: Teachers College Press, 2003), 112–16.

20. Mary C. Boys, "Engaged Pedagogy: Dialogue and Critical Reflection," *Teaching Theology and Religion* 2 (1999): 130.

21. Theresa O'Keefe, "Learning to Talk: Conversation across Religious Difference," *Religious Education* 104 (2009): 197–213.

22. Kenneth A. Bruffee, *Collaborative Learning: Higher Education, Interdependence, and the Authority of Knowledge*, 2nd ed. (Baltimore: Johns Hopkins University Press, 1999), 3–9. He later describes "transition communities" as "small, new, temporary communities made up of people who also want to undergo the same sort of change" (74); that is, a change from one subculture's ways to knowing to that of a more expansive knowledge community.

23. Judith A. Berling, *Understanding Other Religious Worlds: A Guide for Interreligious Education* (Maryknoll, NY: Orbis, 2004), 32; emphasis added.

24. Berling, *Understanding Other Religious Worlds*, 25. Note that "bell hooks" is intentionally in lower case, following this author's own usage. Also see Maureen R. O'Brien, "Disciplined Conversations, Faithful Practices: Practical Theology and the Education of Lay Ecclesial Ministers," in *Religious Education as Practical Theology*, ed. Bert Roebben and Michael Warren (Leuven, Belgium: Peeters 2001), 275–308, for an application of Bruffee's work to lay ministry education.

25. Horell describes these strategies in "Cultural Postmodernity," 98–104.

26. See Burbules, *Dialogue in Teaching*, 110–30.

27. *Co-Workers*, 35, quoting CL 63.

28. Another helpful source, though focused more on the dynamics of religious community living than on education per se, is Anthony J. Gittins, *Living Mission Interculturally: Faith, Culture and the Renewal of Praxis* (Collegeville, MN: Liturgical, 2015). See especially his discussion of the distinction between a community of many cultures that takes a radically mutual, "intercultural" approach and one that is merely "multicultural," 180–83.

29. José R. Irizarry, "The Religious Educator as Cultural Spec-Actor: Researching Self in Intercultural Pedagogy," *Religious Education* 98 (2003): 367, emphasis added.

30. Irizarry, "Religious Educator as Cultural Spec-Actor," 371.

31. Irizarry, "Religious Educator as Cultural Spec-Actor," 379.

32. Anne Carter Walker, "Practical Theology for the Privileged: A Starting Point for Pedagogies of Conversion," *International Journal of Practical Theology* 16 (2012): 250.

33. Boyung Lee, "Toward Liberating Interdependence: Exploring an Intercultural Pedagogy," *Religious Education* 105 (2010): 283–98. Also see Katherine Turpin in Mary Elizabeth Moore, Boyung Lee, Katherine Turpin, Ralph Casas, Lynn Bridgers, and Vernonice Miles, "Realities, Visions, and Promises of a Multicultural Future," *Religious Education* 99 (2004): 299, on the inevitability of conflict if we are serious about using liberating forms of religious education.

34. Walker, "Practical Theology for the Privileged," 249.

35. *Co-Workers*, 44.

36. The Alliance for the Certification of Lay Ecclesial Ministers, "National Certification Standards for Lay Ecclesial Ministers," 24, accessed October 2, 2020, https://cdn.ymaws.com/lemcertification.org/resource/resmgr/standards_various/part_2-_the_standards_-_scem.pdf.

37. Sheryl A. Kujawa-Holbrook, *God beyond Borders: Interreligious Learning among Faith Communities* (Eugene, OR: Pickwick, 2014), xxi–xxiv.

38. Kristin Johnson Largen, "A Christian Rationale for Interreligious Teaching and Learning," in *Interreligious Learning and Teaching: A Christian Rationale for a Transformative Praxis*, by Kristin Johnson Largen, Mary E. Hess and Christy Lohr Sapp (Minneapolis: Augsburg Fortress, 2014), 55, http://www.jstor.org/stable/j.ctt9m0spt.7.

39. Largen, "Interreligious Teaching and Learning," 46–66.

40. Largen, "Interreligious Teaching and Learning," 49.

41. Berling, *Understanding Other Religious Worlds*, 64.

42. Mary Hess, "How Do We Understand Student Learning as Adult Learning?" in Largen, Hess, and Sapp, *Interreligious Teaching and Learning*, 67.

43. Hess, "How Do We Understand?" 69.

44. Hess, "How Do We Understand?" 68.

Chapter Eleven

SUPERVISED MINISTRY

Practical Learning as Adults and Professionals

Wayne Cavalier

When I was going through seminary in the late 1980s, the supervised practice of ministry was a well-known, but underutilized, approach to ministry education. At the school where I studied, faculty members were often enlisted to facilitate the reflective aspect of the experience, but they had little understanding of the process of integration that was its goal. The students thought it was a waste of time and an insult to our intelligence.

Today where I practice, the experience is quite the opposite. The supervised practice of ministry is a highly structured, carefully planned experience that often leads to growth and transformation on the part of the seminarians. Faculty members are sold on its value and well prepared to engage in their roles. Its integrative strengths are greatly appreciated among faculty. It is a challenging experience for students, but they usually come to appreciate the enduring value of this way of learning.

Much of what has informed the development of this learning practice has come to seminaries through interdisciplinary sources.

However, there is a cluster of relatively recent developments in adult learning theory and professional practice that can contribute further to this approach to learning for the practice of ministry.

BECOMING A MINISTER

The ministerial vocation is a particular way of being a Christian, with shared responsibility for the community's evangelical mission. The minister's vocation is to serve this mission by intentionally fostering the community's practice of it. Therefore, the education of ministers must account for the transformative encounter with Christ that gives rise to this vocation. Authentic Christian ministry aims to bring about transformation on the personal, interpersonal, and societal levels. It is the fruit of the complex conversion dynamic by which the disciple "takes on the mind of Christ" both personally and in an exemplary or witnessing way (see Phil 2:5). The latter means that ongoing conversion shapes the minister's way of being in the world and is not limited to internal processes.

Formation for ministry must account for these processes, and the supervised practice of ministry is the essential integrating component at its center. In the context where I serve, there are two types of supervised ministry: (1) part-time experiences that occur alongside theological study during the academic year, and (2) full-time experiences that occur between either the second and third years of theology ("pastoral year") or during the year of the transitional diaconate ("pastoral internship").

In both the part-time and full-time experiences, various members of diverse ministerial expertise are engaged in the supervised practice of ministry. In the case of full-time experiences, the pastoral year intern may work with a ministry supervisor, lay committee, pastoral staff members, and a director. All are engaged in different, structured ways in the ministry internship or pastoral year.

In this chapter, I propose that this same configuration can be strengthened, and its desired outcomes fostered by consciously integrating the insights of adult learning theory. The result can be characterized as an intentional process by which members of the Christian community move farther into their identity and role as ministers. This is the specific goal of the supervised practice of ministry, and it is parallel to the generic goal of the adult learning theories that I will describe.

The immediate goal of the intentional community of practice by which a baptized member of the Body of Christ becomes recognized mutually as a full and legitimately practicing minister is to foster the practice of "making Christ present."[1] This is done by the adept use of the tools provided by the Christian tradition for "reading the signs of the times in the light of the Gospel."[2] In supervised ministry, collaborative inquiry into the practice by which these tools are used and the situations in which they are needed is at the center of the learning process. It engages the learner at every level of knowledge.[3]

No single adult learning theory can claim to accomplish all of these goals. I propose a framework for the education of ministers based on several contemporary approaches to adult and professional education that suggest an effective response to the contemporary ecclesial context. Such education must be a transformative learning process based on a mutually critical encounter between (1) the ministry candidate's experience and (2) the gospel, as carried into the present by the continually transformed life of the Christian community.

To give an overview, the process has the structure of a *community of practice* seeking *critical intersubjectivity* in a *participatory paradigm* of *collaborative inquiry* engaging together in (modified) *reflection-in-action* over a specified period of time.[4] (These concepts are unfolded in the remainder of the chapter.) The ultimate goal of this process is human flourishing—understood here as knowledge of Christ realized in greater responsibility toward others, reflected in ministerial activity that more faithfully and authentically mediates God's saving activity in a particular context.[5]

In some ways akin to the catechumenal process, but also much more critical and reflective about the transformative aspect of the Christian ministerial vocation, education for ministry is envisioned here as a practical, holistic, and communal process of shared inquiry. It is practical because it flows out of and back into the practice of ministry. It is holistic because it engages the whole being of the minister-in-formation. It is communal because it is ideally accomplished in the context of a community. Its fundamental dynamic is the critical assessment of the assumptions that neophyte ministers bring to their interpretation of the world and of faith, and the consequences for ministerial action to which these assumptions give rise. Such a critical assessment will permit the aspiring minister to address the fundamental variations from or similarities with gospel values made evident in their theory-laden practice of ministry, and, if necessary, to adapt their practice so that it better reflects authentic gospel values.[6] Not coincidentally, this is the dynamic central to practical theology.

PRACTICAL THEOLOGY: CENTRAL PARADIGM OF MINISTERIAL FORMATION

Gerben Heitink suggests that practical theology's primary concern is change. Not only does practical theology aim to understand and explain the praxis of a particular believing community, but it must also be concerned to change that praxis.[7] This is important, Heitnik writes, because "practical theology deals with God's activity through the ministry of human beings."[8] By the means of human ministry, God is constantly and ever-recurringly coming to God's people.[9]

My students of practical theology often first articulate the goal of practical theology as making the Christian faith "relevant" to the context in which it is being lived. That is when they learn that the word *relevant* is banished from the classroom. I explain that what we are seeking through practical theology is something far more significant than the superficial idea of relevance, as important as relevance is. If practical theology is the mediation of God's action through the ministry of human beings, then richer concepts such as "faithfulness" or, better, "authenticity" or "congruence" are more appropriate to describe what we are seeking.[10] In my understanding, it is no less than the endless quest to be more and more faithful to the call to be the continuing incarnation of God's love in a particular context. In other words, it is to be the Body of Christ anointed and animated by the Holy Spirit, present and active here and now.

Heitink describes the need for practical theology as a response to a crisis.[11] In ministry, the crisis has to do with the inadequacy of a particular ministerial praxis in responding to the current needs of the context. A common example of such a crisis is seen in the experience of many mainline Christian denominations today that are seeing an alarming increase of disaffiliation among young people. In a context of increasing alienation from institutions, increasing societal pluralism, and overall declining commitment to denominational affiliation, former practices of youth ministry are no longer effective in keeping young people connected to the life of the Church. Yet, no new paradigms have arisen to address this adequately, and congregational leaders are left wringing their hands in the face of rapidly declining membership.

Another way to express Heitink's understanding of a ministerial crisis is when the challenge of mediating God's action in the present moment is not being met by the actions of the ministering community. Often this is not the consequence of bad faith, but of inadequate understanding of either the context or the available options for action. Critical reflection is necessary to increase one's understanding of the available options—or to discern new options—that faithfully communicate God's saving action in a new context. Neophyte ministers are constantly confronting their limited perspectives in novel ministerial situations. An authentic ministerial response often calls neophytes to transform their foundational perspective on what is occurring so that their practice of ministry more authentically mediates the gospel. While this may sound simple, it is not easy, because such new understandings are often not immediately available to the minister. A genuinely new perspective can only come from a transformation at some level in how the minister perceives the situation. This transformation is a moment of conversion.

JACK MEZIROW AND TRANSFORMATIVE LEARNING THEORY

Jack Mezirow's transformative learning theory intends to identify what is specific to the adult learning process.[12] As a constructivist, he begins with the assumption that the interpretation of experience is central to adult learning.[13] Mezirow does not define how he is using the term *experience*, rather, experience spans a continuum stretching from pure, unmediated sensory input to socially constructed interpretations.[14] It is important to note that, for Mezirow, learning from experience is not *necessarily* a liberating event, nor does it necessarily lead to personal or social change. A certain level of maturity among learners is required for it to succeed. Mark Tennant explains: "The meanings that learners attach to their experiences may be subjected to critical scrutiny. The teacher may consciously try to disrupt the learner's world view and stimulate uncertainty, ambiguity, and doubt in learners about previously taken-for-granted interpretations of experience."[15] Such transformative learning demands an adult capacity to reinterpret experience. For example, when I confessed once to a friend that I was stuck in a self-defeating pattern of relating to an acquaintance, she offhandedly responded, "Hmmm. I wonder what you are gaining from doing that." My anger at the suggestion made me pause. I realized she was on to something, and began to attend carefully to the question. It led to important new insights and changes in my behavior.

According to Mezirow, we have to interpret experience in order to know how to act effectively in response to it. However, sometimes our habits of expectation distort our interpretations. Our habits of expectation are the assumptions into which we have been socialized—assumptions that "powerfully influence" our perceptions and thoughts about our experience. Racism, for instance, is rooted in habits of expectation about a particular group of people. These, often unconscious, habits filter our interpretations. What does not fit into our particular meaning perspective (formed through early socialization) will be ignored, misinterpreted, or otherwise diminished in order to reduce the anxiety that would otherwise surface. I may have a respected friend or colleague who belongs to a group toward which I have racist attitudes, but somehow dismiss this contradiction without reasons that would stand up to close scrutiny. For example, my friendship with this individual might become evidence for the self-deluding claim that "I am colorblind"—a self-justification that reinforces the underlying bias. This tendency to sacrifice awareness for the sake of psychological peace can prove to be a dysfunctional approach to interpreting our experiences. Mezirow believes that overcoming this tendency is central to adult development.[16] Because our habits of expectation guide all our interpreting activity, they shape meaning for us. Therefore, it is not enough to *reflect* on our experience, we must *critically reflect* on this experience. "Critical reflection involves a critique of presuppositions on which our beliefs have been built."[17] The process of evaluating our habits of expectation through critical reflection is at the heart of transformative learning theory.

MEANING SCHEMES AND MEANING PERSPECTIVES

Mezirow separates frames of reference or habits of expectation into two dimensions: meaning schemes and meaning perspectives. He defines the latter thus: "A meaning perspective is a habitual set of expectations that constitutes an orienting frame of reference that we use in projecting our symbolic models and that serves as a (usually tacit) belief system for interpreting and evaluating the meaning of experience."[18] Therefore, a meaning perspective is something as all-encompassing as our conviction about whether the universe is essentially friendly or essentially hostile to our personal existence. Each meaning *perspective* contains a number of meaning *schemes*. Mezirow defines meaning schemes as the particular knowledge, beliefs, value judgments, and feelings that we articulate in an interpretation. Meaning schemes are the concrete manifestations of our habitual orientation and expectations (or meaning perspectives) that translate these general expectations into specific ones that guide our actions. If I am convinced the universe is hostile to my existence, I may enter relationships in a generally competitive mode of operating, convinced that I will only get what I fight for. If the universe is perceived as hospitable, I may tend to enter relationships in a generally collaborative mode of operating. Whatever the case, we are much more likely to examine critically and transform *meaning schemes* than we are to transform *meaning perspectives*.[19] I may successfully become less aggressive in my behavior in the workplace through behavior modification or even therapy, but I may never change my general orientation toward the universe's inhospitality.

CRITICAL REFLECTION

Mezirow argues that we build inadequate meaning perspectives on distorted assumptions into which we were socialized in our early lives. Critical reflection on these assumptions, he theorizes, will help the adult to confirm or negate a meaning perspective or else to restructure it significantly.[20] That makes critical reflection central to transformative learning theory.[21] Mezirow distinguishes among different kinds of reflection but is especially concerned with the critique of premises. He states,

> Reflection involves the critique of assumptions about the content or process of problem solving. Premises are special cases of assumptions. The critique of premises or presuppositions pertains to problem *posing* as distinct from problem *solving*. Problem posing involves making a taken-for-granted situation problematic, raising questions regarding its validity. While all reflection is inherently critical...the term "critical reflection" often has been used as a synonym for reflection on premises as distinct from reflection on assumptions pertaining to the content or process of problem solving.[22]

When the religious authorities confronted Jesus on the question of the authority by which he acted and spoke, rather than addressing the content of their question, he posed another question to them: "Did the baptism of John come from heaven, or was it of human origin?" The hostile authorities understood that Jesus was critiquing their own assumption that they had the authority to pose the question. If they really had such authority, answering the question would not have presented the conundrum that silenced them in fear (Luke 20:1–8). Jesus forced them to reflect critically on this assumption.

Mezirow contends that reflection focused on content or process may change *meaning schemes.* Such change can include their reinforcement, elaboration, creation, negation, confirmation, iden-tification as a problem, or transformation. However, when reflection focuses on premises, then meaning *perspectives* may be transformed. In other words, they become "more inclusive, discriminating, perme-able (open), and integrative of experience."[23] Mezirow believes that meaning perspectives with these traits are more desirable because they assist adults in better understanding the meaning of their expe-rience.[24] Had the religious authorities taken the time to do critical reflection on the experience they had when Jesus posed his coun-terquestion to them, they might have discerned, for instance, that "authority" has many meanings. They might have discerned that they should honor the authority Jesus had with the people and open themselves to the conversion to which Jesus was inviting them. Sub-sequent events suggest that they did not open themselves to this more inclusive understanding of authority, thus eschewing the dif-ficult work of critical reflection on premises. Similarly, the neophyte minister might come to realize through critical reflection that the behavior of parishioners is not the result of an ill-defined sense of doctrine, but instead a well-founded preference for a Church seek-ing unity with other Christians. She might then come to recognize that there are different legitimate models for understanding the Church and become more respectful of those who operate out of a different model. She might even come to recognize that each model helps to complete the other.

In summary, transformative learning theory purports that adult development is fostered by critical reflection on the prem-ises underlying our meaning perspectives. Therefore, fostering such reflection will foster adult development, and this, according to Mezirow, should be the concern of adult education, for one is always called to transform one's present meaning perspective when it is found wanting.

BEYOND TRANSFORMATIVE LEARNING THEORY: PARTICIPATION AND POWER

Mezirow's work has sparked criticism due to its overem-phasis on an individualistic and rationalistic approach to adult learning.[25] Theorists who appreciate what Mezirow is trying to do nonetheless wonder about the social nature of the learning process, especially in relation to the issue of power and its distribution in the learning process. There is already the power differential that almost always accompanies such structured learning contexts. Usually, the student's evaluator is present as the professor or supervisor. Furthermore, rarely are the participants equal in power in relation to one another. These dynamics are exponentially increased in a context where participants are critically reflecting on the meaning perspectives and meaning schemes they bring to their practice.

To address these concerns, theorists have introduced several concepts into the transformative approach to adult learning. In order to consider the challenges of diversity and structural bias that exist in real life, but not in Mezirow's theory, theorists confront the relationship of power to knowledge, in terms of both social structures and the ways these structures intersect with the individual as producer of knowledge.[26] They call for critical awareness regarding epistemological assumptions, the relation of experience to knowledge, and the interaction among learners.[27] In the U.S. context, we tend to put a premium on the production of knowledge that comes through "pure" research, carried out by the lone scholar in a library or lab—as if knowledge could somehow be dislodged from context. We put less value on knowledge that is discovered through a communal process of shared exploration, knowledge that arises from reflection on praxis, or knowledge rooted in the affective domain.

In lifting up these alternative epistemologies, one approach proposed is "connected knowing," an empowering way of relating in asymmetrical groups through positive regard and empathy.[28] Another proposal is the concept of engaged learning, a shared commitment to intellectual and personal growth, rather than a retreat to "safety," which too often serves as a disguised attempt to maintain the structural status quo.[29] Also, problematizing the social position of the educator helps to moderate its potential negative impact on learning dynamics.[30] This can be done simply by recognizing that the presence of the educator introduces such a power dynamic into the situation and acknowledging that the whole group needs to monitor the educator's effectiveness in mitigating its impact.

Another helpful approach to this issue is offered by social teachings of the Roman Catholic Church about the common good.[31] This teaching calls for equal participation of all members of a group, with the ultimate value of promoting human flourishing.[32] In this view, there is a role for hierarchy in fostering the conditions for participation, but this hierarchy must be regulated by the principle of subsidiarity, always favoring more egalitarian, local processes.[33] Therefore, the goal is "to foster relative egalitarian participation by the students in practical inquiry—that is, intellectual inquiry that guides and is informed by praxis for the sake of the common good."[34]

All of this points toward practical theology—understood as a hermeneutical movement that is based on critical reflection about ministerial practice in a particular context and leads to critical correlation with the faith tradition, with the goal of confirming or converting that ministerial practice to promote greater congruence with the faith tradition.

SUPERVISED PRACTICE OF MINISTRY AS TRANSFORMATIVE ADULT LEARNING

How can all of the above be applied to the supervised practice of ministry? I propose that the formation of ministers in and for the Christian community is understood best in terms of situated learning, where neophyte ministers move from legitimate peripheral participation in ministry to full, recognized participation.[35] They do so by engaging with other members of diverse ministerial expertise and levels of experience, and with the tools they have at their disposal to foster the community's participation in its evangelizing mission. The goal for the neophyte minister is to learn how to use these tools effectively, to develop an identity as a minister, and to be recognized as such by the community members—especially by those who are at the center of ministerial practice.

THE PARTNERING RELATIONSHIP

Practically every neophyte minister in the United States engages the process of education for ministry through some form of active, partnered ministry.[36] Their involvement in ministry, depending on the level of experience already gained, will grow from low-risk involvement to higher-risk involvement (i.e., from relatively peripheral involvement to relatively central involvement).[37] Low-risk involvement in ministry might involve serving on a youth ministry team and being present at the weekly meetings. Higher-risk involvement would be developing and facilitating a presentation to the group. A primary source of risk management will be the partnering relationship. In my experience, the ministry supervisor plays this role. The supervisor manages the risk by slowly increasing the neophyte minister's responsibilities and evaluating her effectiveness as her responsibility increases.

The partnering relationship involves pairing the neophyte minister with one or more persons who have ministerial experience, and who are recognized as full, legitimate members of the ministerial community. While the partnering relationship must always be structured, its intensity will depend on the level of experience and capabilities of the neophyte minister. The type of partnering relationship may vary over time, as might the partner. However, the process always must engage neophyte ministers in practices that increasingly bring them to the center of ministerial practice in one or more contexts.

The participants structure the partnering relationship in a variety of ways, depending on the resources available. Minimally, it requires a primary partner who has some responsibility for the overall ministry within which the neophyte serves. She or he has knowledge of the local context and will be able to intervene effectively when necessary. The partner will also be close enough to the neophyte minister's situation to permit direct observation, as well as to gather impressions from others who are a part of the situation. The participants might enrich the partnering relationship by involving other stakeholders at the ministry site, such as fellow on-site ministers and trusted members of the faith community.

The primary purpose of the partnering relationship is to serve the inquiry of the larger *community of practice*—usually the pastoral staff, a lay committee, and select members of the parish. This community of practice is concerned especially with practical knowledge and the experiential knowledge to which it gives rise. It is attentive also to dilemmas of practice that become sources for reflection-in-action.[38] Partnering as an aspect of the community of practice is concerned less with answers than it is with identifying and helpfully formulating the questions that will feed into the collaborative inquiry of the community of practice.

The partnering relationship operates with awareness that the participants in the relationship are stakeholders who are coinquirers. Neither is expected to be the "answer person." Each can grow in terms of one's practice. This is important in view of the nature of the learning situation in such a participatory paradigm, and it must be given explicit and ongoing attention.[39] This should be addressed in the orientation to the learning experience. While there is the expectation that those more experienced in ministry will be guiding the learning experience for the neophyte ministers, they should remain open to the possibility of learning from them as well.

Ideally, the nature of the relationship with regard to the role of power and of shared participation in ministry can be an early focus of collaborative inquiry for the community of practice. For example, when the neophyte minister is a Catholic seminarian, clericalism might affect the way he relates to the lay committee. He might demonstrate an attitude that he has nothing to learn from them or that he is there to teach them rather than to share an inquiring stance with them. The lay committee should raise this as a matter for reflection in the group.

One of the main purposes of the partnering relationship is to explore the practice situation in terms of the four levels of knowledge—experiential, presentational, propositional, and practical—in an intentional manner. In this way, the coinquirers (partner, neophyte, and others) develop a full description of the practice situation (not limited to propositional statements) that will be useful to the community of practice. For example, a seminarian might be asked to analyze and reflect on a ministerial experience from a number of different perspectives, including psychological, spiritual, theological, affective, and sociological perspectives, encouraging the neophyte minister to look at the situation from a variety of viewpoints. It also calls for a decision about how the ministerial situation might be approached differently after critical reflection on the ineffective way she or he approached it the first time.

CREATING COMMUNITY IN THE COMMUNITY OF PRACTICE

The nature of learning in the community of practice requires that the dominant Enlightenment model of competition as the motivation for excellence be replaced with collaboration as the facilitator of excellence. With the goal of connected knowing, there is the recognition that everyone is not equal in their ability to participate in the learning process, due to differences in experience, background, and role.[40] In the community of practice, such diversity is first recognized, and then recognized as an asset rather than a liability. Honoring the desire of all those present to learn according to their own preferences and abilities, the members of the community empower participation by all through positive regard and empathy.[41] That is, they intentionally call forth and affirm the contribution of each member, recognizing that while each may not be able to contribute at the same level, all contributions enrich the collaborative inquiry, which is diminished to the extent that a member refrains from offering their perspective and insights. This is accomplished, however, without sacrificing openness to appropriate challenges or a sense of rigor about the inquiry. This is managed by maintaining a strict focus on the shared goal of inquiry: to increase responsible practice in ministry.[42] Sometimes, these two aspects of positive regard and openness to challenge will be in tension, and it is important to acknowledge that such tension can be appropriate and useful in the pursuit of truth.[43]

Since a constant goal in the background of the inquiry of the community of practice is the transformation of the meaning perspectives of members, the community will have to have some sophistication to understand this aspect of their inquiry. While not all may be required to have the same level of understanding, there has to be some understanding that the result of the critical reflection is ideally a transformation of perspective. In Christian terms, this means that the members are open to conversion to a perspective on their experience that is more congruent with the world rendered by the gospel. This understanding should be developed in the early inquiry called for above.

Some means for assessing where participants are in terms of meaning perspectives or epistemological forms (in Robert Kegan's terms) may prove helpful. Understanding the history of the perspective out of which they presently practice may help community members recognize how deeply embedded they might be in their particular perspective. Coming to terms with human limitations in relation to epistemological stances, as well as the necessity of operating out of a particular perspective that is nonetheless never complete, will assist members in recognizing the relation between their critical inquiry and the need to remain open to transformation. The current tension between the cultic understanding and the relational understanding of priestly identity in the Catholic community serves as a good example. If the seminarian is introduced to these two perspectives as viable options in Catholic doctrine and helped to see the historical context in which each developed, he might be able to take a stance toward that identity that permits greater critical reflection than might be possible if he believed that his understanding of priestly identity were the only viable one.

THE INQUIRY OF THE MINISTRY COMMUNITY OF PRACTICE

While engagement in the community of practice fosters neophyte ministers in their development as ministers, this is not the exclusive interest of the group. Rather, the group is interested in collaborative inquiry[44] into the effective contemporary practice of ministry, that is, service to the evangelizing mission of the Christian community. In an evangelizing community, all the members recognize that a commitment to continued growth in practicing the presence of Christ is both necessary and desirable. While the conditions for such growth are not limited to the concerns and questions of the practice of ecclesial ministry, this particular community of practice has this focus for inquiry. Growth in practicing the transforming presence of Christ takes place for all as a consequence of collaborative inquiry.[45]

The community of practice comes together over a particular period of time to inquire into dilemmas of practice. An early focus would be the role of religion in human society, part of which would deal with the three areas of research on reflection-in-action identified by Donald Schon: (1) frame analysis, that is, stepping back from the immediate issue of a specific ministerial practice to consider the whole context in which that practice is taking place, so as to look critically at the perspective through which one is considering the questions; (2) development and analysis of the usefulness of one's repertoire of media, language, images, and metaphors gained through earlier experience, especially through one's education and formation for ministry; and (3) effective means of approaching reflection-in-action, considering how the group wants to approach the task of critical reflection, with the neophyte minister's practice as the primary focus and catalyst of reflection.[46]

It is important that all participants realize that they operate out of a chosen theological or religious framework, and therefore they can change that framework, with the understanding that their work as a community of practice will in part be the development or confirmation of effective theological frames out of which they will practice ministry. This includes the perspective that fundamental to any human framework, let alone Christian framework, is responsible action toward the other.

THE CYCLE OF INQUIRY

The members of the community of practice, therefore, begin their shared inquiry by focusing on the role of theological frames and the fact that each member is operating out of a particular frame. They are made aware that there are alternative frames that might be chosen, some already developed and some that may be developed. Their inquiry, therefore, focuses on their theological frame as it is expressed in practice. This might be achieved by using an exercise based on Avery Dulles's *Models of the Church.* Helping members take a step back from their convictions about the Church to see that those convictions are shaped by an a priori frame ("model") will make them more skilled at critically reflecting on the frame itself. They become aware that (1) there are different viable frames by which the Church can be understood theologically; (2) their preferred frame minimizes their ability to see real aspects of the Church that might be more visible when looking at it through a different frame; and (3) their frame is a preference rooted in their experience and context.

The most likely, but not exclusive, place the cycle of inquiry might begin is the partnering relationship. In the partnering session, ministers identify areas where the practice situation resists the frame being applied by the neophyte, the partner, or both.[47] The larger community of practice also may assist in this reflection, since it is not always easy to determine the cause for the resistance of situations to a particular frame. In terms of collaborative inquiry, this lack of fit represents incongruity between the learners' propositional knowledge, practical knowledge, and experiential knowledge. Inquiry begins with the desire to establish greater congruity among various ways of knowing.[48] For example, at the start of the pastoral year, a seminarian might be convinced that the only social justice cause worth pursuing is the right to life of the unborn. However, he soon discovers that participation tapers off in his social justice group focused on that question, despite strong initial interest. He comes to learn that for these parishioners, the dignity of life is understood in a comprehensive way, and they find his focus on the single issue of abortion to be narrow-minded and tone-deaf at a time when prisons are filled with nonviolent offenders and immigrants are deprived of their basic rights. By the end of the pastoral year, his understanding of social justice, after some reflection individually and communally, has expanded to include all aspects of life.

Thus, the first step is to attend to the "back-talk" from the situation, that is, participation tapering off despite general interest in social justice; murmurings heard about dissatisfaction with the group. What information can the learner gain about the incongruity between frame and reality? This requires gathering information about the situation, surfacing the frame the learner has tried to impose on the situation, and examining the ways in which the frame was brought to action on the situation.[49]

Then the learner reflects on this information. This reflection can be done alone, with one's partner, with others, or with the whole community of practice. Ideally, it is done in all these variations. In my practice, this reflection is encouraged through a guided reflection known as the process note (alone), which is used to continue and deepen reflection with the supervisor (partner); it may be brought to reflection with a pastoral staff member, the whole pastoral staff, or a trusted parish member; finally, it may become the focus of reflection at the monthly meeting with the lay committee (community of practice). The intentional learning and reflective nature of the supervised practice of ministry experience encourages this, but it can be made much more intentional through a shared understanding of transformative learning dynamics.

Since the community of practice is engaged in intentional and conscious, critical reflection upon the premises on which their theological perspectives are built, questions about ministerial practice that at first seem very specific and isolated are seen rather in terms of their connection to a consistent theological perspective. For instance, a minister may be trying to determine whether or not to include communion under the species of wine at the eucharistic liturgy. At first, this may seem merely to be a disciplinary and practical question. However, critical reflection on the premises underlying the decision raises issues related, for example, to the role of the Holy Spirit in the ecclesiology of the community. Thus, the minister is brought to a deeper awareness of the intimate links between the practice of liturgy and theology of the sacraments, the Church, and God. Critical reflection raises hermeneutical issues about the interpretation of tradition and its application in the present. It demonstrates that "merely practical" questions have deeper meanings in a symbolic universe, meanings that are dismissed at one's own peril. Such recognition will spare the neophyte much grief in his future practice of ministry!

257

EROS AND THE COMMUNITY OF INQUIRY

It may serve as a good reminder to point out the role of eros in this situation.[50] First, neophyte ministers (or any member of the community of practice) are often aware at the level of feeling when their practice is not congruent with the situation, even if they cannot articulate why this is the case. This affective or emotional response is often the catalyst for bringing the experience to reflection. If they are not aware, another person, often the partner, may bring it to their attention. In response, the neophyte minister will have a desire to understand the cause of the incongruity and the inner tension it creates. This emotional desire will stimulate and motivate learning. The role of the community of practice includes promoting attention to these affective responses, helping the minister articulate them, and reverencing the minister's desire to learn from them. The neophyte minister might discuss her experience of a gay teen coming out to her, and how she sees his trust as a great confirmation of her effectiveness in working with youth. If someone from the community of practice observes that her recognition of this joyful fact is expressed with marked sadness, it might be an occasion for the neophyte minister to see that she is connecting the encounter with her own memories of a gay friend's suicide. Reflection leads to the recognition that such emotional connections affect how we respond to others in ministry and need to be addressed. Such a recognition might be new to the neophyte and could open up a completely new way of understanding the relationship between the minister's inner emotional world and the outer world of ministerial practice.

While the community of practice is concerned primarily with critical reflection on the premises on which the learners' theological frame is built, the community's ultimate goal is to assist the individual minister to achieve greater congruity among the four ways of knowing. They attempt this by codeveloping on-the-spot experiments for trying out a new frame in a particular situation.[51] This is when the lay committee might propose a different way of looking at a situation or tell a story that leads to insights about how to approach the situation in a new way. This is supplemented by the work of the partnering relationship, where strategies for new practice based on a new frame are reflectively applied and assessed. Often this is accomplished by sharing a similar experience from the partner's ministerial practice. Another effective way this happens is through the extensive questioning that such a partnering relationship allows. As the neophyte scans the choices among these different perspectives and attempts to apply them to the ministerial situation, this provides renewed experience that gives rise to new experiential learning that reenters the cycle of cooperative inquiry. In supervised practice of ministry, it becomes new learning that may be reflected on in a process note, supervisory session, or meeting of the lay committee. The inquiry cycle is repeated until the acceptable level of congruity is achieved.[52]

THE MINISTERIAL FOCUS OF THE COMMUNITY OF PRACTICE

A criterion for identifying the kind of ministry on which the partnering relationship focuses is that the minister meets "God the stranger" there.[53] When all is congruent with the neophyte minister's premises, God is never a stranger. However, when incongruence enters in, God becomes a stranger, and occasionally an enemy, until congruence is restored. Transformation happens when the source of congruence is not the neophyte's former premises and frames, but newly embraced ones. This kind of ministry will always be on the edge of the minister's "comfort zone." It should challenge, but not overwhelm. The role of the partnering relationship is key to helping the neophyte minister manage the stress of being stretched. However, it is essential that the goal for this is not to make things easier for the minister, so much as to foster his or her ability to befriend the situation. This is accomplished in such a way that the questions to which it gives rise become potential sources of transformation, so that he or she ultimately meets "God the friend" there.[54] In particular, the minister's attempt to control the situation in order to tame it according to his or her needs should be challenged. This is important especially for the community of practice, who generally prefer to tread lightly in these situations due to the tensions often present.

This is where the community-building work of the members becomes key. The community of practice must be a place where members feel validated enough that they can freely share their uncomfortable emotions without feeling ashamed, while at the same time remaining open to having their assumptions challenged. The community can challenge the clericalism evident in a seminarian's tendency to dismiss their ideas, but at the same time remain open to reevaluating their assumptions about the seminarian's attitude toward eucharistic adoration, for instance. The members might see that they are not respecting what the seminarian actually thinks about the practice, but instead are basing their assessment on the assumption that adoration is an attempt to negate Vatican II and return to earlier practice. They will be challenged to identify mechanisms that ministers might use to avoid or deny the difficult emotions associated with such challenges.[55]

CONCLUSION

While the methods described above represent an ideal, they suggest ways to maximize the potential of the supervised practice of ministry. In so doing, these methods promote conversion toward greater fidelity and authenticity in mediating the action of God through the practice of ministry. While many who are already promoting growth among ministry candidates understand much of this intuitively, a conscious focus on these dynamics may promote even greater success in helping neophyte ministers develop a critical approach to their ministry. It opens up new levels of understanding by bringing pertinent aspects of the faith tradition into critical conversation with the practice of ministry.

NOTES

1. See, e.g., Hannah Brockhaus, "A Good Priest Makes Christ Present to His People, Pope Says at Chrism Mass," CNA/ EWTN News, March 29, 2018, https://www.catholicnewsagency

.com/news/a-good-priest-makes-christ-present-to-his-people -pope-says-at-chrism-mass-18181.

2. See *Gaudium et Spes* 4 and 11, accessed November 7, 2019, http://www.vatican.va/archive/hist_councils/ii_vatican_coun cil/documents/vat-ii_const_19651207_gaudium-et-spes_en.html.

3. According to Heron and Reason, there are four interdependent ways of knowing that relate to four modes of functioning of the human psyche. Through the *affective mode*, we come to experiential knowing, the direct encounter between the knowing subject and the given cosmos. The knower also interprets the reality encountered, creating or shaping a world by imaging the object through perception and other means. Thus, through the *imaginal mode* comes presentational knowing, grounded in experiential knowing. Through the *conceptual mode* comes propositional knowing. This mode involves attempts to describe the given cosmos we encounter in experiential knowing. Propositions depend on presentational forms ultimately grounded in experiential knowledge. Finally, through the *practical mode*, we come to practical knowing, demonstrated in skills and competence. This form of knowledge is the fruition and consummation of all the other forms of knowing and depends on them. John Heron and Peter Reason, "A Participatory Inquiry Paradigm," *Qualitative Inquiry* 3, no. 3 (1997): 282.

4. Each technical term in italics represents a distinctive aspect of various theories that will be further explained and integrated into the educational framework described in this chapter. I develop the framework based partially on the following theorists: Virginia Buysse, Karen L. Sparkman, and Patricia W. Wesley, "Communities of Practice: Connecting What We Know with What We Do," *Exceptional Children* 69, no. 3 (2003): 262–77; Heron and Reason, "Inquiry"; Jean Lave and Etienne Wenger, *Situated Learning: Legitimate Peripheral Participation, Learning in Doing* (Cambridge: Cambridge University Press, 1991); Donald A. Schon, *The Reflective Practitioner: How Professionals Think in Action* (New York: Basic Books, 1983); Lyle Yorks and Elizabeth Kasl, "Toward a Theory and Practice of Whole-Person Learning: Reconceptualizing Experience and the Role of Affect," *Adult Education Quarterly* 52, no. 3 (2002): 176–92.

5. In addition to practical theology, my thinking here is influenced by the radical phenomenology of Emmanuel Levinas.

See, e.g., Emmanuel Levinas's essays, "Ethics as First Philosophy," "Revelation in the Jewish Tradition," and "Substitution," in Sean Hand, ed., *The Levinas Reader* (Cambridge, MA: Blackwell, 1989; repr., 1998), 75–125, 190–210. I also draw on the critical anthropology of Roberto Goizueta. See Roberto S. Goizueta, *Caminemos Con Jesus: Toward a Hispanic/Latino Theology of Accompaniment* (Maryknoll, NY: Orbis Books, 1995).

6. All practice reflects an underlying theory (or several) that consciously or unconsciously informs that practice. This is the basis for a praxiological approach to practical theology, the goal of which is to first bring that theory to consciousness and second to critically assess that theory in relation to the desired practice—in this case, practice that more and more authentically makes Christ present.

7. Gerben Heitink, *Practical Theology: History, Theory, Action Domains; Manual for Practical Theology*, trans. Reinder Bruinsma, Studies in Practical Theology (Grand Rapids: Wm. B. Eerdmans, 1999), 6. I use the term *praxis* to mean practice and the theory that informs that practice, consciously or not.

8. Heitink, *Practical Theology*, 6.

9. Heitink, *Practical Theology*, 8.

10. Heitink, *Practical Theology*, 10.

11. Heitink, *Practical Theology*, 2–5.

12. According to Mezirow, "This is a generic process of adult learning, usually undertaken without the help of a professional educator. If an educator assists the learner, whole new dimensions of adult development and action are opened up." Jack Mezirow, *Fostering Critical Reflection in Adulthood: A Guide to Transformative and Emancipatory Learning*, The Jossey-Bass Higher Education Series (San Francisco: Jossey-Bass Publishers, 1990), xv. My premise is that adult Christian conversion is one context in which the generic process of transformative adult learning (described in this section) takes place. For a contrary view, see Michael Newman, "Transformative Learning: Mutinous Thoughts Revisited," *Adult Education Quarterly* 64, no. 4 (2014): 348.

13. Jack Mezirow, "Transformation Theory and Cultural Context: A Reply to Clark and Wilson," *Adult Education Quarterly* 41, no. 3 (1991): 58.

14. E. Michelson, "Usual Suspects: Experience, Reflection

and the (En)Gendering of Knowledge," *International Journal of Lifelong Education* 15, no. 6 (1996): 439.

15. Mark C. Tennant, "The Psychology of Adult Teaching and Learning," in *Adult Education: Evolution and Achievements in a Developing Field of Study,* ed. J. M. Peters, P. Jarvis, and associates (San Francisco: Jossey-Bass, 1991), 196–97.

16. Jack Mezirow, *Transformative Dimensions of Adult Learning,* The Jossey-Bass Higher and Adult Education Series (San Francisco: Jossey-Bass, 1991), 5.

17. Jack Mezirow, "How Critical Reflection Triggers Transformative Learning," in Mezirow, *Fostering Critical Reflection in Adulthood,* 1.

18. Mezirow, *Transformative Dimensions,* 42.

19. Mezirow, *Transformative Dimensions,* 44.

20. Mezirow, *Transformative Dimensions,* 8.

21. Mezirow bases his approach to critical reflection on Jürgen Habermas's assertion that, in Mezirow's words, "the very nature of [human] communication implies the existence of a set of optimal [or ideal] conditions for participation in rational discourse." Mezirow, *Transformative Dimensions,* 77. See also Mezirow, *Fostering Critical Reflection,* 11; Mezirow, "Reflection Triggers Transformative Learning," 13–14.

22. Mezirow, *Transformative Dimensions,* 105, emphasis in original.

23. Mezirow, *Transformative Dimensions,* 111.

24. Mezirow, "Reflection Triggers Transformative Learning," 14.

25. See Newman, "Transformative Learning," 348.

26. Mezirow, *Transformative Dimensions,* 8. Mezirow adopts Habermas's theory of the ideal communicative situation as the foundation for the critical reflection carried out in adult learning contexts.

27. See Elizabeth J. Tisdell, "Poststructural Feminist Pedagogies: The Possibilities and Limitations of a Feminist Emancipatory Adult Learning Theory and Practice," *Adult Education Quarterly* 48, no. 3 (1998): 139–56.

28. Mary Field Belenky and Ann V. Stanton, "Inequality, Development, and Connected Knowing," in *Learning as Transformation: Critical Perspectives on a Theory in Progress,* ed. Jack Mezirow,

The Jossey-Bass Higher and Adult Education Series (San Francisco: Jossey-Bass, 2000), 71–102.

29. This concern is an explicit way that the values of participation and of holistic learning (discussed below) become connected.

30. Tisdell, "Poststructural Feminist Pedagogies," 147–50.

31. In *Gaudium et Spes*, the Catholic bishops at Vatican II defined this phrase as follows: "The sum of those conditions of social life which allows social groups and their individual members relatively thorough and ready access to their own fulfillment" (no. 20).

32. See Pope Paul VI, *Octogesima Adveniens* (OA), May 14, 1971, accessed February 21, 2005, http://www.vatican.va/holy_father/paul_vi/apost_letters/documents/hf_p-vi_apl_19710514_octogesima-adveniens_en.html. In that apostolic exhortation, Paul VI states, "Without a renewed education in solidarity, an overemphasis of equality can give rise to an individualism in which each one claims his own rights without being answerable for the common good" (OA 23).

33. Todd D. Whitmore, "Practicing the Common Good: The Pedagogical Implications of Catholic Social Teaching," *Teaching Theology and Religion* 3, no. 1 (2000): 14.

34. Whitmore, "Practicing the Common Good," 14. bell hooks, coming out of a critical education, feminist, and African American cultural perspective, comes to a similar conclusion. See bell hooks, *Teaching to Transgress: Education as the Practice of Freedom* (New York: Routledge, 1994), 152.

35. Lave and Wenger, *Situated Learning*, 34–37. For a helpful view of how Lave and Wenger's theory of practice-based learning complements transformative learning theory, which will be discussed below, see Steven Hodge, "Transformative Learning as an 'Inter-Practice' Phenomenon," *Adult Education Quarterly* 64, no. 2 (2014): 165–81.

36. Understanding the "ministry supervisor" as being in a "partnering relationship" moves this relationship from that of authority to a more collaborative position in the community of practice. Perhaps the most common terminology used to describe this kind of relationship is mentoring. My choice to use "partnering" instead has to do with problematizing the asymmetrical

power in the relationship and, more importantly, emphasizing the mutuality of the learning process. Both must be equally open to learning from one another and from their shared inquiry into the practice of ministry for the good of the whole community. Placing this aspect first may distort the fact that it is not the primary relationship. Rather, the partnering relationship serves the primary relationship, the community of practice described below. The nature of the partnering relationship is determined by the nature of the community of practice, in which all participants are fellow inquirers. Therefore, the partnering relationship is not correctly understood outside the context of the community of practice. It is described here first because it provides a way to connect the ministerial practice of the ministers (minister partner and neophyte minister alike) to the inquiry of the community of practice.

37. See Lave and Wenger, *Situated Learning*, 34–37.

38. See Schon, *Reflective Practitioner*, 49.

39. See Goizueta, *Caminemos Con Jesus.* See also Mary V. Alfred, "The Politics of Knowledge and Theory Construction in Adult Education: A Critical Analysis from an Africentric Feminist Perspective," in *41st Annual Adult Education Research Conference*, ed. Thomas J. Sork, Valerie-Lee Chapman, and Ralf St. Clair (Vancouver: University of British Columbia, 2000), 2; Roberto S. Goizueta, "The Symbolic Realism of U.S. Latino/a Popular Catholicism," *Theological Studies* 65, no. 2 (2004): 255–74; Whitmore, "Practicing the Common Good," 3–19. See also Heron and Reason, "Inquiry," 278.

40. See Mary Field Belenky et al., *Women's Ways of Knowing: The Development of Self, Voice, and Mind* (New York: Basic Books, 1986); Mary Field Belenky and Ann V. Stanton, "Inequality, Development, and Connected Knowing," in *Critical Perspectives*, 71–102.

41. See Belenky and Stanton, "Inequality, Development, and Connected Knowing," 71–102.

42. See hooks, *Teaching to Transgress*, 39.

43. hooks, *Teaching to Transgress*, 39.

44. Collaborative inquiry is described in Heron and Reason, "Inquiry," 286. See also Lyle Yorks and Elizabeth Kasl, "Collaborative Inquiry for Adult Learning," in *Collaborative Inquiry as a Strategy for Adult Learning: New Directions for Adult and Continuing Education*, ed. Lyle Yorks and Elizabeth Swain Kasl (San Francisco: Jossey-Bass, 2002), 3–5.

45. An effective tool for identifying, engaging, and tracking change in these might be the concept map, described in Susan M. Yelich Biniecki and Simone C. O. Conceigao, "Using Concept Maps to Engage Adult Learners in Critical Analysis," *Adult Learning* 27, no. 2 (2015): 51–59. Chad Hoggan describes another useful tool in the form of conceptual metaphors that can be used to promote transformative learning effectively in several ways. See Chad Hoggan, "Transformative Learning through Conceptual Metaphors: Simile, Metaphor, and Analogy as Levers for Learning," in *Adult Learning* 25, no. 4 (2014): 134.

46. Schon, *Reflective Practitioner*, 309–11.

47. Schon, *Reflective Practitioner*, 149–50. See also Heron and Reason, "Inquiry," 284.

48. Heron and Reason, "Inquiry," 286.

49. Schon, *Reflective Practitioner*, 149–50. Examples are given in Yorks and Kasl, "Collaborative Inquiry," 6–7; Yorks and Kasl, "Learning from the Inquiries: Lessons for Using Collaborative Inquiry as an Adult Learning Strategy," in Yorks and Kasl, *Collaborative Inquiry*, 94–96.

50. hooks, *Teaching to Transgress*, 194, 198.

51. See Schon, *Reflective Practitioner*, 149–51; Heron and Reason, "Inquiry," 284.

52. See Heron and Reason, "Inquiry," 286–87.

53. This is one way to name the disorienting dilemma of being surprised by the other, by that of which one's meaning perspective is unable to make meaning. It is the shock of the complacent subject confronted by the insistent Other, as Levinas puts it. The term is attributed to Richard Niebuhr and is used by Robert Kegan and James Loder to signify the kinds of situations that potentially presage developmental movement. See Robert G. Kegan, "There the Dance Is: Religious Dimensions of a Developmental Framework," in *Toward Moral and Religious Maturity*, ed. Christiane Brusselmans et al. (Morristown, NJ: Silver Burdett Co., 1980), 421; James E. Loder, *The Transforming Moment: Understanding Convictional Experiences* (San Francisco: Harper & Row, 1981), 87.

54. Kegan, "Dance," 423.

55. This suggests a role for a counselor and a spiritual director.

CONCLUSION

Nathaniel G. Samuel and
Theodore James Whapham

If ministry formation is to be effective, it requires shaping lives to work in the complex realities of our Church. This is challenging for an organization like AGPIM because universities and their graduate programs excel at describing the ideal—the way the Church ought to be, its best self. The reality of ministerial work too often falls short of that ideal. Turf wars, mixed motivations, poor communication, poorer management, and limited resources frequently plague the work of ministry. Any attempt to form ministers for ministry today must attend to the concrete realities of life and work in the Church. An inductive and contextual approach is needed. Thus the chapters of this volume adopt a practical theological methodology that begins in reality, reflects on the work of building the reign of God that is still to be accomplished, and points toward a future for the Church that is not out of reach.

The opening contributions by William Johnston and Marti Jewell looked at the historical development of lay ecclesial ministry in the United States. These chapters pointed out that the development of a new type of ministry required a new form of ministry formation. They also pointed to tensions that developed along the way—tensions that come about when new realities enter into conversation with established structures, and tensions that come about with growth and development. This history shaped the contemporary context of ministry, and the particular challenges that face ministry formators. These challenges include issues related to diversity and access, interdisciplinarity, countercurrents to graduate ministry formation, and the need for trust and reconciliation. The following reflections point to places in the volume where these challenges were addressed and then move on to indicate areas where more work is needed.

DIVERSITY AND ACCESS

Hosffman Ospino and Maureen O'Brien both addressed the need for ministry formation programs to prepare students interculturally. They pointed to the need for diversity among faculty, staff, and students, the need to help future ministers better understand culture, and the need to prepare for cultural border crossings. We know that the realities of the emerging Catholic Church in the United States require providing opportunities for members of underrepresented communities to have access to theological education and ministerial formation. We also know that we are not yet doing enough to address this need.

Students who are middle-aged, in their late forties, fifties, and sixties, make up an increasing share of our graduate ministry formation programs. In many cases, these students are among the most frequently enrolled because they are more likely to have two of the scarcest commodities in our society: time and money. Far too often, however, older students can only undertake their studies by accumulating massive student debt. An older, more indebted student population needs urgent attention, and the creation of creative and novel models of formation. Younger students are also encumbered by significant student debt and, like their older counterparts, have difficulty finding a stable job that pays a living wage and helps to pay off student loans. These young ministers often leave ministry for financial reasons. In the process, lay ecclesial ministry is robbed of one of the Church's most precious resources—young adults.

To address issues of diversity and access, ministry formation programs need to continue to find resources to make graduate study possible for all those who are called to ministry. While the hard work of fundraising is not something that most theologians signed up for, it is essential for ministry formation. We continue to need to develop outstanding administrators who are able to martial limited resources to develop programs that reach marginalized communities. We should also not expect our salvation to come in the form of support from parishes and dioceses. They too are strapped—especially in the wake of the most recent manifestations of the sex abuse crisis. Instead, lay ecclesial ministers need to provide mutual support for one another. Small dollar donations from alumni of our ministry programs, alongside larger gifts from foundations and supporters that are more affluent, can make a significant difference in providing access.

INTERDISCIPLINARITY

Both the apologists of the second century AD (like Sts. Irenaeus and Justin Martyr) and medieval Scholastics (like Anselm and Aquinas) teach us that theology must always draw upon the best available human knowledge of any age. Plato and Aristotle each needed to be "baptized" by the theologians who drew upon their work, and theologians working in ministerial formation must do the same again today. This interdisciplinary work is already going on in conversation with modern and postmodern philosophical systems, but ministry formators need to expand this interdisciplinarity in at least two ways.

The first expansion of interdisciplinarity in ministry formation involves engaging the social sciences—a dialogue familiar to practical theologians. Advancing such interdisciplinary work, Wayne Cavalier draws on educational theory and psychology (along with theology and philosophy) to articulate ways in which field education and supervised ministry experiences can become loci of transformation. Howard Ebert draws on the work of French sociologist Pierre Bourdieu to understand the *sensus fidelium*. This work of engaging the social and natural sciences needs to continue and expand, especially in the world of Catholic theology. While the truth of revelation always remains primary, the work of theology is to mine and advance this truth through mutually critical dialogue between tradition and human experience. We need to continue to engage in such dialogues.

A second form of interdisciplinarity emerges out of the experience of developing new formation programs for nontraditional ministerial roles. Celeste Mueller's discussion of forming health care executives and other members of the Ascension Health community teases this out. The ecclesiology of Vatican II that undergirds lay ecclesial ministry emphasizes that all of the baptized are called to be ministers of the gospel. Thus, the work of ministry formation cannot afford to limit itself to parish-based lay ecclesial ministries, such as youth minister, catechetical leader, music minister, and so on. This form of interdisciplinarity requires new and innovative programs that form professionals who serve in nontraditional ministerial roles (lawyers, doctors, janitors, and teachers) to serve the mission of the Church—in the pew, at home, and in the workplace. It also requires that members of our parish councils, Catholic school boards, and Catholic Charities offices understand themselves primarily as ministers. We must be more expansive and less parochial in our definition of the professional minister. By placing resources behind an expansive call to the ministry of all the faithful—both *intra ecclesia* and *extra ecclesia*—we may avoid an insidious form of lay clericalism that retards the effectiveness of ministry in changing and complex societies.

COUNTERCURRENTS

Tracey Lamont's reading of the deep culture of adolescents, in the context of the much-cited "rise of the nones" phenomena, helps remind us of countercurrents in the Church. These countercurrents are often found in new and frequently disruptive movements and patterns through which the Spirit often slips into view. timone davis points to the ways that working with the young Church can result in the exchange of narratives that brings new life to our traditions. The youth are a constant countercurrent, as Pope Francis reminds us in his recent document on young adults: *Christus Vivit.* In it he asks the Lord "to free the Church from those who would make her grow old, encase her in the past, hold her back or keep her at a standstill" and challenges the Church to keep "close to the voices and concerns of young people."[1] Encounter with the youth in this sense is a countermovement that asks us to continue to grow in relation to the gospel.

Another countercurrent in ministry formation is the growing number of noncredit certificate programs. AGPIM is an organization that has developed around graduate programs oriented to preparing individuals for professional ministry. Thus many of the chapters in the volume have this model of ministry formation in mind. However, issues related to access discussed above have made clear the need to provide multiple pathways into ministry formation. Over the years, noncredit certificate programs (often sponsored by universities and dioceses) have played an important role in expanding access to quality ministerial formation. While such programs are not generally able to provide the same level of academic depth and rigor as graduate programs, they have helped to expand the number of lay ecclesial ministers and have a profoundly positive impact on the life of the Church.

Nonetheless, the increasing number of noncredit programs raises concerns. First, given the realities of limited resources in the life of the Church, many pastors have come to see graduate-level formation programs as optional. Noncredit programs are increasingly becoming the preferred form of ministerial formation for lay ecclesial ministers. Fewer parishes and dioceses are supporting graduate formation for lay ecclesial ministers. For example, in 2018, the *Christifidelis Laici* program in the Archdiocese of Seattle stopped offering financial support for graduate education to those in formation—including support for those who intend to serve as pastoral administrators for this diverse and geographically widespread local church. In other words, graduate degrees are increasingly less likely to be seen by pastors and bishops as the norm for the professional formation of lay ecclesial ministers. The result is that, in some corners of the Church, theological engagement is being deemphasized within a tradition that has always prided itself on dynamic interplay of faith and reason.

At the same time that noncredit programs are becoming the norm for ministerial formation, a number of trends threaten to undermine the quality of these programs. For example, a desire to make theological education more understandable for a broad public can lead to lowering academic standards. Not long ago, noncredit certificates in lay ministry took two to three years to complete and involved dozens of contact hours. Some institutions now offer certificates for attending a weekend conference or for watching a few videos. In an effort to expand access to theological education, the educational process of entering into the mysteries of the faith under the guidance of one who has spent years in study has been reduced to a series of low and wide hoops, involving little effort and no call to conversion. While the content of such short courses may be good, they tend to make extremely difficult the kind of integration of theory and praxis that Diana Dudoit Raiche shows is a hallmark of such classic means of Christian formation as the RCIA. The best education develops nuance and fosters the desire to continue to learn. However, nuance is too often a casualty of providing formation quickly and inexpensively. Devotional programs that are designed to foster love of God and the Church sometimes come at the expense of watering down the challenge of the gospel and preparing professional ministers for the challenges of working in real ministerial contexts. The need for a deep and balanced formation for lay ecclesial ministry is well attested in *Co-Workers*, and all four of the dimensions of ministerial formation must be kept in mind for any program of ministerial formation.[2]

Moreover, the role of capitalism in American culture and the real financial responsibilities of lay ecclesial ministers have given rise to a for-profit mentality in ministry circles. There are an increasing number of programs and organizations that give the impression that they are more interested in financial gain than the demands of the gospel. Formation programs designed to train team members for a prepackaged confirmation program, for example, use a series of professionally produced videos instead of actual interaction with an instructor. Or the training process for college missionaries dedicates more time to fundraising techniques than being transformed by the gospel. These programs appear more interested in generating revenue than anything else.

272

Conclusion

As the Church in the United States moves through a seismic shift in its business model, lay ecclesial ministers need to be mindful of the evangelical counsels of poverty, chastity, and obedience that have been at the root of every ecclesial renewal in Christian history. A for-profit mentality runs the risk of taking advantage of those who have the least access to ministry formation. A quality education must always be a just education.

Ministry formators need to continue to find ways to strengthen noncredit formation programs. One way to ensure the quality of these programs is to remain attentive to all of the dimensions of formation outlined in *Co-Workers* and the NCS. *Co-Workers* endorsed degree programs as "usually preferable" for formation and it recognized that "inadequate and faulty formation harms rather than helps the mission of the Church."[3] Another way to assess quality is to focus more on the quantity and quality of interaction with instructors and less on branding or church celebrity.

TRUST AND RECONCILIATION

The final aspect of the future of ministry formation that we must prepare for grows out of the present polarization in our Church and our broader society. Nearly every chapter in this volume addresses in some way the "othering" that we are so frequently encounter. By "othering," we mean the all-too-human tendency to pit one idea, person, or movement against another. Christian personalism teaches that recognition with the other is necessary. The relationship between two different persons results in a creative tension that helps to develop identity. Indeed, the Christian tradition has associated the mutual gift of self among persons with the very notion of God. The othering with which we are concerned, however, is often accompanied by unhealthy prejudices, and is symptomatic of a deep moral injury in which we are all caught up. Our ability to trust, especially in the life of the Church, is a common casualty. It is our human woundedness that turns the gift of diversity and difference into fear. Fear erodes trust and relationship—too often among those who ought to be closest to one another. The result is sin and the violence that causes devastating damage in contemporary American society.

The work of ministry formation in the future needs to be empowered by the grace of God to reconcile us to one another. We are convinced that this is what Paul meant when he wrote, "God [is] reconciling the world to himself" (2 Cor 5:19). It seems that at the core of the work of ministry formation in our day is the development of peacemakers and those who hunger and thirst for justice and righteousness—women and men who will help bind the wounds in our Church and our world. We are in need of reconciliation, which does not hide, excuse, or forget injury, but acknowledges it as the site where the painful process of healing may begin and where relationship and trust may be reestablished.

This last insight brings us to what is perhaps the most challenging and perennial aspect of ministry formation—transformation and conversion, which can only come through cooperation with the grace of God. We must strive with all we have to prepare for service to the Church and the world ever challenged by God's refining grace, present and active in all of creation. And so our work goes on.

NOTES

1. Francis I, *Christus Vivit*, 35, 38, accessed August 4, 2019, http://w2.vatican.va/content/francesco/en/apost_exhorta tions/documents/papa-francesco_esortazione-ap_20190325 _christus-vivit.html.

2. *Co-Workers*, 33–50.

3. *Co-Workers*, 34.

ABOUT THE CONTRIBUTORS

Wayne Cavalier, OP, is an ordained friar of the Southern Dominican Province. He is a life-long educator with a particular interest in religious education who has served at every level of education. Presently he assists the formation of ministers from the certificate to the doctoral level. As founding director of the Congar Institute for Ministry Development, he fosters partnerships with resource-challenged churches in the formation of lay pastoral leaders. He is associate professor of practical theology and director of the doctor of ministry program at Oblate School of Theology, where he also works with seminarians in formation during their pastoral year. Wayne serves on the board of the Aquinas Center of Theology at Emory University and of Bethany House Prison Ministries in Millis, Massachusetts. He works with the executive committee of the Association for Doctor of Ministry Education. And in San Antonio, Texas, where he lives, Wayne serves as chaplain to a couple of small Christian communities. He was the recipient in 2016 of the San Juan Diego Award from the National Association for Lay Ministry.

timone davis, PhD, is a cradle Catholic who was a "pewster" until she discovered that the uselessness of the Church was because she was not giving anything of herself. After committing to do something, her life changed. timone's first ministry was with the RCIA, where she not only welcomed others into the Church but also revitalized her own spirituality. After working for the Archdiocese of Chicago as the coordinator of ReCiL—Reclaiming Christ in Life young adult ministry—timone launched PEACE-centered WHOLENESS with her husband, Orlando, where they are blending clinical counseling and spiritual companioning. In addition, timone is an assistant professor in the Institute of Pastoral Studies at Loyola University Chicago. She also serves as the treasurer of the Black Catholic Theological Symposium.

timone uses lowercase letters for her name to indicate her willingness to embody the creedal assertion in John 3:30—Jesus must increase, but she must decrease—in her everyday living.

Howard Ebert, PhD, is professor of theology and religious studies at St. Norbert College, De Pere, Wisconsin. He received his doctorate in religious studies from Marquette University (1992). His recent publications include the essay "The Social Nature of the *Sensus Fidei* in the Thought of Karl Rahner" in *Philosophy and Theology* (2016). Howard's research focus is on Rahnerian studies, theologies of history, the use of the social sciences in theology, and theologies of ministry. In the past, he served as president of the Karl Rahner Society, vice president of the College Theology Society, and secretary for the Association of Graduate Programs in Ministry. He has also served in various administrative roles at St. Norbert College, including associate dean of humanities and fine arts, director of the master of arts in liberal studies and, since 1999, as director of the master of theological studies program. He is married, has three daughters, and lives in De Pere, Wisconsin.

Edward P. Hahnenberg, PhD, is the Jack and Mary Jane Breen Chair in Catholic Theology at John Carroll University in Cleveland. He is the author or coeditor of five books: *A Church with Open Doors: Catholic Ecclesiology for the Third Millennium* (edited with Richard Gaillardetz); *Theology for Ministry: An Introduction for Lay Ministers*; *Awakening Vocation: A Theology of Christian Call*; *A Concise Guide to the Documents of Vatican II*; and *Ministries: A Relational Approach*. He has authored numerous articles in academic and pastoral journals.

Edward served as a delegate to the U.S. Lutheran-Catholic Dialogue and as a theological consultant to the U.S. Bishops' Subcommittee on Lay Ministry in its preparation of the document *Co-Workers in the Vineyard of the Lord*. In 2019, he received the Called and Gifted Award from the Association of Graduate Programs in Ministry in recognition of his contributions to the Church's ministerial life.

Marti R. Jewell, DMin, associate professor emerita, has served as an associate professor of pastoral theology in the Neuhoff School of Ministry at the University of Dallas and was named the University's 2017 Michael A. Haggar Scholar. Previously, Marti served as the director of the Emerging Models of Pastoral Leadership Project, a national research initiative funded by the Lilly Endowment, studying excellence in parish leadership. Her books include *Navigating Pastoral Transitions: A Parish Leaders' Guide, The Changing Face of Church,* and *The Next Generation of Pastoral Leaders*. She has received several national awards, including the Called and Gifted Award from the Association of Graduate Programs in Ministry for her contributions to the field of lay ecclesial ministry, and the *Lumen Gentium* award from the Conference for Pastoral Planners and Council Development for her research with parishes and pastoral leaders. Marti works as an author, researcher, teacher, and trainer. Her doctor of ministry degree is from the Catholic University of America.

William H. Johnston earned his BA, MA, and PhD from the University of Notre Dame. After twenty-seven years in church educational ministry—at Holy Cross Parish in Lynchburg, Virginia, in the Division of Religious Education of the Archdiocese of Baltimore, and as Director of the Secretariat for Christian Life and Ministry Formation in the Diocese of Grand Rapids—he joined the faculty of the department of religious studies of the University of Dayton in 2006. Over his career, William has served in leadership on various boards and commissions, including the Commission on Religious Education of the Diocese of Richmond, the National Advisory Committee on Religious Education, the Board of the National Association for Lay Ministry, the Task Force for the Revision of the National Certification Standards, and the Executive Committee of the Association of Graduate Programs in Ministry. Since 2001, he has served on the advisory board of the Vital Worship Grants Program of the Calvin Institute of Christian Worship at Calvin University, Grand Rapids. At the University of Dayton, he is director of master of arts programs and coordinator of undergraduate studies, and teaches courses in liturgy, sacraments, theology of ministry, Vatican II, and C. S. Lewis. He has authored *Care for the Church and Its Liturgy: A Study of Summorum Pontificum and the Extraordinary Form of the Roman Rite* (Liturgical Press, 2013), and articles in *Worship, Antiphon, New Theology Review, Catechist, Catechumenate,* and *The Living Light.* William is married and has three children and five grandchildren.

Tracey Lamont, PhD, is an assistant professor of religious education at the Loyola Institute for Ministry at Loyola University, New Orleans. She earned her MA and PhD in religion and religious education from Fordham University and specializes in youth and young adult ministry and religious education. Her passion for ministry and teaching has given her a range of experiences serving in parishes as a youth and young adult minister; teaching theology and religion at the undergraduate level; and teaching religion, social studies, and epistemology in high school. Tracey's commitment to her vocation as a religious educator enhances her praxis to see the world around her as a theological and cosmological text, and she teaches her students to envision education as a prophetic act aimed at the transformation of society. Her passion, scholarship, and commitment to teaching and learning has led her to serve in a variety of advisory positions, including her role as vice chair of resources for the United States Conference of Catholic Bishops' National Advisory Team for Young Adult Ministry and as a member of the National Leadership Network for the National Dialogue on Catholic Pastoral Ministry with Youth and Young Adults.

Celeste Mueller serves as vice president of ministry formation for Ascension, a large Catholic health system headquartered in St. Louis.

As a member of the system executive council for Mission Integration, Celeste assures standards of excellence for spiritual and theological formation and organizational spirituality through Ascension. Celeste leads a team of formation leaders and facilitators, researchers and practitioners, who function as an internal and external consulting group. She also serves as faculty for the Ascension Leadership Academy and as executive codirector of the Ascension Leader Institute.

Prior to joining Ascension, Celeste was assistant professor of practical theology at Aquinas Institute of Theology in St. Louis. She founded and directed the Vocare Center at Aquinas Institute (now the Ashley O'Rourke Center for Healthcare Ministry Leadership), which was established to strengthen the capacity of leaders to transform society according to the gospel.

Celeste has taught practical theology, Scripture, and systematic theology at Aquinas Institute and St. Louis University, as well as at the secondary level. She has served parish ministry in catechetical and faith formation programs, in urban ministry in programs for at-risk youth and transitional housing, and in jail ministry. Celeste holds a doctor of ministry in practical theology from Eden Theological Seminary in St. Louis.

Maureen R. O'Brien is an associate professor of theology at Duquesne University in Pittsburgh. Her research interests are focused in practical theology, religious education, and the education of lay ministers. She is coeditor of the collection *Emerging from the Vineyard: Essays by Lay Ecclesial Ministers* (with Susan Yanos), produced through a collaborative writing project. She recently completed field research in West Africa for a qualitative, crosscultural study of lay catechists there. She also engages in research on the pedagogical practices and sensibilities of Spiritans, the founding congregation of Duquesne University. She is a past president of the Association of Graduate Programs in Ministry, as well as the Religious Education Association.

Hosffman Ospino, PhD, is an associate professor of theology and religious education at Boston College, School of Theology and

Ministry, where he is also director of graduate programs in Hispanic ministry. He served as the principal investigator for the National Study of Catholic Parishes with Hispanic Ministry (2014) and as coinvestigator for the National Survey of Catholic Schools Serving Hispanic Families (2015). He is currently advancing a national study on Latino Catholic vocations. He has authored or edited thirteen books and more than a hundred academic and general essays.

Hosffman has received several national awards from academic and ministerial organizations in recognition of his work, as well as his writings. He serves as an officer of the Catholic Theological Society of America (CTSA) and of the Academy of Catholic Hispanic Theologians of the United States (ACHTUS). He is also a member of the board of directors of the National Catholic Educational Association (NCEA). Hosffman is a coeditor of the Horizons book series in religious education, published by Wipf and Stock, and general editor of the New Horizons in Latinx Catholic Theology book series, published by Convivium Press, based in Miami. He is a consultant for various national and international organizations, as well as a recognized speaker in academic and ministerial settings.

Diana Dudoit Raiche, PhD, is associate professor of ministry in the Neuhoff School of Ministry at the University of Dallas. Formerly a team member with the North American Forum on the Catechumenate, she provided training for implementing the catechumenal process for adults and children of catechetical age in the United States and Canada. At The Catholic University of America, her dissertation focused on the essential nature of liturgical catechesis, especially in relation to the Rite of Christian Initiation of Adults (RCIA). Her research and teaching focuses on the link between catechesis and liturgy, and is grounded in her previous experience in pastoral ministry. Diana has served as a teacher in Catholic schools, parish director of catechetical ministry, director of the catechumenate, chair of a diocesan educational commission, executive director of the Religious Education Department at the National Catholic Educational Association, consultant to the Bishops' Committee on Evangelization and Catechesis, and on the planning team for the Diocesan Educational Catechetical Leadership Institute with USCCB and NCCL. In her work, Diana aims to develop a deeper understanding of the catechumenate as the model for all catechesis and formation in faith.

Nathaniel G. Samuel, PhD, is assistant professor of political and liberation theology at the Institute of Pastoral Studies, Loyola University Chicago, and teaches courses in social justice and Catholic social ethics. His research interests converge on issues of Caribbean religiosity and theology and narrative hermeneutics. A trained economist, earning his masters from the London School of Economics, Nathaniel also explores issues at the intersection of faith and economy, particularly with regard to the ethics of economic equality and opportunity. He currently serves as president of the Association of Graduate Programs in Ministry (AGPIM) and secretary of the Black Catholic Theological Symposium (BCTS). He has been engaged in adult religious education ministry for more than twenty years.

Theodore James Whapham, PhD, is associate professor and dean of the Ann and Joe O. Neuhoff School of Ministry at the University of Dallas. He is the author of numerous books and scholarly articles focusing on aspects of contemporary systematic theology and practical theology. His most recent book, *The Unity of Theology: The Contribution of Wolfhart Pannenberg,* provides a historical introduction to the work of one of the most significant theological voices of the twentieth century. In addition to teaching, research, and university administration, Theodore has taught at the secondary level and in diaconal formation for the Dioceses of Dallas and Palm Beach. He currently serves as vice president for the Association of Graduate Programs in Ministry.